Indian Ocean Islands

Islands are intrinsic parts of the Indian Ocean Region's physical geography and human landscape. Historically, many have played substantial roles in the regional cultural and economic networks, as well as in the regional political developments. Today, at least three issues bring these islands back to the forefront of the regional and global affairs, namely geopolitics and strategic matters, environmental conditions and challenges, as well as ocean affairs. However, there has not been yet a lot of research and publications on this phenomenon of islands' growing significance in the specific context of the Indian Ocean Region.

This book provides a rare attempt to cover various issues related to geopolitics, international relations, history, security, anthropology and ocean/environment of Indian Ocean islands and their societies. More specifically, it provides case studies on Sri Lanka (foreign policy), Cocos and Christmas Islands (geostrategy), Chagos archipelago (history), Mauritius ('Indo-Mauritians'), Mauritius and Seychelles (maritime security), European Union and the Indian Ocean Islands (international relations) and Sundarban islands (environment and society).

The chapters in this book were originally published in a special issue of the *Journal of the Indian Ocean Region*.

Christian Bouchard is the coordinator of Environmental Studies (French) at Laurentian University, Canada, a founding member of the Indian Ocean Research Group (IORG) and an associate editor of the *Journal of the Indian Ocean*.

Shafick Osman is a research associate at the Florida International University (USA), deputy editor-in-chief of Outre-Terre (France) and a member of the Society for Indian Ocean Studies (New Delhi) and Indian Ocean Research Group (IORG).

Indian Ocean Islands

Illustrated Cases on Geopolitics, Ocean and Environment

Edited by
Christian Bouchard and Shafick Osman

LONDON AND NEW YORK

First published 2018
by Routledge
2 Park Square, Milton Park, Abingdon, Oxon, OX14 4RN, UK

and by Routledge
711 Third Avenue, New York, NY 10017, USA

Routledge is an imprint of the Taylor & Francis Group, an informa business

© 2018 Indian Ocean Research Group

All rights reserved. No part of this book may be reprinted or reproduced or utilised in any form or by any electronic, mechanical, or other means, now known or hereafter invented, including photocopying and recording, or in any information storage or retrieval system, without permission in writing from the publishers.

Trademark notice: Product or corporate names may be trademarks or registered trademarks, and are used only for identification and explanation without intent to infringe.

British Library Cataloguing in Publication Data
A catalogue record for this book is available from the British Library

ISBN13: 978-1-138-49302-5

Typeset in MyriadPro
by diacriTech, Chennai

Publisher's Note
The publisher accepts responsibility for any inconsistencies that may have arisen during the conversion of this book from journal articles to book chapters, namely the possible inclusion of journal terminology.

Disclaimer
Every effort has been made to contact copyright holders for their permission to reprint material in this book. The publishers would be grateful to hear from any copyright holder who is not here acknowledged and will undertake to rectify any errors or omissions in future editions of this book.

Contents

	Citation Information	vii
	Notes on Contributors	ix
	Introduction *Christian Bouchard and Shafick Osman*	1
1	Balancing and bandwagoning: explaining shifts in Sri Lankan foreign policy *Rajni Nayanthara Gamage*	4
2	Cocos and Christmas Islands: building Australia's strategic role in the Indian Ocean *David Brewster and Rory Medcalf*	26
3	Towards a workers' history of the Chagos archipelago *Marina Carter*	45
4	'Indo-Mauritians' and the Indian Ocean: literacy accounts and anthropological readings *Mathieu Claveyrolas*	66
5	Small islands' understanding of maritime security: the cases of Mauritius and Seychelles *James A. Malcolm and Linganaden Murday*	82
6	The European Union and the Indian Ocean Islands: identifying opportunities for developing a more ambitious and comprehensive strategy *Erwan Lannon*	105
7	Tropical cyclones and coastal communities: the dialectics of social and environmental change in the Sundarban delta *Debojyoti Das*	128
	Index	147

Citation Information

The chapters in this book were originally published in the *Journal of the Indian Ocean Region*, volume 13, issue 2 (July 2017). When citing this material, please use the original page numbering for each article, as follows:

Chapter 1
Balancing and bandwagoning: explaining shifts in Sri Lankan foreign policy
Rajni Nayanthara Gamage
Journal of the Indian Ocean Region, volume 13, issue 2 (July 2017) pp. 133–154

Chapter 2
Cocos and Christmas Islands: building Australia's strategic role in the Indian Ocean
David Brewster and Rory Medcalf
Journal of the Indian Ocean Region, volume 13, issue 2 (July 2017) pp. 155–173

Chapter 3
Towards a workers' history of the Chagos archipelago
Marina Carter
Journal of the Indian Ocean Region, volume 13, issue 2 (July 2017) pp. 213–233

Chapter 4
'Indo-Mauritians' and the Indian Ocean: literacy accounts and anthropological readings
Mathieu Claveyrolas
Journal of the Indian Ocean Region, volume 13, issue 2 (July 2017) pp. 174–189

Chapter 5
Small islands' understanding of maritime security: the cases of Mauritius and Seychelles
James A. Malcolm and Linganaden Murday
Journal of the Indian Ocean Region, volume 13, issue 2 (July 2017) pp. 234–256

Chapter 6
The European Union and the Indian Ocean Islands: identifying opportunities for developing a more ambitious and comprehensive strategy
Erwan Lannon
Journal of the Indian Ocean Region, volume 13, issue 2 (July 2017) pp. 190–212

CITATION INFORMATION

Chapter 7
Tropical cyclones and coastal communities: the dialectics of social and environmental change in the Sundarban delta
Debojyoti Das
Journal of the Indian Ocean Region, volume 13, issue 2 (July 2017) pp. 257–275

For any permission-related enquiries please visit:
http://www.tandfonline.com/page/help/permissions

Notes on Contributors

Christian Bouchard is the coordinator of Environmental Studies (French) at Laurentian University, Canada, a founding member of the Indian Ocean Research Group (IORG) and an associate editor of the *Journal of the Indian Ocean*.

David Brewster is with the National Security College, Canberra, where he is a leading academic expert on Indian strategy affairs and strategy and security in the Indian Ocean Region. He is a regular participant in various 1.5 track strategic dialogues and advises government bodies on policy matters. Major books include *India as an Asia Pacific Power*, about India's strategic role in the Asia Pacific and *India's Ocean: The Story of India's Bid for Regional Leadership*, which examines India's strategic ambitions in the Indian Ocean. His recent work includes *Australia, India and the United States: The Challenge of Forging New Alignments in the Indo-Pacific*, which examines the potential for a trilateral security and defence relationship between those countries.

Marina Carter is a research fellow, and member of AHRC Funded Becoming Coolies team.

Mathieu Claveyrolas is an anthropologist, CNRS research fellow, member of the Center for South Asian Studies (EHESS, Paris). After many years studying Hinduism in Banaras (Uttar Pradesh, India), he turned to Mauritian Hinduism. He recently published Quand l'hindouisme est créole. Plantation et indianité à l'île Maurice (éditions de l'EHESS).

Debojyoti Das is an anthropologist from South Asia. His work focuses on the Bay of Bengal and Eastern India, looking at the lives of marginalised seafaring communities. He has contributed papers to several peer-reviewed journals and his upcoming book is under contract for publication entitled Land's End. He is at present a visiting postdoctoral fellow at the MacMillan Center for International Area Studies, Yale University, USA.

Erwan Lannon is professor at the law school of Ghent University, Belgium. He also teaches at the College of Europe on the Bruges (International Relations and Diplomatic Studies & European Political and Governance Studies) and Warsaw campuses (European Interdisciplinary Studies). He specializes in the areas of external relations of the European Union and international and strategic relations as well as in EU institutional and constitutional law.

James A. Malcolm is a research fellow in Maritime Security at the Centre for Trust, Peace and Social Relations (CTPSR), Coventry University, UK, where he also serves as

NOTES ON CONTRIBUTORS

Postgraduate Teaching Director. His main research interests are in port and coastal security with a particular emphasis on maritime security governance and the implementation of security policy.

Rory Medcalf is Head of the National Security College at the Australian National University, Canberra, where he has extended the College from its academic and training roles into policy engagement and future analysis. He has wide experience across diplomacy, intelligence analysis, think tanks, journalism and academia. He was founding director of the international security program for the Lowy Institute, Sydney. His career in the Australian diplomatic service included a posting to New Delhi, a secondment to Japan's foreign ministry and policy development on Asian regional institutions. He has contributed to three international panels on nuclear arms control and was an adviser to the Australian Government's 2016 defence white paper. He has made a significant contribution to Australia–India relations, including as convener of '1.5 track' dialogues. His research interests include developing an Indo-Pacific concept of the Asian strategic environment as well as major power relations, maritime security and nuclear issues.

Linganaden Murday is a lecturer in the Department of History and Political Science at the University of Mauritius (UOM). He completed his BA in History and International Relations at UOM in 2007 and his MA in International Law and Politics at the University of Hull (UK) in 2008. He has been teaching concepts and theories of international relations, international institutions and human rights since 2009.

Rajni Nayanthara Gamage is a senior analyst in the Maritime Security Programme, Institute of Defence and Strategic Studies (IDSS), S. Rajaratnam School of International Studies (RSIS), Nanyang Technological University (NTU), Singapore. Her research focus is on maritime security affairs in the Indo-Pacific and the foreign policies of Indian Ocean small states. She can be reached at israjni@ntu.edu.sg.

Shafick Osman is a research associate at the Florida International University (USA), deputy editor-in-chief of Outre-Terre (France) and a member of the Society for Indian Ocean Studies (New Delhi) and Indian Ocean Research Group (IORG).

Introduction

In the contemporary research and literature on the Indian Ocean Region, the focus and discourses are very much dominated by the continental rim states, especially India and other large coastal states. Fortunately, the islands are not totally ignored and forgotten, and there is today an increasing interest to get a better understanding of their specific context and contribution to the region. With no doubt, islands are intrinsic parts of the Indian Ocean Region's physical geography and human landscape. Large or small in land areas, such as Madagascar compared to the Seychelles, coastal islands or located farther away at sea, such as the Zanzibar Archipelago compared to Mauritius, islands have been integrated to the Indian Ocean's migration, cultural, commercial and political networks for as long as there have been ocean travellers. Historically, many have played substantial roles in these regional networks, as well as in the Indian Ocean geopolitical and geostrategic developments.

In the past centuries, several islands have served as essential replenishment stops and ports of call for ships sailing throughout the Indian Ocean. As well, under colonial times, many have hosted military facilities and served as fulcrums for the Europeans' ventures in the Indian Ocean. Their strategic importance has been proven again in the course of the Second World War, the Cold War and the recent US military operations in the Indian Ocean Region (such as in Iraq in 1991 and Afghanistan in 2001). In this context, with the development and operation of its large American logistical base[1], Diego Garcia appears as the Indian Ocean archetype of the strategic island. Apart from military functions, economic activities have also been central over the past centuries in linking the islands to their colonial metropole, their continental rim neighbours and the rest of the world.

Today, at least three issues bring the Indian Ocean islands to the forefront of the regional and global affairs, namely geopolitics, ocean and environment. However, there has not been yet a lot of research and publication on the islands' growing significance in the specific context of the Indian Ocean Region. This was the motivation for this special edition of the *Journal of the Indian Ocean Region*, in an attempt to raise the awareness for island issues and island significance to the region.

First, the islands have become of prime interest in terms of geopolitics and geostrategy. Island states and island territories have their own internal political dynamics, and they are strongly involved in regional cooperation and international island networks. Among other things, the sovereignty over some islands is still disputed (as for example, for the Chagos Archipelago), many maritime domains are still in the making (several unsettled maritime boundaries, claims for extended continental shelf), and there is an increase interest to develop their military functions. On this latter point, we can even affirm that many of the islands have been very much involved in the recent regional strategic developments, and island states' military cooperation with foreign powers has increased significantly.

Second, developing stronger links with their surrounding waters is another main issue for the islands. The ocean is seen as providing economic opportunities (blue economy: fishing, aquaculture, tourism, energy, etc.), but also as an environment that needs to be better protected (biodiversity, ocean physicochemical conditions) and controlled (regulation, monitoring, policing, defence). Like the other coastal states, the islands have gained extended rights and duties over larger oceanic spaces, as granted by the United Nations Convention on the Law of the Sea. This made them very relevant in regards to the regional maritime affairs and well positioned in the regional and international programs to develop the blue economy and maritime security.

Third, in regards to the environment, the islands are recognized as being very fragile and facing growing pressures, which are both internal and external. On the one hand, local natural resources and ecosystems need to be exploited and managed in a sustainable manner, with specific efforts to be made to limit the environmental degradation and pollution, as well as to expand conservation. On the other hand, the islands are also going to be greatly affected by global changes, including changes in climate conditions and sea level rise. Overall, environmental sustainability and climate change adaptation have emerged as main challenges for the twenty-first century. Failing to cope with these issues could have significant regional repercussions in terms of migrations and stability.

Considering the importance of these three issues, there is definitively a need to better understand both the islands' general background as well as their respective specific situation, especially in relation to the regional context of the Indian Ocean Region. With this in mind, we realized that we came short in this special edition to browse a comprehensive picture of the islands significance in the Indian Ocean Region. Nevertheless, we propose an interesting mix of papers addressing some of the main issues listed earlier, hoping that this will initiate the development of a much stronger island research agenda feeding both island studies and Indian Ocean studies.

In Chapter 1, 'Balancing and bandwagoning: explaining shifts in Sri Lankan foreign policy', Rajni Nayanthara Gamage explores the key drivers of small state foreign policy and proposes a comprehensive explanation for Sri Lanka's foreign policy changes over three decades (1977–2015). The author shows that 'an interplay of system and domestic-level factors best explains this pattern of foreign policy change', with domestic imperatives and actors playing a central role in the foreign economic policy, and systemic factors being predominant on the foreign security policy. In 'Cocos and Christmas Islands: building Australia's strategic role in the Indian Ocean', David Brewster and Rory Medcalf explore the growing militarization of islands throughout the Indian Ocean and considers the strategic value of Australia's Indian Ocean territories. They argue that 'upgraded facilities on both Cocos and Christmas would provide Australia with valuable leverage in its relationships with regional defence partners and the United States'.

In Chapter 3, 'Towards a workers' history of the Chagos archipelago', Marina Carter addresses the issue of the islanders (*Ilois*) life and working conditions from early settlement to the end of the commercial exploitation of the coco plantations and the population expulsion. She discusses 'the challenges of framing a workers' history characterized by exploitation and marginalization alongside the romanticized collective representation of life in the archipelago which has been adopted as a "narrative of exile" by the Chagossians'. In '"Indo-Mauritians" and the Indian Ocean: literacy accounts and anthropological readings', Mathieu Claveyrolas considers the Hindu descendants of indentured labourers and 'the many and changing narratives of indenture, as a "domesticating paradigm" promoted in both literature and identity discourses'. The chapters explore the links between 'Indo-Mauritians' and India, including the representations and meanings associated to their original migrations, and argue that these links are still of prime significance and are even revitalized today in what is the largest ethnic community in Mauritius.

In Chapter 5, 'Small islands' understanding of maritime security: the cases of Mauritius and the Seychelles', James A. Malcolm and Linganaden Murday discuss the importance of maritime security in the small islands and large ocean states' quest for sustainable development. This work specifically looks after how Seychelles is reacting to maritime piracy and how Mauritius is addressing drug trafficking. Then, in 'The European Union and the Indian Ocean islands: identifying opportunities for developing a more ambitious and comprehensive strategy', Erwan Lannon presents the relationship between the European Union (EU) and the islands in terms of geostrategic, geoeconomical and cooperation perspectives. This chapter discusses the EU's multidimensional and significant involvement in the region and in the islands, and also notes the issues related to its member states (France and United Kingdom) overseas island territories. Finally, in the seventh and last chapter, 'Tropical cyclones and coastal communities: the dialectics of social and environmental change in the Sundarban delta', Debojyoti Das provides an in deep analysis of the relations between social and environmental changes since colonial time and today's vulnerability of coastal communities in the Sundarban delta. The author argues that cyclone-related disasters are embedded in the social and political relations shaping the human habitation on these coastal islands.

Recognizing that this special edition on the Indian Ocean islands is an eclectic mix of chapters, we want to stress that each of these chapters addresses an important issue for the Indian Ocean islands, whether it be foreign policy making, strategic considerations, history and collective memories, indenture and links with India, maritime security, external power action, as well as cyclones and disaster management. Let us just close this foreword by insisting that, as much as the islands can be seen from the outside great powers and larger regional powers as useful – mainly for strategic and economic reasons – , there is a strong need to also consider and better understand the islands' perspectives on the challenges they face today (pressure from global and regional powers, for example), the future they aspire to and their integration and positioning in a vibrant but complex Indian Ocean Region which itself is more and more associated with the African and Asian continents.

This edition of *Journal of the Indian Ocean Region* draws upon the research of a much larger project entitled 'Building an Indian Ocean Region' DP120101166, which is funded by the Australian Research Council (ARC) Discovery Projects Scheme for funding in 2012–2017.

Note

1. Officially: US Navy Support Facility Diego Garcia, operational since 1973 (as Naval Communications Station). However, the presence of this US Base is highly controversial as Mauritius claims that the Chagos Archipelago have been illegally separated from their national territory in 1965 by the United Kingdom prior to its independence, and because the entire population of the archipelago (known as Ilois or Chagossians) was evicted from their homeland between 1967 and 1973.

Balancing and bandwagoning: explaining shifts in Sri Lankan foreign policy

Rajni Nayanthara Gamage

ABSTRACT
Analysis of Sri Lanka's foreign policy over three decades (1977–2015) reveals a pattern of shifts from balancing to bandwagoning, and then back again to balancing. The more salient foreign policy issues during each administration fall broadly within the economic or security spheres. What are the key drivers of small state foreign policy – do systemic factors preside in general, and domestic factors prove inconsequential? Or are domestic factors able to play a decisive role under certain circumstances, within broader structural parameters? Three primary arguments are made in this regard. First, an interplay of system- and domestic-level factors best explains this pattern of foreign policy change. Second, in the domain of foreign economic policymaking, domestic imperatives and actors appear to play a decisive role, although within the broader structural preconditions. Third, systemic factors maintain predominance over domestic-level factors in shaping foreign security policy.

Introduction

In January 2015, Sri Lanka's president-elect Maithripala Sirisena took over the reins of leadership from the outgoing leader Mahinda Rajapaksa. As part of his electoral manifesto, Sirisena pledged to 'correct' the country's foreign relations, allegedly mismanaged during the Rajapaksa administration. The Government of Sri Lanka (GOSL) had tilted precariously towards China since 2005, triggering Indian political and security sensitivities and alienating itself from the West. The Rajapaksa administration, well-known for its firebrand nationalism in its foreign relations, especially in response to international pressures from some quarters for accountability for alleged war crimes, had chartered its own course of foreign policy. This, however, is not an anomaly in the country's history of foreign policy, each administration having drawn closer to some states often at the expense of relations with others.

Important questions result from such a variable foreign policy. First, what are the sources of a state's foreign policymaking? Do systemic forces preside at all times, or do domestic factors play a significant role as well? Second, is the dynamic different for small states' foreign policymaking? An understanding of the international system based on the distribution of capabilities and the maxim that 'the strong do what they can and the weak suffer what they must' hints at the foreign policy of smaller, weaker states being subject to broader, systemic changes within the international system. Finally, is there any discernible pattern or certain conditions under which one set of factors take precedence over the other in explaining a state's foreign policy at a particular juncture of time?

The answers to these questions would facilitate a deeper, more nuanced understanding of the process of Sri Lankan foreign policymaking. Identifying the causal mechanisms and trends within a country's foreign policy has predictive and, therefore, prescriptive value. Therefore, in discernible circumstances where domestic variables are said to have a decisive impact, it is proposed that the state can play a more active role engaging in public dialogue and shaping these domestic factors in line with national interests. On the other hand, in conditions identified as allowing primarily systemic factors to prevail, the prescribed course of action is to 'hedge,' i.e. to develop and maintain healthy and diversified foreign relations.

This article analyzes the dynamics of Sri Lankan foreign policymaking, concentrating primarily on its relations with the key powers engaged in the subcontinent since the 1990s. It was found that although factors at each level of analysis contribute to explaining Sri Lankan foreign policy shifts along numerous administrations, on certain case studies, and in certain points of time, it is possible to rank their importance, although within a predefined context of binding structural factors that constrain. In doing so, it is also important to be cognizant of the interrelationship among the factors at different levels. Although the series of events and persons in these case studies may be the exception that proves the rule, it can generate a more nuanced, yet simple understanding of the conditions under which system- or domestic-level factors' influence is blunted. The research methodology comprises interviews with policy analysts, bureaucrats, military personnel, and academics based in Sri Lanka, Singapore, and the U.S., combined with analysis of secondary sources.

In this paper, three primary arguments are made. First, an interplay of system- and domestic-level factors best explains this pattern of small state foreign policy change. That is, the shifts in balancing or bandwagoning strategy are not driven purely by system- or domestic-level factors, but at various times by one or the other, and sometimes together. It is not, therefore, a matter of identifying 'either-or' factors but rather determining which factors preside on a case-by-case basis. Second, in the domain of foreign economic policymaking, domestic imperatives and actors appear to play a decisive role, although within the broader structural preconditions. Foreign economic policy is commonly characterized as involving issues of 'low-politics' and hence offer greater latitude for domestic factors to influence the decision-making process. Third, systemic factors maintain predominance over domestic-level factors in shaping foreign security policy. Since foreign security policy deals with issues more integral to a country's sovereignty and survival, the capabilities of each state matters and systemic factors preside. Such findings reveal a different dynamic depending on the nature of the issues examined.

In closing, the article suggests three policy recommendations. First, Sri Lanka needs to recognize the indispensability of India as a strategic and economic partner, and avoid any actions that blatantly antagonizes India. Second, Sri Lanka must pursue a foreign policy that is diversified and independent of any one power's influence. Finally, Sri Lanka's foreign policy must be less reactionary and more stable. It is argued in closing that it may be in Sri Lanka's interests too to have an extra-regional balancer such as China, but at the same time developing sound political and economic relations with India.

The first section presents a historical overview of Sri Lankan foreign policymaking, and the different schools of thought and their contribution to understanding the sources of foreign policymaking. Section two analyzes the key literature on the study of Sri Lankan foreign policymaking. The following two sections examine the shift from a balancing foreign policy during the Jayewardene and Premadasa administrations (1977–1989 and 1989–1993) which had pro-Western inclinations and strained relations with India, to a bandwagoning foreign policy during the Kumaratunga administration (1994–2005) which cultivated markedly improved relations with India, illustrated through the case studies of the India–Sri Lanka Free Trade Agreement (ISLFTA) and bilateral strategic linkages (military assistance, Defence Cooperation Agreement (DCA), and the Hambantota Port). This is followed by analysis of the subsequent shift back to a balancing foreign policy during the Rajapaksa administration (2005–2015), this time with China – demonstrated by the Comprehensive Economic Partnership Agreement (CEPA) and the India–Sri Lanka–Maldives Maritime Agreement.

Sri Lankan foreign policymaking: a historical overview

The GOSL has traditionally followed a foreign policy of non-alignment in the interest of avoiding entanglement in superpower rivalries. However, this official aspiration has not for a large extent concurred with political realities, as the two main political parties, the United National Party (UNP) and the Sri Lanka Freedom Party (SLFP) had perceptibly different foreign policy orientations. While the former was generally friendlier towards the capitalist West, the latter had 'historically supported leftist/communist regimes, encouraged welfare policies, and shown a penchant for state-centrism' (DeVotta, 1998, p. 460; Sivarajah, 2003).

The UNP's tilt towards the West at the expense of relations with then-leftist/communist states stems from historical experiences. In the post-independence context, the UNP was in competition with local, oppositional Marxist parties and viewed Soviet expansionism in East Asia with trepidation. It also harboured the memory of the Soviet Union vetoing against the admission of Sri Lanka to the United Nations (UN) in 1955. As a result, from 1945 to 1956, UNP governments refused to establish diplomatic or cultural relations with leftist/communist states (Wilson, 1974, p. 57). In contrast, during the SLFP administrations (1960–1965 and 1970–1977), the country developed closer ties with the Soviet Union, China, and India (De Silva, 1995, pp. 25–27; Hewitt, 1997, p. 70).

Within Sri Lanka's foreign policy calculus, India is perceived as the 'predominant power' due to the latter's proximity, its sizeable ethnic Tamil population in Tamil Nadu (making the Sinhalese a 'majority with a minority complex'), and a historical record of invasions by India as well as more recent instances of hegemonic interventionism (Sikri, 2009, p. 75). The island-state's insecurities in relation to India are largely shaped by the tremendous disparities of bilateral power capabilities in every sector (World Bank, 2016).[1] The sheer magnitude and asymmetry of India's regional power preponderance evokes Sri Lankan anxieties regarding Indian dominance and aggressiveness, whether or not the latter behaves in such a fashion (Sridharan, 2008, p. 15). Feeding further into such anxieties was rhetoric by Indian strategists in the immediate years preceding the island's independence in 1948, including PM Nehru, which hinted at Sri Lanka joining India 'as an autonomous unit of the Indian Federation' (Wriggins, 1960, p. 399 as cited in DeVotta, 2010, p. 38). Such rhetoric has been constantly played up by Sinhala nationalists as evidence of Indian expansionism and many in Sri Lanka, from the political elite to the general public, believe to this day that some in India want to ensure that the island stays destabilized.

'Balancing' as a form of foreign policy behavior refers to aligning with other states *against* a predominant power (within a given geographical grouping). In the context of Sri Lankan foreign policymaking, balancing is therefore tantamount to developing close strategic and economic relations with states other than India, often at the expense of relations with the latter. In contrast, 'bandwagoning' refers to aligning *with* the predominant power, either as a form of appeasement or to share the spoils of victory (Walt, 1987). In the more recent past, such tendencies were most evident during the Kumaratunga administration in the 1990s and early-2000s.

Sri Lankan foreign policymaking has from the onset being personality-driven, owing partly to the lack of an established foreign policymaking body in newly independent, developing states such as itself (Gunaratna, 2016). In fact, it was as late as the Jayewardene administration, in 1977, that an exclusive Ministry of Foreign Affairs (known as the 'Ministry of External Affairs (MEA)') was established. Even then, the ambit of foreign policymaking was largely confined to Jayewardene and two of his close cabinet members – Gamini Dissanayake and Lalith Athulathmudali (Gunasena, 2013, p. 227). In such circumstances, the personal beliefs and preferences of the President 'received even greater weight in [foreign] policy formulation than they do under regular circumstances, with his [or her] personal leadership style becoming even more critical to the implementation of the formulated policy' (Mahdiyeva, 2011, p. 44). This offers greater scope for domestic factors to play a decisive role in foreign policymaking in Sri Lanka (Mara, 2003, p. 27).

In analyzing the forces behind any country's foreign policy imperatives, an understanding of the three 'images' or levels of analysis which fit loosely within the main schools of thought in international relations theory is essential. Realism's primary causal mechanism is at the systemic-level; liberal theory identifies domestic-level factors as the primary determinants of state behavior; and constructivism contends that identities and norms play a foremost role in determining state actions. Thus, while realism's predominant emphasis is on systemic factors, the latter two theories also focus on domestic and cognitive variables in explaining state behavior.

'Neoclassical realism' can be understood as an extension of classical realism, as they both share core assumptions about the state, relative power, and the primacy of the anarchical material structure. The former is, however, critical of the latter's assumption of state behavior being a direct response to structural incentives whatever the internal composition of the state: 'systemic pressures and incentives may shape the broad contours and general direction of foreign policy without being strong or precise enough to determine the specific details of state behavior' (Rose, 1998, p. 147).

Neoclassical realists argue instead that state behavior is a function of systemic factors, as well as cognitive and domestic variables, as 'complex domestic political processes act as transmission belts that channel, mediate, and (re)direct policy outputs in response to external forces' (Schweller, 2004, p. 164). Structural incentives therefore shape the broad contours of foreign policy, 'but the variation between states' foreign policies under similar structural pressures is explained by incorporating the perceptual variable and pressure of domestic commercial interest groups on leaders and decision makers' (Foulon, 2015, p. 654). Neoclassical realism thereby bridges the spatial divide (domestic–international), and also the cognitive (matter-ideas) and temporal divide (present–future). It demonstrates how and why foreign policies are not always in line with structural incentives or domestic interests, and accounts for the foreign policy which we observe in the real world (Foulon, 2015, p. 653).

That the foreign policy of small states has a dynamic of its own has been a matter of contention within the literature. While some scholars reasoned that system-level factors possessed the 'home-court advantage' in explaining small state foreign policy, the post-1990 context witnessed a challenge to this notion and explored the role of domestic factors as a significant, additional lens of foreign policy behavior (Galbreath, 2006; Goldgeier & McFaul, 1992; Handel, 1981; Labs, 1992). To qualify as a 'small state' requires fulfillment of an objective element, with reference to the quantitative and material attributes of a state (e.g. population size, land mass, gross domestic product (GDP)), and a subjective element, i.e. based on the idea of internal and external perceptions of a state's role in the international hierarchy. A state is therefore considered as 'small' 'if a state's people and institutions generally perceive themselves to be small, or if other states' peoples and institutions perceive that state as small,' negating the necessity to decide on rigid objective attributes (Hey, 2003, p. 4).

The study of Sri Lankan foreign policymaking: the theoretical literature

The better part of the existing literature on Sri Lankan foreign policy considers systemic factors as providing the most compelling and sufficient explanations of a range of foreign policy behavior. Such analysis, however, is more often found within studies on India's Sri Lankan (foreign) policy, which are more readily available than literature written from the viewpoint of Sri Lankan foreign policy.

In 'India's Sri Lanka Policy: Towards Economic Engagement,' Orland argues that the dual systemic forces of the end of the Cold War and liberal economic reforms within India resulted in its renewed economic engagement with Sri Lanka since the mid-1990s (Orland, 2008). Likewise, Kelegama contends that the FTA was largely a consequence of the slow pace of regional economic initiatives such as the South Asian Preferential Trade Agreement (SAPTA) (Kelegama, 1999).

On defense- and security-related issues, a number of scholars explain India's inconsistent attitude over the years towards strategic cooperation with Sri Lanka through Tamil Nadu state politics, negative historical experiences upon meddling in the island's internal political affairs, and contrasting nation-building strategies, versus the fear of extra-regional powers gaining a stronghold in the region in its absence (Destradi, 2012; DeVotta, 2010; Jacob, 2010; Sikri, 2009; Sridharan, 2016). In turn, DeSilva-Ranasinghe, Samaranayake, and Ladduwahetty perceive Sri Lanka's strategic drift towards China since 2005 to be the result of a confluence of strategic and economic objectives: China's military aid and armaments allowing Sri Lanka to minimize its dependence on the West (and even India), and Rajapaksa's national development agenda coinciding with China's rising capabilities and strategic interests (DeSilva-Ranasinghe, 2011; Ladduwahetty, 2015; Samaranayake, 2011).

Additional contributions have been made to the literature by a number of authors who highlight the additional influence of domestic factors on specific occasions. De Votta attempts to explain Sri Lanka's post-1977 tilt towards a pro-Western foreign policy through the enactment of domestic structural adjustment policies. This dramatic foreign policy tilt was argued to be largely a function of the legitimacy and survival of the UNP regime, obscuring the geostrategic constraints that a small country is typically cognizant of (DeVotta, 1998). Basrur contends that while Sri Lanka's foreign policy was driven by an essentially structural-realist outlook prior to the 1990s, in the post-1990 context, a shift in foreign relations culminating in the ISLFTA were the result of both systemic *and* domestic developments (Basrur, 2011). Meanwhile, Kelegama and Pattanaik explain the inability of the CEPA to take off through the strong opposition by politically influential segments of the business community, and the economic and political incompatibility of the CEPA with Rajapaksa's domestic-oriented economic ideology and nationalist discourse (Kelegama, 2014; Pattanaik, 2012). On political- and security-related issues, Gunasena highlights the influential role played by Sri Lankan leadership, political parties, and interest groups in the progressive shift in bilateral relations during the Kumaratunga administration (Gunasena, 2013).

This paper seeks to contribute to the existing literature by comprehensively examining system- and domestic-level forces that played a role in determining the pattern of foreign policy shifts in Sri Lanka since 1977 up to the current context (although primary focus is based on the period 1994–2015). It is expected that in doing so, a framework of foreign policymaking can be developed which would provide a more holistic and deeper understanding of Sri Lankan foreign policy behavior over this frame of time. As such, it can also have utility when extended beyond the particulars of the region or case studies to predicting or explaining small state foreign policy shifts elsewhere (in choosing between balancing or bandwagoning) and, in doing so, inform existing theories of foreign policy and enrich the body of small state foreign policy.

Jayewardene and Premadasa administrations (1977–1993): a balancing foreign policy

President Jayewardene gave Sri Lankan foreign policy a decidedly Western orientation for two primary reasons: the desire to secure Western aid and investment to back the national economic liberalization program that he launched in 1977 (in contrast to the preceding administration's inward-looking socialist economic policies) and which was tied to the legitimacy and political survival of himself and his party (Abeyratne, 2015; DeVotta, 1998);[2] and to defeat the emerging ethnic Tamil militancy, which in turn would affect the success of his economic liberalization program and regime survival (Wijesinha, 2015).[3] These developments irked the sensitivities of the corresponding Indian state administration led by PM Indira Gandhi (Gunaratna, 2016). Given the backdrop of the Cold War and strained ties with the U.S., it was feared that the latter 'would gain a new geostrategic foothold [in the island], along India's oceanic flank,' resulting in India's regional dominance and national security being compromised (Homes and Yoshihara, 2008, p. 1000 as cited in Gunasena, 2013, p. 223).

In response, as an instrument of political pressure, the Indian government supported the funding, arming, and training of Sri Lankan Tamil militant groups through its Research and Analysis Wing since 1983 in order to destabilize Sri Lanka (DeVotta, 2010, p. 44). The height of India's hegemonic behavior was in 1987, when the Indian Air Force intervened in the ongoing military siege by the Sri Lanka Army (SLA) in Jaffna by airdropping food and medicine in the North. This was followed by the India–Sri Lanka Accord (ISLA) and the presence of Indian Peace Keeping Forces (IPKF) on the island to enact the terms of the Accord (Sridharan, 2016, p. 59).[4] Bilateral relations reached their lowest during the subsequent Premadasa administration (1989–1993), under whose directive the GOSL provided arms to the Liberation Tigers of Tamil Eelam (LTTE) to attack the IPKF until the latter's eventual withdrawal in 1990 (after sustaining around 1200 casualties) (Orland, 2008, p. 5).

Although the foreign and domestic policies pursued during these two UNP administrations were markedly different in many aspects, they both shared a common sense of antagonism vis-à-vis India. While this could be largely accounted for by India's hegemonic behavior and the non-alignment of Indian and Sri Lankan interests concerning the ethnic Tamil issue during both administrations, developments within Sri Lanka's domestic political landscape also helped determine the eventual decision by its leadership to pursue a balancing foreign policy.

The UNP's pro-Western, economic liberalization ideologies were part of its founding leaders' legacy in contrast to the socialist, autarkic economic policies pursued by India since its independence. Such domestic and foreign economic policies were employed by Jayewardene as an electoral platform to distinguish himself from the socialist opposition party and later to maintain his hold on power. Moreover, hostile personal relations with Mrs Gandhi due to clashes of personality, poor diplomatic foresight that failed to realize the crucial importance of Indian goodwill (Izzadeen, 2015; Jayatilleka, 2015), and antagonism with his domestic counterpart in the SLFP (Sirimavo Bandaranaike) with whom Mrs Gandhi shared a close, personal camaraderie, all made the importance of a diversified and independent foreign policy clearly evident.[5] On Premadasa's part, balancing against India was driven mainly by the electoral capital he gained during his election campaign in 1988 by playing up nationalist and anti-Indian rhetoric which pledged to remove the IPKF from the island (Gunasena, 2013, p. 228; Hewitt, 1997, p. 73). This, however, was not an anomaly in the region, as other small states in the region resorted to similar electoral tactics during this period (Hewitt, 1997, pp. 51, 63; Kelegama, 2016, p. 202).[6]

Kumaratunga administration (1994–2005): the shift to a bandwagoning foreign policy

During the Kumaratunga administration, there was a marked shift in foreign policy to one of bandwagoning, as great importance was placed on establishing good relations with India (as well as in fostering regional cooperation through the South Asian Association for Regional Cooperation or SAARC). Interestingly, some of the changes within the international system that enabled this rapprochement were present even during the Premadasa administration. These included the end of the Cold War (Sridharan, 2016, p. 60);[7] the economic liberalization of India in 1991 (and the resulting shift in its foreign economic policy and South Asian policy from one dominated by ideological power politics to pragmatic security interests) (Orland, 2008, pp. 1, 7);[8] and the painful lesson of the IPKF debacle and the assassination of Indian PM Rajiv Gandhi by an LTTE suicide bomber, which effectively turned the Indian central government and general public opinion against the LTTE (Sridharan, 2016, p. 60).[9] In turn, India adopted a more hands-off policy when dealing with contentious political/security issues connected to the island, but at the same time engaged deeper on matters of bilateral economic integration (Orland, 2008, p. 3).[10] The presumption was that benefits in bilateral trade in favor of Sri Lanka would lead to diminished perceptions of Indian exploitation within Sri Lanka and thereby, greater economic and political engagement (Destradi, 2012, p. 601).

India–Sri Lanka Free Trade Agreement

The ISLFTA was signed in 1998 and has been often identified as the epitome of improving bilateral economic relations under the Kumaratunga administration. India's foreign policy shift from the hegemonic 'Indira Doctrine' to the 'Gujral Doctrine' around 1996–1997 assured smaller regional neighbors that their internal affairs would no longer be interfered with and that regional economic cooperation would be facilitated by India in the form of unilateral concessions (Gunasena, 2013, p. 389). India's rapid economic growth from the mid-late 1990s also enabled it to offer Sri Lanka favorable terms in trade (World Bank, 2016).[11] Moreover, the slow pace of regional economic initiatives such as the SAPTA (and later the South Asian Free Trade Agreement or SAFTA in the 2000s) pushed both states to opt for a faster-paced bilateral agreement by the mid-late 1990s (Mukherji & Iyengar, 2013, pp. 2–3).

While developments at the international and regional levels may have facilitated, to some degree, bilateral economic integration, they fail to hold their own upon deeper scrutiny. Although India agreed to the provision of asymmetrical benefits to regional states under the SAPTA framework (in step with the Gujral Doctrine), Article II of the ISLFTA requests that the contracting parties pay due regard to the principle of reciprocity (Kelegama, 1999, p. 286). Arguably, the ISLFTA did eventually favor Sri Lanka disproportionately, as India's 'negative list' included 429 goods compared to Sri Lanka's 1180, with only three years to reach zero-tariff levels against Sri Lanka's eight (Orland, 2008, p. 11). However, that 97 items India had not listed under the SAFTA negative list were found under the ISLFTA negative list, questions the extent of India's non-reciprocity vis-à-vis its smaller neighbor (Behera & Mukherji, 2013, p. 40). Moreover, this was the first (and remains the only) bilateral FTA India was a signatory to in South Asia, hinting at the lack of systemic forces driving such initiatives at the regional level.[12]

That the slow pace of SAPTA provided the impetus for both sides to pursue a bilateral FTA also appears questionable. India lacked as strong an incentive to push for a bilateral FTA as Sri Lanka did as it had already managed to expand its exports without zero tariffs to become Sri Lanka's largest supplier of imports, accounting for 8–9% of its total imports (Kelegama, 1999, p. 287; Sikdar & Chakraborty, 2012, p. 3). Sri Lanka, on the other hand, viewed an FTA with India as a means of broadening its industrial base by taking advantage of the 'first-mover' access to the large and growing Indian market (Behera & Mukherji, 2013, p. 18). This is evident in the ISLFTA working to even the bilateral trade imbalances from 16:1 in 1998 to 5:1 by 2002. While Sri Lankan exports to India increased by more than three times during the first decade of the FTA, Indian exports to Sri Lanka grew only by 1.25 times during the same period, as 'previously uncompetitive products of Sri Lankan origin gained competitiveness as a result of the FTA and found its market in India' (Behera & Mukherji, 2013, p. 22).

While these systemic elements may have formed a conducive environment for bilateral economic cooperation, the national leadership and topmost policymakers played a foremost role in redefining bilateral relations with India. The push for the ISLFTA came from Kumaratunga and a handful of advisors, mainly bureaucrats from the MEA and the Finance Ministry (Basrur, 2011, p. 251; Hettiarachchi, 2015). While Jayewardene and Premadasa failed to demonstrate serious political will in establishing close bilateral relations with India, Kumaratunga's foreign policy of rapprochement consistently sought to engage India on economic (and eventually, political/security) issues (Dixit, 1992, p. 709 as cited in Gunasena, 2013, p. 228; Jayewardene, 1992, p. 301 as cited in Gunasena, 2013, p. 225).[13]

The administration's positive attitude towards India was reflective of the SLFP's usual foreign policy flavor, traditionally having had close relations with India unlike the UNP. The party therefore provided the broader impetus for initiatives that sought to accommodate and engage with India, in keeping with the maxim that '[a]s the composition of the ruling coalition changes, foreign policy goals will shift as well' (Basrur, 2011, p. 251; Skidmore, 1997, p. 6). Moreover, the close camaraderie that existed between the Nehru and Bandaranaike families since independence influenced, however subtly, President Kumaratunga's decision-making calculus (Jayatilleka, 2015; Wijesinha, 2015). In foreign policy-making then, elite ideas and identities 'constitute the filter through which material and structural threats and opportunities are perceived' (Gvalia, Siroki, Lebanidze, & Iashvili, 2013, p. 100). Even though the influence may have been modest, at times, it is these subtle differences which facilitate significant shifts in ultimate foreign policy behavior.

There were also no significant levels of public opposition within Sri Lanka to the ISLFTA, Sri Lanka having liberalized its economy as early as 1977; a number of years having lapsed since India's behavior as an aggressive, regional hegemon; and India having also had the experience of loss at the hands of the LTTE (Basrur, 2011, p. 251). Kumaratunga had also carried out a successful public information sharing and education campaign on the benefits of economic cooperation with India through the implementation of the ISLFTA (Gunasena, 2013). Interest groups (including religious- and ethnic-based political parties, and business lobby groups) too were generally receptive of the initiative. It is noteworthy that even the *Janata Vimukthi Peramuna* (JVP), a traditionally anti-Indian political party as per its manifesto (and which was in the opposition during this period), did not create any notable or dogged resistance to the FTA (Basrur, 2011, p. 251). All of this stand in contrast to the Jayewardene and Premadasa periods when public opposition to cooperation with India was acute, given the concurrent experiences of the IPKF and Indian-sponsored Tamil militancy in the island (Orland, 2008, p. 4; Wijesinha, 2015).

Bilateral strategic linkages

During Kumaratunga's second term in office (1999–2005), there were three significant foreign security/political issues in relation to India that stood out. In 2000, around 4000 SLA personnel were trapped by the LTTE in the gateway of the Jaffna Peninsula, known as the Elephant Pass. Kumaratunga made an urgent appeal to New Delhi for military assistance, not being prepared for the subsequent refusal by India to involve itself in the ongoing armed conflict. The National Democratic Alliance's (NDA's) decision was a stark reminder to Kumaratunga that regardless of the cultivation of close personal relations with India's political leadership, national interests eclipsed all else in the Indian foreign policymaking calculus (Jayatilleka, 2015).

New Delhi's decision was primarily in response to domestic political imperatives. A surge in public sympathy in Tamil Nadu towards Sri Lankan Tamils due to the influx of refugees around the time of Tamil Nadu assembly and parliamentary elections led even moderate parties in Tamil Nadu to refuse to support another Indian military intervention (Jacob, 2010, p. 94). The *Dravida Munnetra Kazhagam* (DMK), the political party representing Tamil Nadu, was a coalition partner of the ruling NDA, and held considerable clout within the alliance on this issue as its withdrawal would cause the government to collapse. India's hands-off policy with regard to the island's security affairs was also reflective of its past experiences with the IPKF, and of uncertainty of the GOSL's ultimate intentions regarding power devolution to minorities – even if the armed conflict were to be resolved. Moreover, internal instability within India in the 1990s concerning Kashmir, Nagaland, Tripura, Assam, and Manipur resulted in a considerable number of casualties and expenses for the Indian central government. The center's doctrine of national unity as the basis of national security alongside fears of alienation of Tamil Nadu leading to separatist politics, and the dissonance between the inclusive and accommodative nation-building strategy of India and the majoritarian state-building strategy of Sri Lanka all contributed towards its decision to stand clear of any direct involvement in the ongoing conflict (Sridharan, 2016, pp. 61, 62, 65, 70, 71).

Similar domestic imperatives explain why India refused to finalize the second issue of importance, the bilateral DCA which had originally been proposed by Sri Lanka around 2002 and agreed to in principle by India (Orland, 2008, p. 20; DeVotta, 2010, p. 49).[14] The third issue is the Hambantota Port, which although later regarded with concern by India as a form of strategic encirclement by China (i.e. as a naval base in its alleged 'String of Pearls' strategy), was initially rejected by India in 2002 upon Sri Lanka's first offer to develop the Port. Subsequently, the Chinese Harbor Engineering Company and Sinohydro Company were awarded the contract (Ladduwahetty, 2002; Uyangoda, 2015).[15] This was disclosed by Rajapaksa in 2013: 'Now take Hambantota port. It was offered to India first. I was desperate for development work. But ultimately the Chinese agreed to build it' (Velloor, 2013). Although the Hambantota Port was initially perceived by India as an unviable 'economic' project, India's eventual concern of it serving as a strategic base give grounds for the Port being conceived of as a 'strategic' issue.

India's rejection of the Hambantota Port proposal follows a logic distinct from that which explains its non-cooperative attitude towards Sri Lanka in 2000 and regarding the DCA. Miscalculation by Indian policymakers, i.e. not foreseeing China taking up the project, and limited Indian investment capabilities in what was seen as a non-core economic project are foremost (Samaranayake, 2016; Wijesinha, 2015).[16] Such concerns turned out to be well-founded, as heavy losses incurred (approximately Rs. 18.8 billion) by the Port made debt repayment an issue.[17] The Chinese, on the other hand, had much deeper pockets and viewed the Port primarily in strategic terms (Izzadeen, 2015).[18] Moreover, there were also concerns within India's policymaking circles that the Hambantota Port would be a competitor of India's own ports, such as the Visakhapatnam Port in Andhra Pradesh, and therefore antithetical to its national interests (Hettiarachchi, 2015).

The tense backdrop against which the Ceasefire Agreement (CFA) was negotiated and concluded in 2001–2002, and deteriorating relations between India and PM Wickremasinghe over the progress of the CFA, also contributed to the overall climate of distrust and estrangement characterizing bilateral relations during this period (DeVotta, 2010, p. 47; Jayatilleka, 2015). That is, the United National Front (UNF) victory in the 2001 General Elections in Sri Lanka had led to a new 'cohabitation government' headed by Wickremasinghe, alongside the executive leadership of Kumaratunga from the opposition party.[19] Given this unique situation of 'split' government, Wickremasinghe was able to shape Sri Lankan foreign policy to a considerable extent (despite the executive presidency being the more powerful office) (Basrur, 2011, p. 252). Although Kumaratunga, Wickremasinghe, and the New Delhi government converged on bilateral economic integration and the need for a political solution to the ethnic Tamil issue, Wickremasinghe diverged from the other two 'parties' in terms of being willing to devolve significantly larger amounts of power to the LTTE during the ceasefire talks, straining bilateral relations to a considerable degree (Uyangoda, 2015; Wijesinha, 2015).[20]

From bandwagoning to balancing: Kumaratunga to Rajapaksa

Explaining Sri Lanka's foreign policy shift towards China

For the Rajapaksa administration, foreign policy was primarily a means to two key domestic ends – the end of the civil war and post-war reconstruction – which, in turn, would cement the legitimacy of his regime. In the immediate post-2005 context, it committed itself to a non-aligned and diversified foreign policy, reflecting the need for as much external support as possible during Eelam War IV (2006–2009). This strategy was largely successful, precluding external intervention (unlike in 1987) in the progress of the war by India or the West despite severe concerns regarding human rights in the latter stages of the war (Jayatilleka, 2015).

While there was implicit support by India and Western nations for an all-out, decisive military campaign, given the regional (and to some extent, global) destabilizing effects and risks the LTTE posed (Uyangoda, 2015), they were unable to provide actual, concrete assistance beyond intelligence, non-lethal weapons, and economic assistance due to domestic political opposition. This included the ethnic Tamil lobby in Tamil Nadu and the Tamil diasporic lobbies that formed significant voting blocs in many Western countries (Gokhale, 2009, pp. 120–121; Rajapaksa, 2016).[21] From 2004 to 2012, the DMK was the third-largest party in the Indian central government ruling coalition and exerted sustained and high-profile resistance to Indian diplomatic support to or strategic cooperation with the GOSL. This largely limited the extent of effective assistance to the Sri Lankan military campaign (and later forced the Indian central government to adopt a hard-liner stance in the post-2009 context regarding the GOSL's alleged war crimes) (Firstpost, 2013). Rajapaksa had no alternative but to turn towards China as its primary source of armaments, military aid, and diplomatic support (Samaranayake, 2011, p. 133).[22]

By the latter stages of Eelam War IV and in the post-2009 context, the civil war had had a crippling effect on Sri Lankan foreign policy, as the all-consuming priority was on defending the government's human rights record – neglecting the fundamentals of a non-aligned foreign policy, which ideally involves engagement with all major powers. In the post-2009 context, Rajapaksa relied heavily on Chinese diplomatic and economic support to withstand international political pressures and sanctions with regard to alleged war crimes, leading to claims of the President being 'authoritarian' and giving Sri Lanka a pariah image in the international arena. China played a critical role in the UN in March–May 2009 when Western allegations of human rights violations with regard to the civil war were made. Using its weight as a permanent member of the UN Security Council (UNSC), along with support from Russia, it strived to keep Sri Lanka off the agenda on the grounds that the war was an internal matter for Sri Lanka and not a threat to international security (Tekwani, 2010, p. 160). Such efforts also proved to be instrumental in defeating a European-backed resolution in May 2009 which called for a war crimes probe into the GOSL's actions during Eelam War IV (Samaranayake, 2011, p. 136). On the economic front, bilateral trade skyrocketed from $660 million in 2005 to $1.13 billion in 2009 (DeSilva-Ranasinghe, 2011, p. 60); and development assistance from China in the period of 1971–2012 amounted to $5056 million, of which 94% was provided during 2004–2012, to become Sri Lanka's largest source of assistance in 2009 (Amarasinghe & Rebert, 2003, p. 12).[23]

Rajapaksa's decision to shift to a balancing foreign policy was mainly driven by the lack of alternative economic, military, and diplomatic assistance both during Eelam War IV and in the post-2009 context.[24] Chinese commercial interests underlying infrastructure development and investment in the island, and the ease with which it conducted business, further facilitated the partnership (Samaranayake, 2016). The Chinese government also had deep pockets and minimal bureaucratic hurdles, which complemented the largely centralized and quasi-authoritarian Rajapaksa regime (Abeyratne, 2015).[25] China was also keen on establishing close political links with the island, as a critical node in China's Maritime Silk Road initiative. Chinese commercial and strategic stakes in the Indian Ocean Region (IOR) were particularly high, given the sizeable volume of Chinese trade and oil imports that transit these waters and due to anxious interpretations of improving U.S.–India bilateral ties (especially in the strategic/defense realm) as a means of Chinese containment (Albert, 2015).[26] China's assistance could also be perceived as general gestures of goodwill, through building political capital and economic development in Sri Lanka, in step with China's increasing economic and naval capabilities *and* in the interests of portraying itself as a benign rising power (Rajapaksa, 2016).

Complementing these dynamics was President Rajapaksa's need to implement visible domestic infrastructure development and generate national economic growth (though one precariously depending on loans rather than actual GDP growth) so as to ensure popular support and regime survival. This is evident, for instance, by the fact that a majority of Chinese-backed development took place in the 'Hambantota Development Zone' (all the more significant due to this district's renowned lack of potential for economic investment) – the impoverished home district of Rajapaksa (Samaranayake, 2011). The administration further adopted a policy of distancing itself from domestic and international pressures for power devolution so as to consolidate a unitary, centralized state as per the increasingly influential 'neoconservative' elements within the ruling coalition (Uyangoda, 2015). A convergence of interests at the systemic and domestic levels therefore characterized Rajapaksa's foreign policy, with Sri Lanka's domestic political, economic, and defense needs being met by Chinese strategic and commercial objectives (Ladduwahetty, 2015).

Explaining Sri Lanka's foreign policy shift away from India

Comprehensive Economic Partnership Agreement

The idea of a CEPA was floated around since 2002, although negotiations only began in 2005. The proposed agreement sought to address many of the shortcomings of the ISLFTA within a more comprehensive economic framework. However, the CEPA was unable to come into completion by the scheduled date of July 2008 as Sri Lanka backed out of signing the agreement that year. This was primarily in response to reservations expressed by sections of the business community, especially from the service sector, which had strong connections within the government (given their political and economic backing of Rajapaksa's military campaign). The primary concerns of this group of lobbyists were the asymmetrical economies of the two countries and a new clause in the agreement which would include competition in the service sector (Law and Society Trust Sri Lanka, 2010, p. 7; Pattanaik, 2012, p. 197). Feeding such apprehensions have been a lack of information and communication by the state on the actual implications of the CEPA, as its complete contents have not been disclosed to the public, with opposition therefore being based more on ideological supposition than factual evidence.

The CEPA was also incompatible with Rajapaksa's domestic-oriented economic ideology and nationalist discourse. The aftermath of the 2009 military victory witnessed the rise of military triumphalism and anti-Indian, Sinhala nationalist elements within the ruling United People's Freedom Alliance (UPFA) (Pattanaik, 2012, p. 198). Such sentiment was especially found within the more hard-line Sinhala nationalist parties in the alliance besides the traditionally anti-Indian JVP, i.e. the JVP-breakaway faction in 2010 – the *Jathika Nidahas Peramuna* (JNP) – and the *Jathika Hela Urumaya* (JHU), who were against the idea of being dependent on India and therefore vulnerable to exploitation. The increasing influence of such elements within the ruling coalition was partly due to the unexpected candidature of General Sarath Fonseka in the 2010 Presidential Elections, who unlike Wickremasinghe (the Leader of the opposition coalition, the UNF, and the most-likely candidate to compete against Rajapaksa), was able to appeal to the Sinhala nationalist electorate that was Rajapaksa's primary vote base (Wijesinha, 2015). Fonseka having had led the victorious boots on the ground negated the utility of Rajapaksa's constant allusions to ending the war as the crux of his election campaign. Rajapaksa was therefore forced to cater to the more extremist nationalist elements within the UPFA and the electorate in order to ensure electoral victory and regime survival (Jayatilleka, 2015; Wijesinha, 2015).

To block implementation of the CEPA, an initiative first proposed by the UNF government in 2002, was also a sort of knee-jerk reaction by the UPFA in discrediting one's political rivals (Jayatilleka, 2015; Pattanaik, 2012, p. 198). In opposing the CEPA, extremist and inflammatory nationalist rhetoric declared that India (along with the Western powers) did not assist Sri Lanka in its hour of need (Sridharan, 2016, p. 67).[27] They argued that while these states imposed cutbacks or conditions on weapons sales to Sri Lanka, they were only mindful of their national interests, and did not consider the helplessness of a fellow democracy at a grave disadvantage against one of the most formidable terrorist groups in the world, despite their rhetoric of democracy and human rights (Sengupta & Ganguly, 2013, p. 105). It was only China (and Pakistan) who enabled and ensured the *actual* defense of Sri Lanka's sovereignty and territorial integrity (Jayatilleka, 2015;

Wijesinha, 2015).[28] By not caving in to cooperation with India, Rajapaksa's image as a nationalist was strengthened, thereby obviating dependence on India which could have been otherwise leveraged by the latter with regard to the ethnic Tamil issue (Pattanaik, 2012, pp. 198, 207). Although similar concerns had been present during the ISLFTA negotiations, strong political will on the part of Kumaratunga ensured its ultimate completion (Pattanaik, 2012, p. 197). In contrast, the monopolization of the political space following the defeat of the LTTE, coupled with factionalism within the main opposition party (the UNP), provided the latitude for anti-Indian, 'neoconservative' factions within the ruling coalition to dominate the foreign policy decision-making calculus (Pattanaik, 2012, p. 197).

The CEPA's eventual fate demonstrated the link between domestic politics and foreign policy stemming primarily from the domestic imperative of retaining political power. Accordingly, when foreign policy actions are incompatible with domestic priorities and pressures, political leaders may be compelled to adjust foreign policy actions: '[P]olitical leaders in elective office aim to survive. It is contexts and circumstances when fundamental changes in foreign policy serve that ultimate end that fundamental alterations of policy are most likely to occur' (Volgy & Schwarz, 1991, p. 618). This influence of domestic stakeholders on foreign policy is likely to increase in a context of 'hung parliament' which forces undue dependence on smaller, coalition parties and other interest groups, which is very similar to the situation Rajapaksa faced.

India–Sri Lanka–Maldives Maritime Agreement

The India–Sri Lanka–Maldives Maritime Agreement is a trilateral security agreement signed in 2013. The agreement is essentially a roadmap for cooperation in maritime security, comprising initiatives to enhance Maritime Domain Awareness (MDA) through access to systems under the protection of the International Maritime Organization; training and capacity building initiatives in areas of Search and Rescue, and Oil Pollution Response; and joint activities including trilateral maritime exercises, protecting sea lines of communications (SLOCs) from illegal maritime activities, and anti-piracy operations (MEA, 2014). The trilateral initiative was an interesting development – why would a 'pro-China' GOSL that had backed out of the CEPA and an India which had voted against Sri Lanka in the 2012 and 2013 UNHCR resolutions enter into a security agreement that very year?

That strategic cooperation in these maritime waters is a necessity given the Exclusive Economic Zones (EEZs) and SLOCs located in these critical waterways provides part of the answer, as any disruption in activity would most certainly result in severe security and economic implications on a regional, and even global, scale (Samatha, 2015, p. 3). Converging strategic and economic interests of the member states to maintain regional stability, share burdens, and avoid duplicity of operations, with the very nature of transnational non-traditional security threats requiring a coordinated effort, all contributed towards the initiative.

India's apprehensions of Sri Lanka and the Maldives moving closer to China (and Pakistan as well, for Sri Lanka) also led to its support for this trilateral grouping (Izzadeen, 2015; Samaranayake, 2011). Sri Lanka's strategic location, in particular, is critical in the defense of India's southwestern and southeastern coastlines. Its war-time reliance on China's arms had led to the development of post-conflict defense cooperation with the latter, including training exchanges, thereby sustaining Indian insecurities. For instance, in 2007, India protested against Sri Lanka's acquisition of a Chinese-built JY-11 3D radar system on the grounds that it would overarch Indian airspace (DeSilva-Ranasinghe, 2011, pp. 63, 65). Perhaps the epitome of such anxieties was the docking of Chinese submarines twice in 2014 without prior notification of India (Samaranayake, 2015). The maritime agreement could then be seen as part of India's attempts to establish its pre-eminence in the region, especially given the growing maritime presence of external actors in the IOR – such as China, the U.S., and Japan, who were increasing bilateral contacts with littoral states in joint naval exercises and provision of military assistance (Jacob, 2010, p. 95; KDU, 2015). Likewise, the agreement could also be seen as a 'correction' policy on Sri Lanka's part after realizing that they were placing all their eggs in one basket (i.e. China) (Jayatilleka, 2015).

The agreement was also a 'low-key' security arrangement (unlike a DCA) and the very trilateral nature of the agreement served to ameliorate the domestic opposition (from India and Sri Lanka) that may have otherwise emerged (Samatha, 2015, p. 2). Moreover, despite the ups and downs of bilateral political relations, there had existed a considerable degree of assistance and coordination between the two militaries since the 1990s (including military exchanges and intelligence sharing), particularly concerning maritime security (Hettiarachchi, 2015). India too had, in the recent past, being warming up to the idea of increased bilateral military cooperation, as it dropped Sri Lanka from her 'negative list' for defense supplies during the 2002 CFA, after having banned *any* transfer of military supplies to Sri Lanka for the preceding six years (Orland, 2008, pp. 15, 19). The timing of the trilateral agreement being after the civil war had ended also made India–Sri Lanka strategic cooperation less sensitive to domestic constituencies within India (Orland, 2008, p. 19; Wijesinha, 2015). China's non-zero sum attitude towards existing security and economic relations with the smaller states in the region is relevant here as well, as it maintained that these states' bilateral relations with India need not be compromised on account of deepening engagement with China (Jayatilleka, 2015; Wijesinha, 2015).

Explaining shifts in Sri Lankan foreign policymaking

Both the ISLFTA and bilateral security linkages during the Kumaratunga administration illustrate how India was perceived during this period as a source of economic opportunity and an indispensable political and strategic partner. Such overtures would have been inconceivable during the Jayewardene or Premadasa administrations, whose balancing foreign policies stand in marked contrast and clearly demonstrate the shift from a balancing to a bandwagoning foreign policy in the post-1994 context. With regard to foreign economic policy, domestic imperatives and actors within Sri Lanka – that is, the top political leadership and policymakers – played a primary role in shaping the decision to engage with India through economic initiatives such as the ISLFTA. While there were systemic changes which facilitated this foreign policy shift to one of 'bandwagoning,' their timing or limited impact preclude claims of sole responsibility to the FTA. In contrast, systemic factors alone, especially within India's domestic political arena, largely accounted for India's inability to cooperate with Sri Lanka on its government's request for military assistance in 2000, and the DCA and Hambantota Port proposals in 2002. Domestic factors were negligible, as the majority sentiment within Sri Lanka's leadership and policymakers strongly favored strategic cooperation with India.

Table 1. Impact of systemic and domestic factors on Sri Lankan foreign policymaking.

		Type of foreign policy issue	
		Economic-related	Security-related
Key determinant of foreign policy	Systemic-level		X
	Domestic-level	X	

Source: Author (December 2016).

The high levels of strategic, economic, and diplomatic dependence of the Rajapaksa administration on China, in marked contrast to the limited strategic, economic, and diplomatic support by India during this period clearly demonstrate the shift from a bandwagoning to a balancing foreign policy. On foreign economic policy, the CEPA was unable to take off due to reservations expressed by sections of the Sri Lankan business community, as well as incompatibility with Rajapaksa's domestic-oriented economic ideology and nationalist discourse, despite the interest Indian counterparts continue to express in the CEPA.[29] The India–Sri Lanka–Maldives Maritime Agreement, on the other hand, was driven primarily by the dual systemic imperatives of India's need to counter China's increasing influence in the subcontinent and the necessity of multilateral cooperation in securing the SLOCs of the IOR. While domestic-level factors facilitated an environment conducive to the signing of the Agreement, they were for the most part only supporting, secondary influencers. Table 1 illustrates these findings.

A number of policy recommendations follow from the discussion on the sources of foreign policymaking in this paper. First, a state's foreign policymaking calculus has to be aware of geopolitical realities. For Sri Lanka, given its geographical location and capabilities, it needs to recognize the indispensability of India as a strategic and economic benefactor. Any action that blatantly antagonizes India should be avoided as far as possible, even if doing so provides political capital in the domestic arena. Second, while being cognizant of India's importance, Sri Lanka must pursue a foreign policy that is diversified and independent of any one power's influence. While good political relations must be maintained with India, Sri Lanka should realize that India's domestic interests and its global preoccupations may not always allow its interests to be aligned with that of Sri Lanka's. It may therefore be in Sri Lanka's interests to have an extra-regional balancer such as China but to also pursue sound political and economic relations with India. Finally, Sri Lanka's foreign policy must be less reactionary and more stable. While the shifts examined in this paper are for the most part necessities in light of domestic and international developments, at times, some of the changes are driven by knee-jerk political reactions in the interest of political capital. It is also very important that the respective governments do not overtly identify with any state/s since this would then set a precedent; any subsequent corrective measures would only serve to stir the sensitivities of these partners. Furthermore, a constantly shifting foreign policy prevents the development of long-term political relations and their related benefits.

Conclusion

The objective of this paper was to determine if small state foreign policy shifts were driven solely by system-level factors, or whether domestic-level factors had additional utility in providing a more comprehensive explanation and were even able to exert a determinative influence under certain circumstances. Three main arguments were made to this end: first, the shifts from a balancing or bandwagoning strategy are not predominantly driven purely by systemic or domestic factors, but at various times by one or the other, and sometimes together. Second, in the domain of foreign economic policymaking, domestic imperatives and actors appear to play a decisive role, although within the broader structural preconditions. Third, systemic factors maintain predominance over domestic-level factors in shaping foreign security policy.

It is acknowledged that analysis in this paper was bounded by the concepts of 'bandwagoning' and 'balancing.' Although such characterizations of the various administrations' foreign policies were made to the purpose of analytical clarification, and do accurately reflect the overall nature of these administrations' foreign policies, it is also recognized that actual foreign policy is rarely so dichotomous. Therefore, while the analytical utility of such categorization is appreciated, it is also emphasized that actual foreign policy during the period under scrutiny involved attempts at engaging with all major players, i.e. at various degrees of engagement, rather than an 'engagement-no engagement' dichotomy.

This paper also opens up avenues for future research within the ambit of Sri Lankan foreign policy, as well as for small state foreign policy within the region. In terms of the latter category, it would be interesting to examine shifts in small state foreign policy within the region (i.e. of Nepal, Bangladesh, Bhutan, and the Maldives) vis-à-vis India and China (and even the U.S.) and whether they reflect a dynamic similar to that of this study, or embody a different disposition altogether. In terms of the former category, it would be interesting to examine the foreign policy strategies employed from independence in 1948–1977, as well as in the current context. In the post-2015 context, the current Sirisena-Wickremasinghe administration is observed to pursue a different strategy of 'balancing,' comprising strategic maneuvering through pro-active economic and diplomatic engagement with a number of regional and global powers, including India, China, and the U.S. Such adaptive and pragmatic foreign policymaking allows Sri Lanka to overcome the vulnerabilities of its size, while exploiting opportunities that present themselves during great power rivalry. However, its ability to do so is being constantly checked by geopolitical and geoeconomic realities: while the new administration has attempted to engage more with India and the West, especially in terms of political relations (in order to redress the tilt away from them during the preceding administration), this is unviable on the economic front by greater reliance on China for the country's economic survival, as good relations with India and the West do not necessarily translate to commensurate economic benefits (Jayatilleka, 2015). Nevertheless, while heightened engagement with certain states admittedly do not translate to tangible and immediate economic gains, the political goodwill and diplomatic support generated from such associations have an intangible value of their own.

Notes

1. India's total land area is 46 times of its neighboring island; has a population of 1.32 billion against Sri Lanka's 22.27 million; India's GDP (Purchasing Power Parity) is $4.99 trillion in comparison to Sri Lanka's $134.5 billion; and has a defense budget of $40 billion (versus Sri Lanka's $1.5 billion) and a military 8.5 times that of Sri Lanka.
2. The economic liberalization program had significant domestic drivers given the fairly serious domestic economic crisis in 1975–1976.
3. Jayewardene could not turn to India for either of these issues due to India's poor economic performance as a result of its socialist, autarkic economic policies at the time; strained personal relations between Jayewardene and Mrs Gandhi; belief that Western armaments and technology were superior; and anxiety that Tamil Nadu pressures would make Indian assistance

politically impossible. Wijesinha (2015) and Jayatilleka (2015), however, make the clarification that this second objective was a consequence of the first, i.e. securing Western financial assistance to back the national economic liberalization program and the resulting proxy war waged by India via the Tamil militants.

4. Sridharan (2016) argues that it in addition to security concerns, domestic concerns at the center about alienation in Tamil Nadu and Congress revival plans in Tamil Nadu contributed to India's motivations for the 1987 intervention. Uyangoda (2015) states that the 1987 Indian intervention in Sri Lanka defined the tenor of bilateral relations thereafter, as the memory of the intervention is evoked by the latter as a constant reminder of India's aggressive hegemonic potential, and of the need to factor in Indian interests as well.
5. Kumaratunga had her own special relationship outside that of her mother, i.e. her husband Vijaya Kumaratunga who founded the Sri Lanka Mahajana Party (SLMP) which had close links with India.
6. Such anti-Indian sentiment was present in Nepal in response to the stringent economic sanctions imposed by India in the late 1980s. Similarly, the left wing of Bangladesh politics claimed that the country had been reduced to a 'mere satellite, "another Himalayan kingdom"' of India, while the political right charged that 'Bangladesh had escaped from the Punjabi embrace of West Pakistan only to fall under the Hindu juggernaut.' In the Maldives, India's support for the former Maldivian President Mohamed Nasheed caused the successor government to regard India with suspicion.
7. Due to the end of bloc power politics, India was less sensitive of its neighboring states engaging with extra-regional powers, alongside its ties with the U.S. rapidly improving in the post-1991 period, especially since the mid-1990s due to converging economic and strategic interests.
8. In the post-Cold War context, India's chief security concern shifted to the destabilizing presence of the LTTE in the region particularly in terms of the negative security externalities of maritime security and refugee influx in south India. This is especially due to the high economic stakes India has on the SLOC in the IOR, given its 1991 trade-oriented economic reforms and aspirations to be a great power, with nearly 89% of its oil imports and over 70% of its maritime trade arriving via the Colombo Port.
9. Sridharan (2016) discusses the split in Tamil Nadu public opinion in the 1990s following the shock of Rajiv Gandhi's assassination. Following the banning of the LTTE by the center in 1992, the *All India Anna Dravida Munnetra Kazhagam* (AIADMK) led by Jayalalitha in Tamil Nadu swept to power (in coalition with the Congress Party) and cracked down hard on the LTTE, carrying the public opinion with her.
10. Such a policy is in line with the basic tenets of functionalism which posits that cooperation should first be pursued in less-controversial areas of economic and social cooperation, and that through actor socialization, communication, and interaction, this will lead to building of trust and positive spillovers in the more salient areas of politics and security.
11. India's economic growth rates of 3.82% in 1984 and 1.06% in 1991 rose to an annual rate of 7.57% in 1995.
12. Since this, India signed a Preferential Trade Agreement with Afghanistan in 2003, a Trade Agreement with Bangladesh in 2006, and a Treaty of Trade with Nepal in 2009.
13. For instance, Dixit (1992) states that during a discussion between Premadasa and foreign VIPs, Premadasa openly condemned India's dominant, unilateral role in Sri Lanka's domestic crisis; and Jayewardene (1992) stated: 'The fear of Indian dominance is a major characteristic of the security perception of the South Asian countries.'
14. It is important to note that the Indian central government had strong incentives to form a strategic partnership with Sri Lanka – reflected in the joint statement released by Wickremasinghe and then-Indian PM Vajpayee in 2003, indicating mutual interest in working towards a DCA and also a Memorandum of Understanding on joint rehabilitation of the Palaly Airforce Base. However, progress on these fronts were stalled primarily due to domestic opposition from Tamil Nadu.
15. The Hambantota Port has been acknowledged as being largely an initiative by Wickremasinghe, partly accounted for by the fact that although Wickremasinghe did not share the same political

16. rapport that Kumaratunga had with India (and was a classic UNP product that favored pro-Western, free market policies), he recognized the immense economic dividends through cooperating with India and the political costs of alienating India. It was during his term that the Indo-Lanka CEPA negotiations began; Wickremasinghe also proposed a land bridge between the two countries – although none of these initiatives were completed during his Premiership.
16. India realized only later that it had miscalculated and started moving quickly on the Kankesanthurai Port.
17. In December 2016, a Framework Agreement was signed by the GOSL towards the leasing of 80% of the Hambantoota Port to China Merchants Ports Holding Company in a debt-for-equity swap. China Merchants Ports Holdings Company expects to revive the Port, investing around U.S.$1.12 billion in this Public Private Partnership. The Framework Agreement also included the offer of a 99-year lease over 15,000 acres of land to build an economic hinterland for the Port. However, amidst strong public protests over the deal, the Sri Lankan cabinet has decided to re-negotiate the deal – see Balachandran (2017).
18. In addition, although the GOSL reached out to potential U.S. investors, there was no interest reciprocated given the continued viability of the Colombo Port and the ongoing civil war being perceived as a potential financial risk.
19. Both Kumaratunga and Wickremasinghe were aware of the need to engage with India economically, given the high costs of war; instability that results from poor economic conditions; and consequently, regime survival. Due to the war, Western and Japanese economic interests in Sri Lanka had receded, and the Chinese economy had not yet started to venture into offshore engagements on the scale that it did in the post-2000 context.
20. Both Kumaratunga and the New Delhi government feared that devolving too much power to the LTTE would only feed its secessionist ambitions, thereby failing to provide a lasting solution to the ethnic Tamil issue which honoured Sri Lanka's sovereignty. The Indian central government never favored the idea of a Tamil Eelam state as it feared this would lead to regional instability and encourage similar sentiments in its state of Tamil Nadu.
21. This includes a 2007 U.S. arms embargo to Sri Lanka. Gokhale makes the argument that although domestic compulsions forced India to adopt a superficial, hands-off policy, India quietly gifted five Mi-17 helicopters to the Sri Lankan Air Force. He does acknowledge, however, that India 'could not go beyond such meagre and clandestine transfer of military hardware.' Then-Defence Secretary, Gotabhaya Rajapaksa, too alludes to the close bilateral relations during Eelam War IV through the 'Troika' mechanism (comprising three key officials from the Sri Lankan and Indian sides).
22. In 2008, Sri Lanka received $75 million worth of Chinese arms shipments against a mere $10 million in 2006. In contrast, SIPRI data for the U.S. and India indicated empty data cells or declining arms exports to Sri Lanka.
23. This included the $1.4 billion Chinese-financed Colombo Port City; an agreement to create the $28 million Mirigama EEZ; and assistance by way of technical expertise and concessional loans for many high-scale infrastructure projects such as the Norochcholai Power Plant in Puttalam, Hambantota Port, Colombo Port terminal expansion, expressways, railway lines, etc.
24. China also fitted Sri Lanka's requirement for a reliable ally so as to reduce its dependence on the West (and India) as the 2002 peace talks indicated partiality by the West towards the 'pro-LTTE' Tamil diaspora and even the LTTE.
25. This was in contrast to the bureaucratic bottlenecks and limited funding on the part of India which restrained its ability to provide similar levels of assistance to Sri Lanka. China also did not impose the kind of preconditions required by Western entities, such as mandatory economic reforms for economic assistance and loans by the International Monetary Fund.
26. Approximately 84% of China's imported energy resources transit the IOR.
27. Sridharan (2016), however, argues that another reason for India's stance (besides domestic Tamil Nadu pressures) was the 'increasingly blatant reneging on commitments [especially of power devolution] made to India at the highest level by the Rajapaksa regime.'
28. Rajapaksa was led to a false sense of security of Chinese patronage by his close advisors who did not have a good grasp of geopolitical realities and thereby failed to realize the limits of

Chinese support and the necessity of Indian goodwill. Thus, while Rajapaksa had managed to balance well relations with India and China during the war, post-war military triumphalism and the accompanying rise of neo-conservatism within the ruling coalition led to the deterioration of the diplomatic rapport between Sri Lanka and India.
29. Following strong public opposition to the CEPA, the current Sirisena-Wickremasinghe government proposed in 2015 another bilateral economic agreement in place of the CEPA called the Indo-Sri Lanka Economic and Technology Cooperation Framework Agreement (ECTA). Public opposition to ECTA is high as it essentially contains similar contents to the CEPA.

Acknowledgements

The author extends her appreciation to colleagues and the interviewees in this study for their insights and time – namely Dr Rajesh Basrur, Dr Anit Mukherjee, Dr Dayan Jayatilleka, Dr Rajiva Wijesinha, Dr Rohan Gunaratna, Ms Nilanthi Samaranayake, Mr Gotabhaya Rajapaksa, Dr Jayadeva Uyangoda, Mr Chaminda Hettiarachchi, Mr Ameen Izzadeen, Dr Sirimal Abeyratne, and sources from the Ministry of Foreign Affairs (Sri Lanka), the University of Colombo, the Kotelawala Defence University, and the Sri Lankan military. Any errors, of course, are all mine.

Disclosure statement

The opinions expressed in this article are the author's own and do not reflect the views of the Institute of Defence and Strategic Studies, S. Rajaratnam School of International Studies, Nanayang Technological University.

References

Abeyratne, S. (2015, December 22). *Interview by Rajni Gamage*. Personal interview, Colombo.
Albert, E. (2016, May 19). *Competition in the Indian Ocean*. Council on Foreign Relations. Retrieved November 23, 2016, from http://www.cfr.org/regional-security/competition-indian-ocean/p37201
Amarasinghe, D., & Rebert, J. (2003). *Dynamics and trends of foreign aid in Sri Lanka: Exploring space for context-sensitive aid delivery*. International Alert, pp. 1–24.
Balachandran, P. K. (2017, January 5). Sri Lanka re-negotiating Hambantota Port deal with China. *The New Indian Express*. Retrieved January 17, 2017, from http://www.newindianexpress.com/world/2017/jan/05/sri-lanka-re-negotiating-hambantota-port-deal-with-china-1556482.html
Basrur, R. (2011). Foreign policy reversal: The politics of Sri Lanka's economic relations with India. In E. Sridharan (Ed.), *International relations theory and South Asia*. New Delhi: Oxford University Press (Chapter 6).
Behera, S. K., & Mukherji, I. N. (2013). Indo-Sri Lanka Free Trade Agreement: An analysis of merchandise trade. In I. N. Mukherji, & K. Iyengar (Eds.), *Deepening economic cooperation between India and Sri Lanka* (pp. 14–52). Manila, Philippines: Asian Development Bank (Chapter 2).
De Silva, K. M. (1995). *Regional powers and small state security: India and Sri Lanka, 1977–1990*. Washington, DC: Woodrow Wilson Press.
DeSilva-Ranasinghe, S. (2011). Another bead in the 'String of Pearls'? Interpreting Sri Lanka's foreign policy realignment. *China Security*, *19*, 57–67.
Destradi, S. (2012). India and Sri Lanka's civil war: The failure of regional conflict management in South Asia. *Asian Survey*, *52*(3), 595–616.

DeVotta, N. (1998). Sri Lanka's structural adjustment program and its impact on Indo-Lanka relations. *Asian Survey*, *38*(5), 457–473.

DeVotta, N. (2010). When individuals, states, and systems collide. In S. Ganguly (Ed.), *India's foreign policy: Retrospect and prospect* (pp. 32–61). New Delhi: Oxford University Press.

Firstpost. (2013, March 19). *Our way or else ... the DMK's history of threatening the UPA*. Retrieved November 30, 2015, from http://www.firstpost.com/politics/our-way-or-else-the-dmks-history-of-threatening-the-upa-666776.html

Foulon, M. (2015). Neoclassical realism: Challengers and bridging identities. *International Studies Review*, *17*, 635–661.

Galbreath, D. (2006). Latvian foreign policy after enlargement: Continuity and change. *Cooperation and Conflict*, *41*, 443–462.

Gokhale, N. A. (2009). *Sri Lanka: From war to peace*. New Delhi: Har-Anand.

Goldgeier, J. M., & McFaul, M. (1992). A tale of two worlds: Core and periphery in the post-Cold War era. *International Organization*, *46*(2), 467–491.

Gunaratna, R. (2016, January 12). *Interview by Rajni Gamage*. Personal interview, Singapore.

Gunasena, J. T. S. (2013). Neorealism versus two level game theory in explaining Sri Lanka's foreign policy responses towards the external compulsions (1993 to 2005). *Humanities and Social Sciences Review*, *2*(4), 217–233.

Gvalia, G., Siroki, D., Lebanidze, B., & Iashvili, Z. (2013). Thinking outside the Bloc: Explaining the foreign policies of small states. *Security Studies*, *22*(98), 98–131.

Handel, M. (1981). *Weak States in the international system*. London: Frank Cass.

Hettiarachchi, C. (2015, December 30). *Interview by Rajni Gamage*. Personal interview, Colombo.

Hewitt, V. (1997). *The new international politics of South Asia*. Manchester: Manchester University Press.

Hey, J. A. K. (2003). Introducing small state foreign policy. In J. A. K. Hey (Ed.), *Small states in world politics: Explaining foreign policy behaviour*. Boulder, CO: Lynne Rienner (Chapter 1).

Izzadeen, A. (2015, December 22). *Interview by Rajni Gamage*. Personal interview, Colombo.

Jacob, H. (2010). Neoclassical realism and Indian foreign policy. In A. Mattoo, & H. Jacob (Eds.), *Shaping India's foreign policy: People, politics and places*. New Delhi: Har-Anand (Chapter 3).

Jayatilleka, D. (2015, December 23). *Interview by Rajni Gamage*. Personal interview, Colombo.

Kelegama, J. B. (1999). Indo-Sri Lanka Free Trade Agreement. *South Asian Survey*, *6*(2), 283–296.

Kelegama, S. (2014). *The India–Sri Lanka Free Trade Agreement and the proposed Comprehensive Economic Partnership Agreement: A closer look*. ADBI working paper series, no. 458, pp. 1–16.

Kelegama, S. (2016). China as a balancer in South Asia: An economic perspective with special reference to Sri Lanka. In T. Fingard (Ed.), *The new great game: China and South and Central Asia in the era of reform*. Stanford: Stanford University Press.

Kotelawala Defence University (KDU) Sources. (2015, December 21). *Interview by Rajni Gamage*. Personal interview, Colombo.

Labs, E. (1992). Do weak states bandwagon? *Security Studies*, *1*(3), 383–416.

Ladduwahetty, N. (2015, February 18). *Revisiting Sri Lanka's foreign policy*. One Text Initiative. Retrieved December 11, 2015, from http://www.onetext.org/revisiting-sri-lankas-foreign-policy/

Ladduwahetty, R. (2002, June 18). Hambantota Port will attract 36,000 ships annually – Ananda Kularatne. *Daily News*. Retrieved December 11, 2015, from http://archives.dailynews.lk/2002/06/18/bus04.html

Law and Society Trust Sri Lanka. (2010). *'An act of faith'? Ten years of the India–Sri Lanka Free Trade Agreement (ISLFTA)*, pp. 1–19.

Mahdiyeva, N. (2011). *Power games in the Caucus: Azerbaijan's foreign and energy policy towards the West, Russia and the Middle East*. New York, US: L. B. Tauris.

Mara, F. O. (2003). Paraguay: From the Stronato to the democratic transition. In J. A. K. Hey (Ed.), *Small states in world politics: Explaining foreign policy behaviour*. Boulder, CO: Lynne Rienner (Chapter 2).

Ministry of External Affairs. (2014, March 6). *NSA level meeting on trilateral maritime security cooperation between India, Sri Lanka and Maldives*. Ministry of External Affairs, Government of India. Retrieved April 21, 2016, from http://www.mea.gov.in/in-focus-article.htm?23037/NSA+level+meeting+on+trilateral+Maritime+Security+Cooperation+between+India+Sri+Lanka+and+Maldives

Mukherji, I. N., & Iyengar, K. (2013). Introduction. In I. N. Mukherji, & K. Iyengar (Eds.), *Deepening economic cooperation between India and Sri Lanka* (pp. 1–13). Manila, Philippines: Asian Development Bank (Chapter 1).

Orland, B. (2008). *India's Sri Lanka policy: Towards economic engagement*. IPCS Research Papers, pp. 1–25.

Pattanaik, S. S. (2012). Sri Lanka: Challenges and opportunities for India. In R. Dahiya, & A. K. Behuria (Eds.), *India's neighbourhood: Challenges in the next two decades*. New Delhi: IDSA (Chapter 9).

Rajapaksa, G. (2016, January, 15). *Interview by Rajni Gamage*. Personal interview (telephone conversation), Colombo.

Rose, G. (1998). Review: Neoclassical realism and theories of foreign policy. *World Politics*, *51*(1), 144–172.

Samaranayake, N. (2011). Are Sri Lanka's relations with China deepening? An analysis of economic, military, and diplomatic data. *Asian Security*, *7*(2), 119–146.

Samaranayake, N. (2015, March 31). India's key to Sri Lanka: Maritime infrastructure development. *The Diplomat*. Retrieved February 15, 2016, from http://thediplomat.com/2015/03/indias-key-to-sri-lanka-maritime-infrastructure-development/

Samaranayake, N. (2016, January 18). *Interview by Rajni Gamage*. Personal interview (Skype conversation), Washington, DC.

Samatha, M. (2015, July 8). *India, Sri Lanka and Maldives trilateral maritime security cooperation: Political and economic constraints in implementation*. Retrieved February 15, 2016, from http://www.icwa.in/pdfs/PB/2014/IndiaSriLankaMaldivesPB08072015.pdf

Schweller, R. L. (2004). Unanswered threats: A neoclassical realist theory of underbalancing. *International Security*, *29*(2), 159–201.

Sengupta, D., & Ganguly, R. (2013). Diffusion, mediation, suppression: India's varied strategy towards the Tamil insurgency in Sri Lanka. *Journal of South Asian Development*, *8*(1), 105–125.

Sikdar, C., & Chakraborty, D. (2012, June 24–29). *Bilateral trade between India and Sri Lanka – Does factor content matter?* 20th IIOA conference, Slovakia, pp. 1–25.

Sikri, R. (2009). *Challenge and strategy: Rethinking India's foreign policy*. New Delhi: SAGE.

Sivarajah, A. (2003, November 28–30). *Sri Lanka's foreign policy since 1994*. Paper submitted for the 9th international conference on Sri Lanka studies, Matara, Sri Lanka.

Skidmore, D. (1997). *Contested social orders and international politics*. Tennessee: Venderbilt University Press.

Sridharan, E. (2016). Indo-Sri Lanka relations: Geopolitics, domestic politics, or something more. In S. Ganguly (Ed.), *Engaging the world: Indian foreign policy since 1947*. New Delhi: Oxford University Press (Chapter 2).

Sridharan, K. (2008). *Regional organisations and conflict management: Comparing ASEAN and SAARC*. Working paper 33. Regional and Global Axes of Conflict, NUS, pp. 1–29.

Tekwani, S. (2010). Sri Lanka: Transnational security and postinsurgency issues. In D. Fouse (Ed.), *Issue for engagement: Asian perspectives on transnational security challenges* (pp. 154–166). Asia Pacific Centre for Security Studies.

Uyangoda, J. (2015, December 18). *Interview by Rajni Gamage*. Personal interview, Colombo.

Velloor, R. (2013, October). 'A man who loves his country,' Mahinda Rajapaksa's interview to the *Strait Times*.

Volgy, T. J., & Schwarz, J. E. (1991). Does politics stop at the water's edge? Domestic political factors and foreign policy restructuring in the cases of Great Britain, France, and West Germany. *Journal of Politics*, *53*(3), 615–643.

Walt, S. M. (1987). *The origin of alliances*. Ithaca, NY: Cornell University Press.

Wijesinha, R. (2015, December 24). *Interview by Rajni Gamage*. Personal interview, Colombo.

Wilson, A. J. (1974). Sri Lanka's foreign policy – Change and continuity. *CJHSS, n.s., IV*(1&2), 52–61.

World Bank. *Public data*. Retrieved February 19, 2016, from https://www.google.com.sg/publicdata/explore?ds=d5bncppjof8f9_&met_y=ny_gdp_mktp_kd_zg&idim=country:IND:PAK:USA&hl=en&dl=en#!ctype=l&strail=false&bcs=d&nselm=h&met_y=ny_gdp_mktp_kd_zg&scale_y=lin&ind_y=false&rdim=region&idim=country:IND&ifdim=region&hl=en_US&dl=en&ind=false

Cocos and Christmas Islands: building Australia's strategic role in the Indian Ocean

David Brewster and Rory Medcalf

ABSTRACT
Australia's Cocos Islands and Christmas Island are remote islands with potentially great significance for Australia's strategic role in the eastern Indian Ocean region and the wider Indo-Pacific. This paper explores the growing militarization of islands throughout the Indian Ocean in the context of growing strategic competition in the region. It then considers the strategic value of Australia's Indian Ocean territories and makes recommendations about the further development of defense infrastructure to potentially support Australian air operations in Southeast Asia and the eastern Indian Ocean. Upgraded facilities on both Cocos and Christmas would provide Australia with valuable leverage in its relationships with regional defense partners and the United States.

Introduction

Australia's Indian Ocean territories – the Cocos Islands and Christmas Island – are remote tropical islands with small populations and potential as tourist destinations. But they also potentially have great significance for Australia's strategic role in the eastern Indian Ocean region (IOR) and the wider Indo-Pacific. This paper explores the growing militarization of islands throughout the Indian Ocean occurring in the context of growing strategic competition between major powers in the region. It then focuses on the strategic value of Australia's Indian Ocean territories and makes recommendations about their future defense use. It concludes that Australia's willingness to commit defense resources, related infrastructure investment and diplomatic utility to its Indian Ocean islands will, beyond pure military considerations, be an important signal of Australia's strategic intent in the region.

The strategic changes we are now witnessing across the Indo-Pacific region will likely include a period of strategic instability and change in the IOR. An uncertain strategic environment in the IOR will have significant consequences for Australia, including for the importance to Australia of its Indian Ocean territories. Among other things, it provides strong reasons for Australia to further develop infrastructure on both the Cocos and Christmas Islands, for use by Australian defence forces and potentially by allied or like-minded forces also. This paper argues that such infrastructure should be developed by Australia to be available to support Australian air operations in Southeast Asia and the eastern Indian Ocean, including in case facilities currently used by Australia in the region become unavailable. We also argue that upgraded facilities on both Cocos and Christmas would provide Australia with valuable leverage in its relationships with regional defense partners and the United States.

This paper first provides an overview of the coming period of strategic change and uncertainty in the Indo-Pacific region. Second, it discusses the growing strategic importance of defense infrastructure on islands throughout the Indian Ocean, including moves by the United States, China and India to develop infrastructure in the region. Third, it will discuss the strategic importance of the Cocos Islands and Christmas Island for Australia. Fourth, it will consider the value of Australia's Indian Ocean territories for its regional defense partnerships.

The coming period of strategic change and uncertainty in the indo-pacific region

Over the coming decade, we are likely to see significant strategic changes occurring right across the Indo-Pacific region (Medcalf, 2014b). The changing balance of economic and military power in East Asia and the western Pacific, including the South China Sea, and its potential consequences for Australia has been the subject of considerable public debate. There has been considerably less public discussion about the IOR, which is also likely to experience the greatest period of strategic change seen in about 50 years. These changes and uncertainties in Southeast Asia and the IOR will create strong imperatives for Australia to further develop defense infrastructure on its Indian Ocean territories.

Australia has long relied on 'great and powerful friends' as the dominant security providers in the Indian Ocean. From the early nineteenth century until the late 1960s, except for a brief interregnum in the early 1940s, the Royal Navy held virtually undisputed dominance of the Indian Ocean, more or less making it a 'British lake.' From the late 1970s, the United States became the dominant naval power in the Indian Ocean. The regional dominance of Australia's allies allowed it to underinvest in its contribution to maritime security in the IOR, including drastically underinvesting in defense infrastructure in Western Australia and Australia's Indian Ocean Territories.

The last major power change in the Indian Ocean occurred in the 1970s, triggered by the decolonization of Britain's Indian Ocean colonies and the withdrawal of the British military forces from east of Suez. At that time, Australia played a role in encouraging a transition from Britain to the United States as dominant naval power in the Indian Ocean, in a manner quite favorable to Australia. This included, among other things, supporting the development of Diego Garcia as a major US military base that could extend the reach of US forces throughout the IOR. Although the Soviet Union and radical Islamism presented some challenges after the late 1970s, US military predominance in the IOR has never been in serious doubt since that time.

In the coming decade, we are likely to see a new period of strategic change in the IOR which involves several new factors and players. This an important reason why Australia is giving greater recognition of the strategic importance of the IOR and the need for it to play a more active role there. As the Australian Defence White Paper 2016 notes:

> The Indian Ocean region is also likely to become a more significant zone of competition among major powers, with China, India and the United States all increasing their levels of military activity in this region. (Australian Government, 2016, paras 292–293)

Importantly, this new transition in military power is unlikely to be as smooth as the transition between two Anglo-Saxon powers in the 1970s and will likely require significantly more attention and investment by Australia in order to maintain a favorable strategic environment. Among other things, the multipolar nature of this coming change makes the outline of the coming regional order relatively uncertain.

Although the United States is likely to continue to be the strongest military power in the IOR for some years to come, there is a significant risk that there will be a reduction of US defense resources committed to the region. Such a development would only accelerate the trend towards declining US influence, strategic instability and competition. Some in the region, particularly Indian analysts, have for some time expected (or hoped for) a gradual 'withering away' of US military power analogous to the gradual withering away of British military power in the Indian Ocean that occurred in the decades after 1945 (Brewster, 2015b). While it is likely to be in Australia's interests to seek to extend US military dominance in the IOR for as long as possible, the Trump administration could create new risks for the region and for Australia. One risk arises from perceptions of reduced US credibility as a reliable ally, which could undermine US influence with regional partners. Another risk arises from the potential for unpredictability of US policy under the new administration which has been suggested by Trump's rhetoric and actions. That remains to be seen but, indeed, there is a realistic possibility that the United States could become a cause of strategic uncertainty and unpredictability in the region, rather than an unalloyed pillar of stability. This could occur, for example, in case of a significant deterioration in US relations with countries such as Saudi Arabia, Iran or China. Any such development would be of significant concern to Australia.

In conjunction with these uncertainties surrounding the role of the United States in the IOR, other powers are playing an increasingly important role in the region. This will almost inevitably make it a much more multipolar region involving at least three major economic and military powers and perhaps others. Among Indian Ocean states, India is emerging as the largest economic and military power. Although we are now relatively early in India's growth trajectory, it seems likely that India will become an ever more powerful and perhaps more assertive power in Australia's western neighborhood. It seems clear that it would be in Australia's interests in coming decades to have a strong and productive relationship with a powerful, democratic and friendly India. But although India and Australia share many interests in the IOR, their relationship has historically been relatively thin. This means that Australia will need to pay greater attention to the relationship and think innovatively about how to develop new forms of cooperation with India in conjunction with traditional defense partners (Brewster, 2016c).

The other big factor is the likelihood that China will become a major player in the IOR. China has strong imperatives to develop capabilities to protect its vital sea lines of communication in the Indian Ocean, particularly those carrying energy from the Persian Gulf and Africa to China's Pacific coast. China's role throughout the IOR is also growing in connection with its 'Belt & Road Initiative' involving major investments in road, rail and power infrastructure in several Indian Ocean countries. For these reasons, China's naval presence will almost certainly continue to grow in both the western and eastern Indian Ocean, with significant consequences for Australia. To date, China's growing naval presence has been mostly focused on the western Indian Ocean. This initially occurred in connection with semi-permanent anti-piracy operations in the Gulf of Aden since 2008, but has more recently involved the establishment of a permanent naval and air presence in Djibouti (announced in December 2015) and quite likely also in Gwadar, Pakistan. But China also has strong strategic imperatives in the central and eastern Indian Ocean which one day could involve the establishment of a naval presence in or near the Bay of Bengal. Chinese submarines have visited the Indian Ocean a number of times in recent years and are likely to continue to do so on a regular basis. The ability to detect and monitor foreign naval activity in the Indian Ocean will provide significant advantages to resident powers such as Australia.

The changing strategic dynamics in areas close to Australian territory has been emphasized on at least three occasions since 2014 when Chinese naval task forces have entered the Indian Ocean and conducted exercises in or near the Christmas Island EEZ (CMO, 2016; Wroe, 2014, 2017). Official Chinese media described the 2014 exercise as involving 'quick response training for electronic war in the Indian Ocean' (CCTV, 2014). There is no indication that the Australian Government received formal advance notification of either combat-simulation exercises (in 2014 and 2017) or counter-piracy exercises (in 2016) conducted by Chinese forces close to Australia's Indian Ocean territories (Medcalf, 2014a). These could be unfortunate precedents for expanded Chinese unilateral military activity in waters close to Australian territory, at odds with China's professed aspirations to strategic partnership with Australia.

Although China has so far been relatively reluctant to become a major military factor in the IOR, any significant drawdown of US defense resources in the Indian Ocean could cause Beijing to fundamentally rethink its military role in the region and accelerate the development of its military presence. Any material growth in China's military presence in the IOR could also trigger a phase of Sino-Indian strategic competition, again with potentially adverse consequences for regional stability.

These and other developments will increasingly require Australia to reexamine its role in the Indian Ocean order and its defense capabilities in the eastern Indian Ocean. The adoption in Australia of the idea of the Indo-Pacific as a strategic construct is also leading Australia to take a more integrated view of its strategic interests right along the Asian littoral between the Korean peninsula in northeast Asia to India in the west (Medcalf, 2015). Among other things, the Indo-Pacific concept is likely to lead to Australia to give greater priority to its defense relationship with India and its maritime security role in the eastern Indian Ocean.

The importance of island territories in the Indian Ocean balance of military power

The strategic significance to Australia of its Indian Ocean island territories also needs to be understood in the context of the growing strategic importance of island territories throughout the Indian Ocean. Australia has in fact been slower than other countries that are active in the Indian Ocean to use island territories to its strategic advantage. Australia's Indian Ocean territories is now premium strategic real estate and needs to be invested in as such if Australia is serious about protecting and advancing its interests in the new multipolar Indo-Pacific security environment.

The vast distances across the Indian Ocean and the very few islands between the major landmasses creates a considerable premium for those countries that can gain access to airfield and port facilities on well-placed Indian Ocean islands – possibly even more so than is the case in the Pacific theater. Despite the long ranges of surveillance aircraft (Australia's AP-3C Orions for instance operate out of South Australia) and the existence of air-to-air refueling, the option of mid-ocean staging points remains extremely important in extending the range and effectiveness of aircraft operations. Similarly, access to onshore logistical facilities in appropriate locations is extremely important in maintaining a naval presence.

When Britain was the dominant power in the Indian Ocean, the Royal Navy operated a string of naval and air facilities around the Indian Ocean rim and islands. Important bases and staging points included Singapore in the east; Trincomalee (Sri Lanka) and Gan (Maldives) in the central Indian Ocean; and Aden, Mauritius and Cape Town in the western Indian Ocean. As the Royal Navy drew down its resources in the Indian Ocean in the 1960s and 1970s, other powers sought to fill the vacuum. This led to considerable jostling between the Soviet Union, United States and others to gain access to port and/or airfield facilities throughout the IOR, including at Trincomalee (Sri Lanka), Gan (Maldives), Port Victoria (Seychelles) and Socotra (Yemen). However, it was the United States that, with the assistance of Britain, developed Diego Garcia as one of its most important military facilities in the Indian Ocean.

The role of Diego Garcia in US defense strategy

The US military base at Diego Garcia has a crucial role in the US military strategy in the Indian Ocean. The United States identified Diego Garcia in the 1960s as a future hub for its base network in the Indian Ocean. It has many advantages as a military base, including its geographical centrality, its position on the territory of a close ally, its isolated location and its lack of local population. The United States developed Diego Garcia through the 1970s and 1980s in part as a response to the growth of a Soviet presence in the Indian Ocean. Diego Garcia was a launch point for B-52 bombers in the event of nuclear war with the Soviet Union, and after the Cold War it was used as a major base for US attacks on Iraq in 1990 and 2003 and Afghanistan from 2001.

Today, the base has four main functions: a semi-permanent anchorage for a fleet of ships that can deliver prepositioned equipment sufficient for Army and Marine Corps Brigades to be deployed anywhere in the IOR within one week; a hub for fast attack submarines and surface ships operating in the Indian Ocean; an airbase that supports the 'Global Strike' concept under which the US Strategic Command can make conventional strikes anywhere on the earth's surface; and the regional hub for communications, signal intelligence (SIGINT) and satellite tracking capabilities (Erickson, Ladwig, & Mikolay, 2010). The base has been upgraded to host a nuclear-powered cruise missile submarine which, with the cruise missile firepower of an entire carrier strike group, will be a key part of the America's 'over the horizon' strategy in the Indian Ocean in coming years. Along with Guam in the Pacific Ocean, Diego Garcia, is now a crucial element in a system that allows the United States to pivot military power throughout the world.

The US military presence at Diego Garcia has been controversial in part because of the dispute between Mauritius and Britain over ownership of the Chagos Archipelago. Some other Indian Ocean states, including India, also disputed the US military presence there, seeing it as an unwanted interloper. While New Delhi formally continues to challenge Britain's territorial claims, Indian rhetoric about Diego Garcia has softened considerably in line

INDIAN OCEAN ISLANDS

with improvements in US–Indian relations and there is now an acceptance of the stabilizing role that Diego Garcia currently plays in the region.

Recent developments in the Indian Ocean

Over the last decade or so there has been growing competition between India and China to develop new naval and air facilities all over the IOR, particularly on island territories. According to one Indian defense analyst:

> Small islands dotting the Indian Ocean are emerging at the centre stage of great power politics unfolding in the Indian Ocean Region. These islands are critical in sustaining a credible presence in the vast Indian Ocean outreach, encompassing the key SLOCs forming the backbone of the global economy. (Baruah, 2015)

The following map shows major sea lines of communications and a selection of recent or potential infrastructure developments in and around the Indian Ocean (Figure 1).

Chinese infrastructure development in and around the Indian Ocean

As is well known, in recent years China has engaged in an aggressive program of developing a series of artificial islands in the South China Sea for use as airfields and naval forward operating bases. Despite their apparent vulnerability to attack, these could eventually facilitate China's military dominance of that area and would also be useful staging

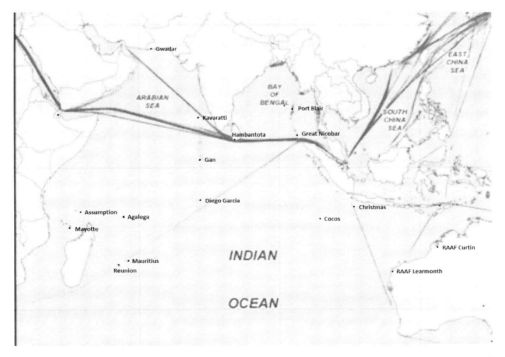

Figure 1. Major Indian Ocean Sea lines of communication and some existing or potential military infrastructure developments. Map of 'The Indo Pacific sea lanes,' Defence White Paper 2013, Department of Defence, Australian Government, with modifications.

points for China as it projects power into the eastern Indian Ocean. Some analysts also claim that China is following a 'String of Pearls' strategy in the Indian Ocean – developing a string of 'dual-use' ports across the northern Indian Ocean that would potentially be available for use by the Chinese navy. Chinese port developments in Myanmar (Kyaukpyu), Sri Lanka (Hambantota and Colombo) and Pakistan (Gwadar) are often held up by some analysts as putative Chinese naval bases. Although some analysts point to the vulnerability of these ports as full scale naval bases in the event of major conflict (Holmes & Yoshihara, 2008; Kostecka, 2011), there can be little doubt that they could be highly useful logistics points for Chinese naval vessels and aircraft operating in the region.

In December 2015, China crossed its own Rubicon when it announced its intention to build its first overseas military base: naval and military facilities at Obock in Djibouti. This is ostensibly to provide logistical support for China's anti-piracy operations in western Indian Ocean and peacekeeping operations in Africa, but is also well placed next to the sea lines of communication that transit the Gulf of Aden and the Suez Canal (Brewster, 2015c). Beijing is also pushing ahead with plans to construct overland links between western China and the Pakistani port of Gwadar as part of its Belt & Road Initiative and according to recent reports, which have not been denied by Beijing, China intends to station naval vessels and troops at the port (PTI, 2016). The location of Gwadar, some 600 km east of the Strait of Hormuz, would significantly enhance China's capabilities to respond to contingencies in and around the Persian Gulf and the Arabian Sea. Importantly, the new Chinese facilities at both Obock and Gwadar will not only include port and logistics facilities, but also new airfields with long runways that could significantly extend China's maritime surveillance and strike reach in the Indian Ocean.

In coming years we are likely to see the development of further Chinese military facilities in the IOR as China seeks to enhance its capabilities to defend its interests in the western and eastern Indian Ocean (You, 2016). There has been speculation that China might seek access to infrastructure on the East African coast perhaps, for example, in Tanzania. There is also a realistic possibility that China might develop naval and other military facilities in the central and eastern Indian Ocean, and as noted above, some analysts have flagged possible Chinese naval bases in locations such as Hambantota in Sri Lanka (Kostecka, 2011), or even on reclaimed/artificial islands in the Maldives (Keck, 2015).

Indian military infrastructure development in the Indian Ocean

India has also stepped up its moves to expand its naval and military presence throughout the region. Since the late 1980s, India has been developing its military capabilities in its Andaman and Nicobar Islands, much of it focused on enhancing India's maritime surveillance capabilities in the Malacca Strait and Southeast Asia. In December 2015, India's Navy chief, Admiral R K Dhowan acknowledged that the Andaman and Nicobar Islands are what he called a 'very very important aspect' of India's security (Raman, 2016). This is largely driven by the proximity of these islands to the Malacca Strait, one of the few routes between the Indian and Pacific Oceans, and one of the busiest waterways on earth.

India's main base in the Andaman and Nicobar Islands is at Port Blair on Great Andaman Island, which includes a naval base and a naval air station with a 3300 m runway. In 2016, the Indian Navy began staging its new P-8I Poseidon maritime surveillance and strike aircraft based on the Indian mainland through Port Blair (Brewster, 2016a). The Indian

Air Force also maintains a facility at Car Nicobar Island with a 2700 m runway that could be used for staging of aircraft based on the Indian mainland for air operations in Southeast Asia. In 2012, the Indian Navy opened a new naval air station on Great Nicobar Island, which overlooks the Six Degree Channel, one of the main shipping channels through the Malacca Strait. The airfield, with a 1100 m runway, is used for the Dornier Do 228 reconnaissance aircraft and Unmanned Aerial Vehicles (UAVs).

Access to facilities in the Andaman and Nicobar Islands is highly valuable not just for India, but potentially also for its defense partners. In 2013, a RAND report prepared for the US Department of Defense argued that in the event of a conflict the US Navy would seek to deploy a detachment of broad area maritime surveillance UAVs to Port Blair airport in the Andaman Islands, to increase surveillance over the Strait of Malacca (Lostumbo et al., 2013). Although Australia currently has access to facilities in Singapore and Butterworth, Malaysia as part of the Five Power Defence Arrangements (FPDA), in some circumstances access to facilities in the Andaman and Nicobar Islands might also be useful.

India has also been very active in developing island infrastructure elsewhere in the Indian Ocean. In the central Indian Ocean, India has long aspired to the old British air and naval base at Gan Atoll, in the southernmost group of islands in the Maldives. Gan has a 2650 m runway and a deepwater port with refueling facilities, all of which are in the process of being modernized and improved. Like Diego Garcia, which lies a further 700 km to the south, Gan can potentially be used to dominate the central Indian Ocean. After the British departed Gan in 1976, Iran, the Soviet Union and even Libya tried to acquire use of the base, which was only prevented through Indian pressure on the Maldivian government. Currently Indian aircraft and naval vessels use facilities at Gan on an occasional basis but India does not yet appear to have a significant permanent presence there (DeSilva-Ranasinghe, 2011; Dutta, 2009). One senior Indian official commented that Gan 'could eventually provide the Indian Navy with a listening post to monitor the movements of Chinese vessels as they sail to and from Africa, ferrying oil and gas' (Bedi, 2009).

In the western Indian Ocean, in 2012 the Indian Navy opened a small forward operating naval base at Kavaratti Island in India's Lakshadweep Islands off the southwest coast of mainland India, which is valuable in helping to further extend the navy's reach in the Arabian Sea. Several other small forward operating naval bases have also been established in the Lakshadweep Islands (Sen Gupta, 2016).

India has also been active in developing its presence in the southwestern corner of the Indian Ocean, especially near the sea lanes that carry oil from West Africa around the Cape of Good Hope to East Asia and at the northern end of the Mozambique Channel near the major offshore hydrocarbon deposits that are being developed off Mozambique and Tanzania. India has long maintained close defense relationships with the island states of Mauritius and Seychelles which it uses to facilitate Indian defense access throughout the western Indian Ocean (Brewster, 2010). The infrastructure in Mauritius and Seychelles currently available to India or in the process of planning or construction will considerably enhance India's maritime surveillance and strike capabilities in the southwest quadrant of the Indian Ocean and along the East African coast.

India has long had a very close defense relationship with the island state of Seychelles, which is located around 2000 km off the coast of Tanzania. A former Seychelles President once described his country to a US official as 'an aircraft carrier in the middle of the Indian Ocean without the planes' (Brewster, 2014, p. 76). In 2016, the Indian Navy began experimenting with the deployment of its P-8I Poseidon maritime surveillance aircraft to the main island of Seychelles, ostensibly to help police its EEZ (Gady, 2016). In early 2015, New Delhi also announced that it would be developing infrastructure on Seychelles' remote and virtually uninhabited Assumption Island located near the north end of the Mozambique Channel. This infrastructure, which is due to be completed in 2017, will include the radar and SIGINT capabilities, an improved airstrip for use by the Indian Navy and a forward operating naval base (Johny, 2016).

India has extremely close relations with Mauritius, including providing Mauritius' National Security Advisor and effectively operating the Mauritian coast guard and maritime air wing. This means, among other things, that the Indian defence forces have more or less guaranteed access to infrastructure in Mauritius. In 2015, India reportedly reached an agreement in principle to develop infrastructure on the remote Agalega islands, around 1000 km north of the main island of Mauritius, near the north end of the Mozambique Channel (Brewster, 2015a). Although work has not yet commenced, the infrastructure will likely include signal intelligence capabilities, an improved airstrip and a jetty (Karnad, 2016).

These are all early moves which likely presage a long period of strategic competition in the Indian Ocean (Brewster, 2016b). In particular, China's naval strategy in that theater is still evolving. In the short term China is probably focused on developing limited and asymmetric sea denial capabilities in the Indian Ocean, but in the medium to long term this could evolve into a strategy of limited sea control – and the state of the Sino–US relationship will be an important driver of this. For its part, India is developing its own naval capabilities, with US assistance. In the future, one of Delhi's likely key focus areas will be on developing India's maritime surveillance capabilities over a broad area running from the Indonesian archipelago in the northeast Indian Ocean to the Persian Gulf in the northwest and the Mozambique Channel in the southwest. Given the distances involved, this will almost certainly require enhanced collaboration with other regional partners (Baruah, 2016). For example, while India owns the Andaman and Nicobar Islands near the Malacca Strait, its surveillance reach across the other key straits through the Indonesian archipelago is limited.

The strategic importance of the Cocos and Christmas Islands for Australia

Australia's Indian Ocean islands lie far from the Australian mainland (Cocos is around 2750 km northwest of Perth, the closest Australian city, and Christmas Island is around 2600 km from Perth) and have long been on the periphery of Australia's strategic considerations.[1] They are small in both area and population: Cocos consists of two coral atolls with a total area of 14 km^2 and a population of about 600; Christmas is a single volcanic island with a total area of 135 km^2 and a population of about 2000. Cocos and Christmas were transferred to Australian control in the 1950s as Britain sought to shed responsibility for many isolated and marginal colonial territories. Having just experienced possible Japanese invasion during the Pacific War, Australia sought to acquire the islands principally to deny their potential use against Australia by hostile powers.[2] Since that time, Australia has generally taken little interest in its Indian Ocean territories and they were only fully legally integrated with mainland Australia in the early 1990s. But the islands are now coming under increased scrutiny as part of a renewed focus on Australia's defense capabilities in the Indian Ocean.

Cocos and Christmas, being the only landmasses in the eastern Indian Ocean south of the Southeast Asian archipelago, potentially have considerable significance for Australia's strategic reach into Southeast Asia and the eastern Indian Ocean. As shown in the table the location of the islands means that they could potentially be used provide excellent air coverage of much of the eastern Indian Ocean and Southeast Asia, as well as the potential for use as forward naval bases (Table 1).

The strategic importance of Cocos first came to the fore in 1944–1945, when Allied forces no longer had access to air bases in Southeast Asia, which had come under the control of Japan. For this reason, the airfield at West Cocos Island was developed for use as a strategic forward operating base by the royal air force and Royal Australian Air Force (RAAF) for attacks on Japanese forces in Burma, Sumatra, Java and Singapore, much of which was effectively out of reach from air bases in India and Ceylon. The airfield at Cocos may have become an important element in the retaking of Southeast Asia by Allied forces during the course of 1945 and 1946, although the war ended before that became necessary.

In the 1950s, both Christmas and Cocos were viewed by Australia as potentially valuable staging points for civilian and military aircraft crossing the Indian Ocean. Cocos was used in the 1960s for Australian military aircraft transiting to Malaysia during the Indonesian Confrontation, and by Qantas between 1952 and 1967 as a staging point for flights to Africa. However, advances in the range of civilian aircraft made both Cocos and Christmas unnecessary for use by normal civilian traffic.

Australia's Indian Ocean territories again became of strategic interest in connection with increased Soviet naval activity in the Indian Ocean during the 1970s and 1980s, particularly after the Soviet intervention in Afghanistan in 1979. These developments led Australia to better integrate itself with US military activities in the Indian Ocean, particularly in maritime air surveillance. Australia launched Operation *Gateway*, which included regular surveillance of the Malacca Strait area and the South China Sea, with Australian aircraft frequently staging through Butterworth in Malaysia. Australia and the United States also began operating joint reconnaissance patrols out of or staging through the Cocos Islands, Diego Garcia and Singapore (Tow, 1978). It is also believed that Christmas Island

Table 1. Distances between Australian Indian Ocean territories and other locations (in nautical miles).

Location	Distance from Cocos Is.	Distance from Christmas Is.
Cilicap, Java	770	270
Colombo	1535	1865
Darwin	1995	1490
Diego Garcia	1475	1980
Jakarta	700	280
Perth	1995	1490
Port Blair, Andaman Is.	1450	1535
RAAF Curtin	1595	1140
RAAF Learmonth	1150	845
Singapore	920	725
Christmas Is.	525	

Source: Bateman & Bergin, 2017.

was used, at least experimentally, for a US operated Sonar Surveillance System (SOSUS) to track Soviet submarines transiting the Indonesian archipelago (Ball, 1980).

Since the turn of this century, Christmas (and, to a lesser extent, Cocos) became a favored arrival points for irregular arrivals by sea. This caused them to become important nodes for support of Australian border protection operations, including air surveillance and naval vessels, and Christmas is also the site of a large offshore immigration detention center. Although there has been a sharp decline in irregular arrivals to Australia by sea in recent years due to Australia's tough policies on illegal migration, the risk of new surges of boat arrivals in the future will likely guarantee the importance of Christmas and Cocos in support of border protection operations.

The strategic value of Australia's Indian Ocean territories, and Australia's ability to defend those territories, was considered by Ross Babbage in the 1980s (Babbage, 1987, 1988) and it is worth summarizing his conclusions:

The strategic value of Cocos Islands

- Access to Cocos could be critical in supporting air operations to assist in the defense of Indonesia, Malaysia or Singapore from external attack. Cocos would also be useful for supporting air operations westwards in the Bay of Bengal area.
- Should the straits through the Indonesian archipelago be obstructed, commercial shipping between the Indian and Pacific Oceans would be forced to transit Torres Strait or pass south of Australia, greatly increasing shipping densities near Cocos Island. This would substantially increase the significance of Cocos for surveillance purposes.
- The location of Cocos may also lend itself to other strategic purposes, particularly for intelligence collection, for example, a satellite ground station, as part of an over-the-horizon radar system or even (to some extent) for conventional radar.
- Australia has a strong negative interest in denying the Cocos to an adversary, which could use them to threaten Australia's western approaches.

The strategic value of Christmas Island

- Christmas Island would be potentially useful for supporting air operations in Southeast Asia and further north.
- Christmas Island would be a valuable site for intelligence collection, including for surveillance of submarines transiting the Java Trench.
- Australia has a strong negative interest in denying the Christmas to an adversary, which like Cocos could be used to threaten Australia's western approaches.

Australia's ability to defend Cocos and Christmas

- It would be possible, with substantial investments, to defend Cocos and Christmas from low level contingencies.
- Were either or both of Cocos and Christmas to be attacked by a major force it would be difficult for Australian forces operating from the mainland to provided effective and timely support.

- The cost of making of substantial forward deployments of Australian forces to defend the islands may be disproportionate to their strategic significance. However, the islands could also be defended in strength as part of a first line of defense strategy of diverting an adversary's attention from the mainland.

Babbage's, 1987 conclusions (Babbage, 1987, pp. 11–26) probably remain more or less valid today, with the possible exception of his comments about the possibility of using the islands as a first line of defense for mainland Australia.[3] However, the contemporary strategic landscape probably makes it even more imperative than in previous decades for Australia to develop independent capabilities to support air operations in Southeast Asia and the eastern Indian Ocean, and to potentially allow allies and partners access to such facilities on appropriate conditions. The substantial problems in defending the islands against attack by major forces remain unresolved, although this issue is common with many island defense facilities.

It is also worth noting that in a new era of undersea competition, with a proliferation of submarine capabilities across the Indo-Pacific, strategically-located islands may play useful roles in future seabed sonar networks analogous to the vast SOSUS arrays of the Cold War era. The expense and ambition of such arrangements makes them essentially hypothetical at present. Australia's Indian Ocean territories are also located close to the submarine cables that provide internet and telecommunications connectivity from Western Australia to Asia and beyond.

However, both Cocos and Christmas are subject to considerable constraints, some of which can be overcome with relatively little cost and others that would require major investments.

The infrastructure in the Indian Ocean territories (including a single 2440 m runway on West Cocos and 2100 m runway on Christmas Island) is not well suited to support Australia's impending defense needs. While the Cocos airfield could support Australia's current RAAF maritime surveillance aircraft, the AP-3C Orion at full load, the Christmas airfield is not currently able to. Neither airfield would be able to support the RAAF's new P-8A Poseidon maritime reconnaissance and strike aircraft at full load without lengthening and strengthening and the development of supporting infrastructure. (It should be noted that there are also limitations on the size of civil aircraft that are currently able to use the Cocos and Christmas airfields. Upgrading of these airfields would also be required if they are to be available for larger civil aircraft carrying tourists from the Australian mainland or from Asia.)

Nor is there much naval infrastructure on either Cocos or Christmas to support operations by the Australian navy. Although West Cocos Island bears some similarities to Diego Garcia, it is much smaller and its lagoon is too shallow for large ships. As Bateman and Bergin note, 'Major dredging and reclamation works would be required to overcome these [depth] problems and make the lagoon accessible to large vessels, but these would be expensive and environmentally unsound' (Bateman & Bergin, 2017, p. 6). Christmas Island (which is volcanic rather than an atoll) does not have any sheltered anchorage and seasonal weather means for several months a year there may be week-long periods in which ships are unable to berth at its exposed jetty. Although improvements can be made to berthing facilities at both Cocos and Christmas to partially ameliorate these problems, without major expenditure there are very significant limitations on the use of the islands as a forward naval operating bases.

Despite these constraints, the availability of a suitably upgraded (strengthened and lengthened) airfield at West Cocos Island would significantly extend Australia's ability to project air power westwards throughout the eastern and central Indian Ocean as well as northwards into the Southeast Asian archipelago, the South China Sea and the Andaman Sea/Bay of Bengal. An upgraded (strengthened and lengthened) airfield at Christmas Island would also provide Australia with a very useful additional staging point for extending Australian air operations through the Southeast Asian archipelago. However, due to the physical geography, lengthening of the airfield at Christmas would require major expenditure. In addition, the relative strategic vulnerability of Christmas Island means that facilities also need to be available on Cocos. Australia has long used facilities in Singapore, Malaysia and Diego Garcia for operations in the eastern Indian Ocean and Southeast Asia. However Australia must also plan for capabilities in the event of the unavailability of those traditional facilities.

Proposed upgrades of infrastructure on Cocos and Christmas

The pending retirement of Australia's AP-3C Orion surveillance fleet and their replacement with P-8A Poseidon maritime surveillance and response aircraft has forced the issue of whether the airfield at West Cocos should be upgraded. In 2012, an Australian Defence Force Posture Review recommended among other things, the development of infrastructure at the northwest ports of Exmouth, Dampier, Port Headland and Broome to allow greater use by warships; the upgrading of the airbase at Exmouth for greater use by maritime surveillance and strike aircraft; and the upgrading of the existing airfield at Cocos (Hawke & Smith, 2012, p. 26). The 2016 Defence White Paper committed the Government to upgrading the facilities on Cocos Islands to support the activities of P-8A Poseidon aircraft (Australian Government, 2016, p. 101), and as a result plans for the strengthening and lengthening of the Cocos airfield are now under way.

Australian defence analyst, Dr Carlo Kopp, has proposed an ambitious plan of transforming the West Cocos into a Strategic Forward Operating Base for the Australian Defence Forces (Kopp, 2012). This would potentially include parallel runways and hardened shelters and Kopp suggests that may also be possible to build a naval replenishment facility at nearby Direction Island. This level of development of military infrastructure may not be required by the current strategic environment. However, if the strategic environment in the Indian Ocean changed significantly to Australia's disadvantage, such facilities could be extremely valuable.

The upgrading of defense infrastructure on Christmas Island receives relatively less attention than Cocos. As noted above, it would be expensive to lengthen the Christmas airfield. In addition, its close proximity to Java (some 270 nm) would make it significantly more vulnerable to air attack than Cocos from an adversary operating out of Indonesian territory. But its proximity to Java should not, of itself, be regarded as negating the overall strategic significance of Christmas Island. On the contrary, the proximity of Christmas Island to Southeast Asia can increase its strategic value in many circumstances and for many purposes. In particular, its location near the Sunda and Lombok Straits and the Java Trench make it ideal for supporting surveillance activities being conducted by Australia and/or its partners. As China has demonstrated with the development of well-placed artificial islands in the South China Sea, even relatively vulnerable defense infrastructure can have significant political and strategic consequences.

The value of Australia's island territories for its regional defense partnerships

As noted, infrastructure at Cocos and Christmas should be primarily developed to provide Australia with capabilities in the eastern Indian Ocean, including as a hedge against any circumstances in which Australia did not have access to other facilities in the region. That being said, an important secondary consideration would be the strategic value for Australia in potentially granting access to such infrastructure, on appropriate terms, to its regional defense partners, including the United States, India and potentially other partners. The mere existence of such facilities would increase Australia's value as an Indian Ocean partner.

Australia's principal defense partnership in the IOR is of course with the United States. The authors have previously argued that Australia should also promote the incremental development of a defense and security partnership with India (Brewster, 2016c). Japan also has significant interests in the IOR and, in a multipolar Indo-Pacific, it is in Australia's interests to promote Japan's role in the region. The availability of facilities in Australia's Indian Ocean territories could potentially play an important role in such partnerships.

Strategic uncertainties in the IOR give Australia a very direct interest in promoting India's role as a complement to that of the United States. For more than a decade the United States has encouraged India to take a more active role in the IOR, reflecting several objectives: to develop India as a balance to China across the Indo Pacific; to encourage India to make a greater contribution to regional security; and to use India's huge military establishment to supplement scarce US defense resources. Some argue that this as part of a new US 'Nixon doctrine' of supporting friends and allies taking greater security responsibilities in their own regions (Ladwig, 2012). Like Washington, Australia sees considerable value in encouraging India to assume an expanded regional security role to supplement the United States.

The interests of the three countries are converging. New Delhi is becoming increasingly concerned about the growth of China's military presence in the Indian Ocean and sees the US and Australian military presence in the IOR as important stabilizing factors. Indian concerns have been heightened by developments such as the deployment of Chinese submarines to the Indian Ocean and the development of a Chinese naval presence at Djibouti and potentially at Gwadar. There is a strong view among many Indian strategists that China is challenging India's aspirations in the region, and this will require India to play a much more active security role in the Indian Ocean (Medcalf, 2016). Nevertheless, most Indian strategists understand that India simply does not have the material capabilities or facilities to address this threat on its own and it will not have sufficient capabilities to do so for years to come.

Despite a number of caveats and sensitivities in the Australian and US relationships with India, there is much that can be achieved among the three countries in the IOR, including in joint exercises, intelligence and cyber cooperation, shared maritime domain awareness and humanitarian assistance and disaster relief (HADR) and search and rescue (SAR). A key area for potential trilateral cooperation is in intelligence, surveillance and reconnaissance (ISR) to improve maritime domain awareness and Australia's Indian Ocean territories could have considerable value for such cooperation. The vastness of distances across the Indian Ocean makes tracking of vessels and aircraft a difficult task and beyond the resources of any single country. It is a field in which India has shown particular interest in cooperating with both the United States and Australia. The recent signing of 'white shipping' information sharing agreements between India and Australia, and India and the United States may be steps towards broader information sharing arrangements which could ultimately include the shared use of facilities around the IOR.

The finalization of the India–US Logistics Exchange Memorandum of Agreement may ease the way for similar facilities sharing arrangements between Australia and India. There is potential for Australia to allow India access to facilities in Australia's Indian Ocean territories as part of a mutual arrangement in relation to Indian facilities in the Indian Ocean. Some influential Indian security thinkers are supportive of such initiatives to advance practical cooperation, which would signal a major advance in strategic trust and practical cooperation between these two Indian Ocean powers (Mohan, 2017). The United States, India and Australia are all making major investments in ISR capabilities, which will include Boeing P-8 maritime aircraft as a key element in maritime ISR capabilities. The use of common platforms could also create important opportunities for cooperation in training, support and maintenance.

Military infrastructure in Cocos and/or Christmas could be valuable to Australia's defense partners in different ways. For several decades, the United States has used facilities at Cocos as an important alternate airfield to fill the gap between its major bases at Diego Garcia and Guam (a distance of some 8300 km), as a partial alternative to Paya Lebar Air Base in Singapore. For India, access to Cocos (or even Christmas) could potentially allow it to extend an effective maritime air surveillance system to the major southern straits through the Indonesian archipelago (Sunda and Lombok) that are located several thousand kilometers from India's facilities in the Andaman and Nicobar Islands. Other defense partners such as Japan could also find staging facilities at Cocos or Christmas highly useful in moving defense assets around the IOR in the event of contingencies. Australia's ability to provide valuable or essential defense facilities to its partners could enhance its role in such partnerships, thereby enhancing Australia's influence in the region.

Conclusion

Growing strategic uncertainties in the IOR are forcing Australia to give greater recognition to the strategic importance of the Indian Ocean and the need for it to play a more active role in that region. Access to defense infrastructure in Indian Ocean islands is at a significant strategic premium. India and China, in particular, are actively developing dual-use or military infrastructure on Indian Ocean islands or elsewhere along on the Indian Ocean rim.

Australia has been slower than some other countries to recognize the full strategic value of infrastructure on Indian Ocean coastal or island territories. Australia is in the process of building on its commitments in the 2016 Defence White Paper to further develop infrastructure in both the Cocos Islands and Christmas Island to help it extend its surveillance and operational reach in Southeast Asia and throughout the eastern

Indian Ocean. Australia should be willing to carry the principal cost of such development and ensure that this infrastructure principally reflects Australia's strategic requirements.

Facilities in the Cocos and Christmas Islands could potentially form an important part of a shared maritime security and monitoring system in the Indian Ocean. In addition to their use as nodes for maritime air surveillance, this could include as anchor points to a network of seabed sensors for submarine detection, as China's and others' submarine presence in the Indian Ocean increases. The development of surveillance infrastructure has obvious benefits for the alliance with the United States, including potential access to runways and other facilities by US forces. Already Australia's capabilities in maritime surveillance and other elements of C4ISR (command, communications, control, computers, ISR) may be the most important contribution it makes to the US alliance (Goldrick, Fruehling, & Medcalf, 2014). Greater use of Australia's Indian Ocean territories in this regard, given their proximity to key Indo-Pacific sea lanes and isolation from mainland Australia, would further enhance Australia's value to the alliance in quiet and relatively uncontroversial ways. It would also create options for Australia to offer emerging partners such as India and Japan access to such facilities on appropriate terms. As a matter of regional diplomacy, Australia's FPDA partners, Malaysia and Singapore, as well as with Indonesia, should as far as possible be informed of significant developments.

The military significance of defense infrastructure on Cocos and Christmas should not be overstated: the islands are unlikely to become new Diego Garcias. However, Australia's willingness to commit defense resources to these islands will be an important statement of Australia's strategic intent in the Indian Ocean. The development of facilities on Cocos and Christmas will be an important signal of Australia's aspirations and commitment to be a major strategic player in the Indian Ocean, and to develop useful capabilities that will be available for use by Australia's defense forces and, potentially, those of its regional partners.

Notes

1. Australia's Indian Ocean territories also include the uninhabited Ashmore and Cartier Islands, low-lying reefs and islands around 150 km south of the Indonesian island of Rote. They are not currently considered as having military value.
2. For a few years after the World War II, a few Australian planners even dreamed of acquiring a protective wall of island colonies to the north, east and west of the Australian continent as part of a strategy of defense in depth. This theory was quickly overtaken by the reality of the end of the colonial era (Goldsworthy, 2002).
3. These arguments may reflect the Defence of Australia doctrine that was adopted at that time and are unlikely to be attractive to contemporary strategic planners.

Disclosure statement

No potential conflict of interest was reported by the authors.

References

Australian Government, Department of Defence. (2016). *Defence white paper 2016*. Canberra: Australian Government.

Babbage, R. (1987). *Christmas and Cocos Islands: Defence liabilities or assets?* Canberra: Strategic and Defence Studies Centre.

Babbage, R. (1988). *Should Australia plan to defend Christmas and Cocos Islands?* Canberra: Strategic and Defence Studies Centre.

Ball, D. (1980). *A suitable piece of real estate: American installations in Australia*. Marrickville: Southwood Press.

Baruah, D. M. (2015, February 24). The small Islands holding the key to the Indian Ocean. *The Diplomat* Retrieved from http://thediplomat.com/2015/02/the-small-islands-holding-the-key-to-the-indian-ocean/.

Baruah, D. M. (2016). Expanding India's maritime domain awareness in the Indian Ocean. *Asia Policy*, 22, 49–55.

Bateman, S., & Bergin, A. (2017, January 9). Defence capability issues with the Indian Ocean territories. Submission to joint standing committee on the national capital and external territories inquiry into the strategic importance of the Indian Ocean Territories. Retrieved from http://www.aph.gov.au/Parliamentary_Business/Committees/Joint/National_Capital_and_External_Territories/StrategicImportanceIOT/Submissions

Bedi, R. (2009, August 21). India strengthens military co-operation with the Maldives. *Jane's Defence Weekly*.

Brewster, D. (2010). An Indian sphere of influence in the Indian Ocean? *Security Challenges*, 6(3), 1–20.

Brewster, D. (2014). *India's Ocean: The story of India's bid for regional leadership*. London: Routledge.

Brewster, D. (2015a, March 17). Modi builds India's sphere of influence in the Indian Ocean. *Lowy Interpreter*. Retrieved April 24, 2017, from http://www.lowyinterpreter.org/post/2015/03/17/Modi-builds-Indias-sphere-of-influence-in-the-Indian-Ocean.aspx

Brewster, D. (2015b). Indian strategic thinking about the Indian Ocean: Searching for leadership. *India Review*, 14(2), 1–16.

Brewster, D. (2015c, December 2). China's announcement of its first overseas military base is the taste of things to come. *Lowy Interpreter*. Retrieved from http://www.lowyinterpreter.org/post/2015/12/02/Chinas-first-overseas-military-base-in-Djibouti-likely-to-be-a-taste-of-things-to-come.aspx

Brewster, D. (2016a, January 26). India beefs up maritime surveillance near Malacca Strait. *Lowy Interpreter*. Retrieved April 24, 2017, from http://www.lowyinterpreter.org/post/2016/01/26/India-poised-to-dominate-western-approaches-to-key-shipping-lane-and-Australia-may-help.aspx

Brewster, D. (2016b, August 12). India and China: Playing 'Go' in the Indian Ocean. *Lowy Interpreter*. Retrieved April 24, 2017, from http://www.lowyinterpreter.org/post/2016/08/12/India-and-China-Playing-Go-in-the-Indian-Ocean.aspx

Brewster, D. (2016c). *Australia, India and the United States: The challenge of forging new alignments in the Indo-Pacific*, United States Studies Centre, University of Sydney. Retrieved April 24, 2017, from http://ussc.edu.au/publications/Australia-India-and-the-United-States-The-Challenge-of-Forging-New-Alignments-in-the-Indo-Pacific

CCTV. (2014, February 2). Combat vessels training for quick response in electronic war. CCTV.com. Retrieved April 24, 2017, from http://english.cntv.cn/program/newsupdate/20140202/100068.shtml

CMO. (2016, May 5). Chinese naval taskforce conducts anti-piracy drill in Indian Ocean. *China Military Online*. Retrieved April 24, 2017, from http://english.chinamil.com.cn/news-channels/china-military-news/2016-05/16/content_7057720.htm

DeSilva-Ranasinghe, S. (2011, June 17). China-India rivalry in the Maldives. *The Jakarta Post*.

Dutta, S. (2009, August 20). Indian Navy eyes Maldives. *The Telegraph* (Calcutta).

Erickson, A. S., Ladwig, W. C., & Mikolay, J. D. (2010). Diego Garcia and the United States' emerging Indian Ocean strategy. *Asian Security*, 6(3), 214–237.

Gady, F.-S. (2016, March 22). India deploys submarine-hunting surveillance aircraft to Seychelles. *The Diplomat*. Retrieved April 24, 2017, from http://thediplomat.com/2016/03/india-deploys-submarine-hunting-surveillance-aircraft-to-seychelles/

Goldrick, J., Fruehling, S., & Medcalf, R. (2014). Preserving the knowledge edge: Survelliance cooperation and the US-Australia alliance in Asia. *Strategic Insight, Australian Strategic Policy Institute*.

Goldsworthy, D. (2002). *Losing the blanket: Australia and the end of Britain's empire*. Carlton South: Melbourne University Press.

Hawke, A., & Smith, R. (2012, March 30). *Australian defence force posture review*. Canberra: Australian Government.

Holmes, J. R., & Yoshihara, T. (2008). China's naval ambitions in the Indian Ocean. *Journal of Strategic Studies*, 31(3), 379–380.

Johny, S. (2016, June 8). We're working with India to ensure security in Indian Ocean: Seychelles. *The Hindu*. Retrieved April 24, 2017, from http://www.thehindu.com/news/international/were-working-with-india-to-ensure-security-in-indian-ocean-seychelles/article8705917.ece?css=print

Karnad, B. (2016, March 21). Nothing major in Mauritius. Retrieved April 24, 2017, from https://bharatkarnad.com/2016/03/21/nothing-major-in-mauritius/

Keck, Z. (2015, July 29). Get ready: China could build new artificial Islands near India. *The National Interest*.

Kopp, C. (2012). Strategic potential of the Cocos Islands and Christmas Island. *Defence Today*, 9(4), 18–21.

Kostecka, D. (2011). Places and bases: The Chinese navy's emerging support network in the Indian Ocean. *Naval War College Review,* 64(1), 59–78.

Ladwig, W. (2012). A neo-Nixon doctrine for the Indian Ocean: Helping states help themselves. *Strategic Analysis*, 36(3), 384–399.

Lostumbo, M. J., McNerney, M. J., Peltz, E., Eaton, D., Frelinger, D. R., Greenfield, V. A., Halliday, J., Mills, P., Nardulli, B. R., Pettyjohn, S. L., Sollinger, J. M., & Worman, S. M. (2013). *Overseas basing of US military forces: An assessment of relative costs and strategic benefits*. Santa Monica, CA: RAND Corporation.

Medcalf, R. (2014a, February 7). China makes statement as it sends naval ships off Australia's maritime approaches. *The Interpreter*. Retrieved April 24, 2017, from https://www.lowyinstitute.org/the-interpreter/china-makes-statement-it-sends-naval-ships-australias-maritime-approaches

Medcalf, R. (2014b). Mapping the Indo-pacific: China, India and the United States. In M. Malik (Ed.), *Maritime security in the indo-pacific: Perspectives from China, India and the United States*. New York, NY: Rowman and Littlefield.

Medcalf, R. (2015, June 26). Reimagining Asia: From Asia-Pacific to Indo-Pacific. *The Asan Forum*. Retrieved April 24, 2017, from http://www.theasanforum.org/reimagining-asia-from-asia-pacific-to-indo-pacific/

Medcalf, R. (2016). The western indo-pacific: India, China and the terms of engagement. *Asia Policy*, 22, 61–69.

Mohan, C. R. (2017). Australia in the Bay of Bengal. *Indian Express*, 11 April.

PTI. (2016, November 30). China deflects queries over naval deployments at Gwadar port in Pakistan. *The Economic Times*. Retrieved April 24, 2017, from http://economictimes.indiatimes.com/news/defence/china-deflects-queries-over-naval-deployments-at-gwadar-port-in-pakistan/articleshow/55706511.cms

Raman, S. (2016, January 3). The strategic importance of Andaman and Nicobar Islands. *The Diplomat*.

Sen Gupta, M. (2016, June 7). India increasing Naval presence in Lakshadweep, Andaman and Nicobar Islands for IOR Security. *Topyaps*. Retrieved April 24, 2017, from http://topyaps.com/naval-presence-in-lakshadweep

Tow, W. T. (1978). ANZUS: A strategic role in the Indian Ocean? *The World Today*, 34(10), 401–408.

Wroe, D. (2014, February 15). China's new military might is Australia's new defence reality. *Sydney Morning Herald*.

Wroe, D. (2017, March 10). Chinese naval ships close to Australia? 'Get used to it', experts warn. *Sydney Morning Herald*.

You, J. (2016). China's emerging indo pacific naval strategy. *Asia Policy*, 22, 11–19.

Towards a workers' history of the Chagos archipelago

Marina Carter

ABSTRACT
The article presents a critical investigation of the historiography of the Chagos archipelago and in particular the expelled islanders, known as Ilois, and more recently as Chagossians. A brief survey of the discovery and settlement of the atolls is provided, along with a more detailed summary of key events in the history of workers on the archipelago from the late-eighteenth to mid-twentieth century. Finally, the paper discusses the challenges of framing a workers' history characterized by exploitation and marginalization alongside the romanticized collective representation of life in the archipelago which has been adopted as a 'narrative of exile' by the Chagossians.

Introduction

The Chagos archipelago, located some 1200 nautical miles from the island of Mauritius in the southwestern Indian Ocean, was until 1965 administered as a dependent territory of the latter. It was then controversially reconstituted as part of the newly created British Indian Ocean Territory (BIOT), for the defense purposes of Britain and the United States. Over the following eight years, the population of the archipelago was removed and construction of what is now a major air and naval base on the island of Diego Garcia begun. The expulsion of the islanders from coral-fringed atolls now viewed as idyllic has unsurprisingly led to repeated invocations of a 'Paradise Lost.' (Abraham, 2011; Jeffery, 2007; Snoxell, 2008). The extensive post-1965 literature of the Chagos archipelago has focused on expulsion and resettlement of the islanders [known as Ilois and, more recently, as Chagossians][1] while the history of these isolated islands, and more specifically of workers' lives on the archipelago, has been comparatively neglected.[2] The framing of a 'narrative of exile' by and on behalf of Chagossians is an important factor in understanding this lacuna (Jeffery, 2011; Pilger, 2004). This paper endeavors to set the closure of the Chagos islands' coconut plantations and the expulsion of their inhabitants in their long-term historical context. A discussion of how and by whom the islands were utilized, how introduced workers were exploited, initially as slaves and later as contractual labor, is presented. The gradual emergence of an island-born community – then known as Ilois – is recounted, along with the consolidation of individually held concessions into a single company having proprietorial rights over the whole archipelago. In the 1960s, economic difficulties led to further transfers of managerial control, but it was the US military plans for the archipelago and the British decision to create the BIOT to accommodate those demands, that led to the expulsion of the Ilois. The history of the Chagos archipelago is one in which geographical isolation, managerial incompetence and capitalist greed, administrative neglect and repeated episodes of strategic rivalry have been key factors.

Around the same time that cold war geopolitics was fixing the fate of the Ilois, a British historian, E. P. Thompson, was framing his monumental study *The making of the English working class*, published in 1963. Labor history flourished in the decades that followed, with influential studies depicting the struggles of 'third world workers' both generally, and in meticulous detail, by historian Charles Van Onselen (1976), among others. More recently, labor historians have stressed the need for working-class history to be placed in a broader international context, to become transnational (Dubofsky, 2000; Linden, 2003). Indian Ocean focused workers' histories have proliferated, heavily influenced by subaltern studies, assessing linkages between slavery and other forms of unfree labor and emphasizing transcolonial labor migration (Carter, 2006; Hurgobin & Basu, 2015; Spivak, 1988). The historian, confronted with the limitations of the colonial archives, with its emphasis on government dispatches and magisterial reports that underplay the creative agency of the subaltern, now has the tools to read against the grain of the official discourse and to work with alternative sources when these become available [such as oral histories and workers' memoirs]. Equally, writings about dispossessed, subaltern groups need to avoid the trap of creating idealized 'deserving' individuals and essentialized communities (O'Hanlon, 1988; Zeitlyn, 2008). The following sections provide an overview of the history of the Chagos archipelago, highlighting key aspects of workers' struggles, followed by a discussion of the challenges of reconciling a pre-expulsion narrative of exploitation and marginalization with a post-expulsion romanticized 'narrative of exile.'

Chagos from discovery to settlement: A brief survey

There is no clear evidence of human settlement on the archipelago prior to the early sixteenth century, however, it is likely that Arab and/or Persian navigators were aware of a few islands to the east of Madagascar (Toorawa, 2007). The so-called Cantino map, dated to 1502, shows, very indistinctly, a group of islands in the position occupied by the Chagos archipelago, the larger of which are named Arissam, Tranom and Sapom. The lack of recorded evidence of early visits to these atolls is no doubt related to the dangers presented by the inter-tropical convergence zone along with the more lucrative attractions of monsoon trading to the north. Early navigators were more preoccupied with avoiding treacherous reefs than naming tiny atolls, and it is no surprise that two separate areas of danger were identified by the Portuguese as the Baixo das Chagas and the Pero dos Banhos.

Dutch shipping is also likely to have passed close to the Chagos islands in the late-sixteenth and early-seventeenth century, and broken Ming pottery dating from this period, found on the reefs off Egmont island, may have originated from a wrecked Dutch vessel. As with the Portuguese, however, Dutch trade routes would have steered them away from Chagos, and it is probable that their only encounters with the archipelago would have been the result of being blown off course by adverse winds and cyclonic conditions. However acquired, Dutch charts indicate accurate knowledge of the position of the Three Brothers and Eagle islands (Wenban-Smith & Carter, 2016).

A British sailing guide published in 1618 includes information on how to avoid or manoeuver carefully through the shoals known as the 'Baixos dos Chagas.' Successive voyagers, in the early eighteenth century, continued to skirt the Chagos islands, according to surviving log books. It was left to the French, who had established settlements at Madagascar, the Mascarene islands [Mauritius, Réunion and Rodrigues] and the Seychelles, by the mid-eighteenth century, to investigate the Chagos islands. In 1757, for example, a French ship, *Le Favori*, on her way from Mauritius to India, encountered Salomon atoll. This was not a happy experience for those involved, as a group of French and 'lascar' seamen found themselves castaway on the atolls, surviving on a diet of coconuts, fish, occasional seabirds and turtle for several weeks before fashioning a raft which successfully carried them to India (Wenban-Smith & Carter, 2016).

Within a few decades of French settlement on the Mascarenes, the supply of turtles [considered to have useful medicinal properties] began to dwindle and their known abundance on the Chagos islands was one of the reasons for growing interest in their exploration and settlement from the mid-eighteenth century onwards. Abbé Rochon and the Vicomte Grenier were among several well known Frenchmen to further the discovery of the best sailing route to the archipelago. By 1780, the French had detailed knowledge of the harbor and products of Diego Garcia:

> This island has the exact shape of a coiled snake, whose head and tail lie close to each other, enclosing a vast bay in which many vessels may anchor safely. The island is four leagues long from north to south and has a maximum width of two leagues. The entrance to the bay is no wider than 400 yards, and capable of being defended easily, while the continuous reef which surrounds the outer rim of the island prevents access to it from any other point. Even the largest vessels can anchor in the bay and be careened there. If the island were productive and had a greater land area, Diego Garcia would merit greater attention from the European nations that trade with India, on account of the size and security of its harbour. It lacks fresh water; or rather, water is obtained by digging wells in the earth, but the product is nothing but filtered seawater.
>
> The island's soil consists of sand on a base of corals and limestone, and covered by trees; the only kind of any utility as timber is a sort of beech, not very tall or thick, and suitable only for minor marine purposes. Otherwise, there are just vast numbers of coconut trees. The island abounds in turtles, fish and two sorts of lobster – marine and terrestrial.
>
> The flesh of the abundant coconuts could be used as fodder for goats, pigs and poultry.
>
> On the eastern side, there are some slightly higher sand dunes, up which, it appears, quantities of turtles climb to lay their eggs; and we observed some huge specimens of these on the reef, as well as many Hawksbills in the lagoon. This island is unsuited to occupation, given that there is hardly any fresh water and no species of land mammal other than rats, which are present in vast numbers; there are however big land crabs which are good eating and plenty of sharks and other fish.[3]

The first recorded French attempt to maintain a settlement on Chagos dates from 1778 when Dupuis de la Faye, commander of *l'Europe*, was sent to Diego Garcia to set up an establishment in the 'Northern Bay' where he raised the French flag.[4]

Chagos: towards a labor history

By the 1780s, arrangements were in place to maintain a French presence on Diego Garcia and to supply the Mascarene islands with the produce obtained there. The unnamed workers who were disembarked at Chagos to establish this early settlement were almost certainly slaves, and must have encountered difficult conditions. The archipelago quickly became an entrepot for newly captured slaves. Deschiens de Kérulvay, a French trader born in Lorient in 1745, is said to have made several stop-overs at Diego Garcia with slaves purchased at Madagascar and the east coast of Africa. On one such occasion, a group of five slaves – four men and one woman could not be located when those ashore were rounded up to re-embark; presumably they absconded and hid in brushwood. What became of them is unknown (Hebert, 1984, p. 235). This is the first recorded act of resistance by workers; over the next two centuries, the 'weapons of the weak' would be employed time and again to escape or violently oppose the oppressive and inhumane conditions of life on the archipelago (Scott, 1985, 1992).

In 1783, Mr Le Normand took over the establishment and along with it the responsibility for maintaining the flagstaff on Diego Garcia. A group of slaves along with a *commandeur* [overseer], François, arrived at Chagos in early 1784. François, nicknamed Jolicoeur, was a Malagasy man. Four of his team, slaves of Le Normand, – Hyacinthe, Jaso, Thomas and Domingue – were Mozambicans, while three others – Casimir, Etienne and Henri – were Isle of France born, known as creoles.[5] Another, Sephir, was a Malagasy. There were also two Mozambican women – Luni and Susanna – the latter having a daughter, Rose. The group settled in the southern bay, where a warehouse, huts for a manager and slaves, and enclosures for pigs, chickens and turtles were erected by the workers. Among the products of Diego Garcia which Le Normand intended to exploit were coconuts and wood, including *tatamaka* and *bois blanc* described as good for building boats.[6] The work schedule for the slaves was to fish for two months [the daily catch was dried in the sun] then switch to gathering 120,000 coconuts to be collected in heaps on the sea shore. After this number had been gathered, the slaves would return to fishing, and to catching turtles on the sea shore, and gathering and packing turtle shells. They were also expected to work for any visiting ships as required, to supply them with coconuts or undertake other jobs as required. The slaves shared the island with a group of lepers, sent there to 'convalesce' on account of the supposed restorative properties of turtle meat.[7]

Unfortunately for Le Normand and the slave workforce, a British expedition was then being prepared at Bombay to 'to take possession of and settle the island Chagos or Diego Garcia.' Two British officers, a detachment of artillery and another of Indian sepoys were sent aboard two ships with instructions that

> any straggling French who may be accidentally there without authority as any settlement of that nation, or any post or pillar, or such like trifling marks of possession left there with an evil design to debar other nations (profiting from its situation) should not be considered an impediment.[8]

On 27 April 1786, the British expedition arrived at Diego, and anchored in the lower bay on the east coast. A canoe approached them with five 'caffrees' on board who showed them three papers. One of the papers provided information about the settlement, but the leader of the British expedition, Richard Price, chose to interpret the document as evidence only of a temporary fishing establishment. François offered to pilot the British ships to a secure anchorage and the British disembarked at the 'French village,' described as 'a dozen huts of the meanest appearance covered from top to bottom with dried branches of the cocoa[nut] tree' in a small clearing. A path had been cut from the clearing to the seashore, everywhere else was covered in coconut trees, some very tall, and 'impenetrable underwood.' In bad weather, and with some difficulty, the expedition cleared a patch of ground large enough to erect their tents. The first interactions with the slaves were not encouraging; they informed the new arrivals that 'the surface of the ground was frequently covered with water from heavy rains [and] that the place swarmed with rats, worms and dangerous insects.' Prospects for a viable settlement did not improve: the 'caffrees' reported 'that all they sow comes up a few inches and then dies' and that their sheep and goats had died in six weeks. By July, Price was noting in his diary that their own supplies of sheep, goats, poultry and pigeons had died, while swarms of rats demolished any vegetables which had managed to survive. The tents were rotting, and the store was full of rats 'which our utmost vigilance cannot prevent till we can build stone walls and better roofs.' The slaves brought from Mauritius were not faring much better. The island had yielded little more than a 'bare subsistence' for them. Price noted, 'they had had no rice, maize, biscuit or any of the commonest food produced in other countries for nearly 2 years before we arrived' and lived mainly on turtle meat, fish and coconut water. On 8th August, a French vessel called the *Petit Cousin* in the British records arrived from Mauritius and proposed to take off Le Normand's workers and his utensils.

Back in Bombay, the Diego Garcia dispatches were being perused. The President in Council concluded that the island was not fit to sustain life so that any settlement would be dependent on external resource. Moreover,

> its distant situation, the want of tides, the badness of the bottom and lowness of the land will render it of less value as a rendezvous for shipping, and more so still as they could here meet with no supplies beyond water, fish, turtle and coconuts.

By November 1786, the British had abandoned the settlement.[9] The slaves having been removed by the *Petit Cousin*, one may speculate that only the lepers and any runaways remained on Diego Garcia at this time.

Despite the evident vulnerability of these remote settlements to British attack, French colonists continued to request permits to exploit the produce of the Chagos atolls and to ship out slave working parties. The early French settlements were reportedly de facto arrangements made with French Governors of the Mascarenes rather than formal concessions, and along with Le Normand, another settler, Dauguet, was authorized to set up a fishing establishment.[10] Coconut oil production, particularly in times of conflict with Britain, when supplies were scarce on the Mascarenes, was becoming a valuable commodity produced by Chagos, and in 1793, another French settler, Lapotaire, endeavored to establish an oil production facility there. In June of that year, however, visiting British frigates plundered the settlements again, setting fire to the huts and carrying off the slaves.[11] In July 1808, Victor Duperrel obtained a concession (*jouissance*) to exploit the Egmont atoll [Six Islands], while on 2 May 1809, Napoleon's emissary appointed

Captain General of the Mascarene islands, Charles Decaen, formally accorded three concessions on Diego Garcia to Messrs Lapotaire, Cayeux and Didier, fixing the limits of their respective establishments (in order to prevent argument between them) and imposing on them the cost of maintaining the leper establishment there. The proliferation of concessions led to increasing numbers of slaves being employed at Chagos, probably amounting to several hundred. In wartime, this was highly risky, and in April 1810, two British navy ships destroyed the settlements on Diego Garcia and again took a large number of slaves away with them, some of whom, it was reported, 'voluntarily' came on board. A detailed list of the slaves taken away from Chagos survived, together with some account of their fate. One hundred and three men and 23 women are enumerated. The number of children varies in the accounts between 45 and 8 and were not individually listed. The surviving slaves were disembarked at Colombo [present day Sri Lanka] and the able-bodied men were recruited to serve in the 3rd Ceylon regiment (Wenban-Smith & Carter, 2016, pp. 74–84).

Visiting Diego Garcia in 1811, shortly before the British arrived to claim possession, following the December 1810 conquest of the Mascarenes, a French naval officer, St Cricq, described it as 'a place of pain,' adding, 'the unhappy beings exiled to this parcel of earth live very miserably; all they have for subsistence are coconuts, some chickens and turtles, it being impossible to glean anything from the sandy earth – all attempts at cultivation having been fruitless' (Lepelley, 1992, pp. 142–144). With the end of the Napoleonic wars, however, new concessions were granted to the French colonists on Mauritius by the first British Governor of the island, Robert Farquhar and deliveries of coconut oil and copra recommenced to the Mascarene islands with renewed vigor. Maurits Ver Huell, the commander of a Dutch warship, the *Admiraal Evertsen*, wrecked off Diego Garcia in 1819, wrote a useful account of life on Chagos in the early nineteenth century, remarking, 'the whole island is divided into 5 settlements (*établissements*) – Mini Mini, le Parc, Pointe de l'Est, Anse David and Pointe Marianne, governed by individuals of mixed race … .The number of negro slaves, shared amongst the 5 settlements, amounted to around 300.' Describing the daily routine of those slaves who worked on the collection of coconuts and their conversion to oil, he wrote:

> Early in the morning, after the slaves have been woken by the crack of a whip they went out into the woods to pick the ripe coconuts and take off the outer husk by skilful use of the pointed end of a large shell. Towards midday, each brought his collection to the headquarters. Here the nuts were broken up and left for 4–5 days in the sunshine until the flesh became separated from the hard shell, and was thenceforth called copra, and left another 4–5 days. It was then ready for pressing and a special kind of mill is used, consisting of a hollow cylinder five or six feet high and about two feet in diameter, narrowing into a skittle shape at the bottom and provided with a hole through which the oil dripped. The cylinder was filled with copra, a round pole like a rolling pin put into it, squashing the contents against the sides of the cylinder, by means of a lever 10–12 feet long attached to the top end of the 'rolling pin' which was in turn chained to a horizontal beam turning in a groove at the bottom of the cylinder. At the end of this 'boom', on which a weight is placed to increase the pressure and to rub the 'rolling pin' with force against the side of the skittle-shaped inside of the cylinder, ran a negro, or sometimes a donkey, at a steady pace. (Fraassen & Klapwijk, 2008)

Verr Huell's depiction of a slave and the oil-making machinery at East Point

The 'mixed race' managers or *régisseurs* mentioned by Ver Huell were blamed for various incidents involving maltreatment of slaves and lepers, tales of which trickled back to Mauritius during these years. It being evident that matters could not effectively be managed from Port Louis, Captain Greville, commander of HMS *Espoir* and his surgeon T. T. Jones were requested by the British Admiralty, at the behest of the Colonial Office, to visit Chagos and provide reports on conditions for workers and lepers prevailing there. These 1828 accounts are the first in a long list of official reports detailing the unglamorous and often distinctly unpleasant working and living conditions of laborers on the archipelago in the nineteenth and early twentieth centuries. Greville pointed to cases of overworking, describing the work assigned to the slaves as 'laborious and distressing' and at East Point, 'the greatest discontent prevails, many of the slaves bear dreadful marks of very severe punishment.' At Egmont, after a woman slave showed Greville her scars, the son of the *jouissance* holder there admitted to having ordered her to receive 150 stripes with the stalk of a coconut frond for making 'false allegations' against him. The 68 slave lepers were even worse off, living in 'very uncomfortable, wretched conditions' and 'in want of every common necessary either for the amelioration of their dreadful disease or to make life even a tolerable burthen.' Sixty one of them were 'without clothing, without medicines or medical aid, and without the smallest rag to cover their sores'; the remaining seven were government slaves who annually received a supply of clothes from Mauritius.[12] Slave registration laws and later claims for compensation provide some details of the names, ages, and ethnic status of the Chagos workforce at this time and indicate that the majority were Malagasy and Mozambicans, with a smaller number of Indians and several Creoles.[13]

Following the passing of the Slave Abolition Act in February 1835 and the transition to apprenticeship, Sir William Nicolay, Governor of Mauritius, proposed that the lesser dependencies be occasionally visited by a peripatetic 'special justice.' At this time, the number of apprentices on the Chagos was recorded as 142 on Diego Garcia, 93 at Peros Banhos, 114 on Six Islands and 31 at Trois Frères.[14] In the event, nothing was done about this until 1838 when Special Justice Anderson visited the Chagos islands. Whilst caution must be exercised when considering the subjective views of these individual rapporteurs, Anderson concluded that the lot of apprentices in the dependencies was rather better than on Mauritius itself. He attributed this to the fact that they had more free time to employ 'to their own advantage,' to their 'limited intercourse with strangers' and to the difficulty of obtaining 'spirituous liquors.' At this time, the total population of ex-slave apprentices and their free children was enumerated at 302 [259 adults and 43 children].[15]

The dependencies were virtually ignored by the British administered Government of Mauritius as the island went through the major changes of slave abolition and mass Indian immigration. Astonishingly, no official reports were made about working conditions on the Chagos during the 1840s and for most of the 1850s. For occasional insights, historians are dependent on the casual observations made by whaling ship captains or reports of surveyors which make scant reference to the lot of the working classes. With no one to hear their complaints on the archipelago, workers with grievances to report had to wait months or years until they were shipped back to Mauritius and could address petitions to the authorities there. One group of workers managed to put together a petition in September 1851 complaining that they had worked for between two and three years at Diego Garcia and Peros Banhos respectively and were owed arrears of wages which their erstwhile employers had refused to pay.[16]

In mid-1856, a whaling ship from the United States, cruising in the Indian Ocean, spotted a canoe floating in the sea. In it were six Indian men and a woman, all in a debilitated condition. They were landed at Salomon and eventually brought to Mauritius by a ship which happened to stop off there. The story they told revealed that *jouissance* holders on Six Islands had been in the habit of employing laborers illicitly recruited from Cochin, India. Having embarked voluntarily, in the belief that they were being recruited for work on Mauritian sugar plantations, they were forcibly kept on the Chagos archipelago, and subjected to harsh treatment for no wages. This unholy scheme was meanwhile unravelling with devastating consequences on Six Islands, where the manager Paul Hugon was murdered by the Indian laborers who had then taken forcible possession of the Alexandre Auguste and compelled the captain to convey them back to Cochin. The murderers were rounded up and brought to Mauritius for trial. Statements were obtained from the individuals who had escaped in the pirogue. One of them, Chaccoo, gave a graphic account of their exploitation and ill treatment:

> We left Six Islands because we had been 2 years and 8 months there without receiving any wages and because we were beaten nearly every day by Mr Hugon the overseer. He used to beat us with a rope's end which he generally carried in his pocket. He made four men hold the arms and legs of those that were beaten. The arms and legs being extended spread eagle position. … men were beaten till they fainted.[17]

The disquieting stories of the escapees from Six islands prompted the dispatch of Commander Lumley Peyton of HMS *Frolic* to the Chagos archipelago to investigate this particular case and to enquire into the conditions of workers more generally. At Six Islands, he found 14 Creole laborers and 3 Malagasys. All complained of ill treatment and expressed a wish to go to Mauritius. At Peros Banhos [population 60], Salomon [89], Eagle Island [35] and Diego Garcia [299], Peyton found no other cases of illegally introduced workers but argued that a magistrate and police force was urgently needed for the archipelago.[18] The Indian workers on Six Islands had successfully highlighted the inhumanity of their treatment but at great cost to themselves; this would be a recurring theme as violent resistance erupted over and over again at flashpoints of history when conditions for workers on the Chagos archipelago became unbearable: imprisonment for the resistors; virtual impunity for the malefactors.

A Commission of Inquiry was subsequently ordered to investigate matters in the lesser dependencies of Mauritius, headed by Lieutenant Henry Berkeley, Captain of HMS *Lynx*, who visited the archipelago, accompanied by the Anglican Bishop of Mauritius, Vincent Ryan, in 1859. The voyage brought forward evidence that laborers worked according to verbal agreements, there being no formal contracts, that punishments included banishment to deserted islets, and that supplies were sometimes scarce. The population of the archipelago was enumerated at 338 of whom 16 were managers and their families. Bishop Ryan was concerned about the lack of educational facilities, himself helping to set up a school on one island.[19]

Despite the Commission of Inquiry, little changed, and the periodic cruises of Royal Navy ships to the islands were subject to other demands. Once again, the next intervention was scandal-driven. In 1861, 20 Malagasys were recruited to work in Six Islands on a three-year contract. Two years later, eleven of them fled in a pirogue, reaching Eagle Island where they were sent on to Mauritius. Their application for unpaid wages eventually led to an investigation headed by the Procureur General. The litany of complaints included insufficient rations, failure to pay wages and corporal punishment including beatings with a rattan cane and being shackled in stocks. It was left to the acting Governor of Mauritius, Major Johnstone, to state the inevitable: 'plainly, it is not possible to afford protection by sending cruisers once perhaps every 2 or 3 years, and then only after the perpetration of some heinous crime.'[20] In the short term, HMS *Rapid* was deployed to visit the archipelago in November and December 1864 with a magistrate from Seychelles deputed to report on working conditions. This was duly executed and remarkable only for its blandness. Another decade of neglect followed as Mauritius was plunged into a succession of catastrophes: an outbreak of cholera in 1866, a devastating malaria epidemic which carried off one tenth of the population [32,000 deaths in 1867 alone] and an exceptionally damaging cyclone in 1868, all of which left little time for supervision of the dependencies.

It would not be until a decade later, in 1874, that the Acting Governor, Edward Newton, decided that the administration in Mauritius must itself take responsibility for improving the governance of its dependencies. His successor, Sir Arthur Phayre, quickly secured the appointment of a special magistrate who set out in July 1875 to tour Chagos, Agalega and Coetivy. The population of the Chagos archipelago had increased only marginally, now numbering 623 persons. At Six Islands, the magistrate found the laborers on strike, with the supply of foodstuffs inadequate and irregular. At the other islands, he reported cases of illegal fines, and cases of incarceration of workers for petty offences, and wages diminished by forced purchases in over-priced 'management shops.' Governor Phayre enumerated the principal grievances of workers as follows:

1. Irregular settlement of wages at long intervals instead of by the month.
2. Excessive deductions from wages on account of absence from work.
3. Inferior quality of rice furnished in some instances.
4. Exorbitant charges for necessary articles of food, the price being deducted from wages.
5. The absence of written Engagements and of a scale of rations.
6. The prohibition against fishing, or any occupation for acquiring an independent supply of food; apparently with the object of forcing the laborers to buy salt fish, salt and other articles at the Store kept by the Manager.
7. Detaining laborers at the islands, long after they have expressed a wish to leave and go to Mauritius.[21]

In 1877, the next magistrate to visit Diego Garcia's East Point estate recorded wage rates varying from two and three rupees a month for boys and girls, six to ten rupees a month for women and eight to nine rupees per month for men. Overseers could earn up to 12 rupees.[22]

A local ordinance had meantime been drafted to authorize the appointment of a magistrate with jurisdiction over the lesser dependencies who would make periodic visits, partially subsidized by the proprietors. John Henry Ackroyd held the post until the early 1880s, followed by Ivanoff Dupont, and Arthur Boucherat in 1887. Their reports provide detailed information about workers' lives but are confined to discussions of work, pay, rations, accommodation, discipline, health and related matters with virtually no analysis of their extra-curricular activities or opinions as to their conditions and treatment. These weighty official missives nevertheless point to changes in the ethnic status of workers which reflect larger patterns in the Mascarenes. The proportion of Mozambicans fell and that of Indians increased. The numbers of single Malagasy men suggest that recruitment from that region continued. The heavy preponderance of men over women was noted alongside cases of domestic violence. The regular visits of magistrates may have prevented some abuses, but the health of workers on the Chagos archipelago, without access to proper medical care, continued to be a cause of concern. Perinatal mortality was high, especially on Six Islands where over a three-year period between 1875 and 1878, eight out of twelve newborns [aged up to two weeks] died.[23] However, the absence of major scandals led to a certain complacency and after 1884, the frequency of magisterial visits declined and a period of neglect of the islanders' well-being followed. Meantime, economic difficulties led the proprietors of the 'oil establishments' to reorganize and mergers followed. Copra (dried coconut kernels) became the dominant export, rather than coconut oil, while little was done to improve the conditions for the working population.

At the turn of the twentieth century, the workers on the Chagos continued to live in huts built of timber, lined with coconut leaves, they reared poultry and fished, to supplement the meagre rations imported for them, and while infant mortality remained high – almost half of children born on Chagos dying before their twelfth birthday, those who reached adulthood had a better chance of survival than on Mauritius where epidemic disease continued to claim many lives. New arrivals were less fortunate – recruits from Anjouan in the Comoros were diagnosed with *beriberi* [symptoms caused by vitamin B1 deficiency] in 1900 and several died. Malnutrition, aggravated by the lack of fresh vegetables, afflicted many of the inhabitants and a continuing disparity between the sexes was a feature of all the atoll populations. Nevertheless, distinctive Ilois communities were in the process of formation and the statement of Petit Jean, in 1908, is reflective of this.[24] Despite having contracted tuberculosis he declined to leave Salomon, declaring that he had been born there and 'all my relatives are on that island. I do not wish to leave a place where I am contented and happy.'[25]

By 1911, the population of the Chagos archipelago had reached 1183 and in the years leading up to the World War I, mortality levels improved, a probable benefit of the appointment of dispenser-stewards, one of the few concessions made by proprietors towards the social improvement of their workers. War, in 1914, and again in 1939, brought disruptions in supplies, especially rice, and consequent hardship for the island residents. During the interwar period, magistrates Geneve and Berengeragain found much to criticize. By now, two distinct groups were becoming visible in the archival record – new arrivals who suffered from the low wages and minimal supplies and were anxious to return to Mauritius, as distinct from the longer established populations who had become accustomed to the regime and asked for little more than occasional visits to Mauritius to vary their routine. Child mortality remained high and the prevalence of ancylostomiasis [hookworm] was noted. The lack of welfare provisions and poor sanitation coupled with derisory pay all testified that productivity not infrastructure remained the priority of owners.[26]

In June 1930, visiting magistrate W. J. Hanning was struck by the failure of management to make the best of the resources of Diego Garcia. He wrote that the machinery was 'old-fashioned and inadequate, and every building and apparatus breathes of stagnation.' He followed up on previous magistrates' reports with what was becoming a repetitive complaint – that insufficient care was being taken to recruit a suitable workforce, observing that 'habitual criminals' were being sent while another, Berenger, claimed that on Diego Garcia 'the majority' of the men and 'many women' spent more than 50% of their pay on a very low quality imported 'wine.' When he left, 18 men, 10 women and 16 children requested to return with him to Mauritius.[27]

The average price per tonne of copra imported to Mauritius from Chagos fell from 231 rupees/tonne to 195 rupees in 1930–1932 and as managers sought to reduce workers' bonuses, labor difficulties increased. On Peros Banhos in 1931, a full-scale rebellion erupted, and serious loss of life was only narrowly avoided.[28] By 1935, the plantations on Egmont and Eagle islands had been abandoned. Père Roger Dussercle, a French Catholic missionary who chronicled the oil islands in the 1930s, summed up the situation of the Ilois when he wrote of those who travelled to Mauritius hoping to find a better life, only to turn up at his door asking for help, having gone without food for days. The depressed conditions of 1930s Mauritius meant that the Ilois were effectively between a rock and a hard place (Dussercle, 1934, pp. 101–102).

The written memoirs of Roger Dussercle and those of Marcelle Lagesse, daughter of Raoul Caboche, manager of Salomon, 1931–1952, offer perspectives of the cultural and social lives of the Chagos islanders which serves as useful counter-narratives to the official reports of visiting magistrates. Dussercle (1934, p. 56) visited Ilois homes which he described as

> rooms separated by partitions made of matted palm leaves and furnished in much the same way as those of the poorest Creoles – at least those living in rural areas – back home in Mauritius: a straw pallet [for a bed], clothing in tumbled heaps or hung up by string … knick-knacks fight for space with purely ornamental containers and, occasionally, a common-or-garden wind-up gramophone. Drums, covered in tightly tensioned goatskin and so essential to setting a séga going, are usually tucked away under the rafters.

Marcelle Lagesse (1967) provides an account of the women workers' usual daily routine on the Chagos which is insightful. They would be woken by a bell at 5 am, go to the copra kiln to fetch charcoal to relight cooking fires, collect water in buckets from the well, and prepare a breakfast of grilled cooked rice and hot sugared water. Then their official working day would begin, and might involve weeding, making roofs with coconut fronds, or more commonly, breaking up a daily quota of 700 de-husked coconuts.

During the World War II, disruption to supplies was again experienced, and further upheaval was occasioned from mid-1941 when Diego Garcia was garrisoned by soldiers from Mauritius, and an RAF flying-boat base was established there. While some islanders found it advantageous to sell fish and chickens to the garrison, there were also complaints that the soldiers stole the already scarce resources of fresh fruit and vegetables. In October 1944, when a group of Ilois broke open the jail and threatened to riot, eight soldiers helped to restore order (Jackson, 2001). After 1945, the troops were able to leave, but the Chagos islanders were left with the negative consequences of neglected infrastructure and investments foregone. It would be an uphill struggle to restore pre-war levels of production let alone achieve a level of prosperity that had always eluded the Chagos (Duyker, 1986, p. 186).

In the mid to late 1940s, a series of recommendations for 'drastic changes' with a view to bettering the lives of both overseers and laborers were put forward. Improved management was deemed to be essential in order to effect much needed ameliorations regarding health, nutrition, housing, education, amenities and wages.[29] Of course, the islanders were not worse off than the Mauritians in many respects at this time and indeed epidemics of whooping cough, measles and influenza which proved fatal to some Ilois, were generally introduced by those who had returned from visits to Mauritius. Illnesses which originated in the Chagos tended to be related to poor sanitation, poisoning from fish or alcohol, and the difficulty of providing proper nutrition for newborns.[30]

Memory and the Ilois: pre and post-Expulsion experiences & narratives

From the 1950s onwards, the experiences of the Ilois are no longer wholly mediated by memoirs of managers, magistrates, sailors and priests, as we begin to have access to the testimonies and recollections of Chagossians, compiled through interviews and research studies. This was also a decade which saw the first visits to the archipelago by successive Governors of Mauritius, improvements in education, and an influx of new workers from the Seychelles.

Of exceptional value are the recently published memoirs of the sadly now deceased Chagossian, Fernand Mandarin (Richon, 2016; Wenban-Smith & Carter, 2016).[31] Growing up on Peros Banhos, he did not benefit from the school which was set up in time for his younger brother to attend but instead recalls a lifetime of hard work:

> I was working already at 12/13 years of age, in 1955–6, in the boiler room of the factory. I had a two-part salary, one given in money: Rs 7 monthly and the other given weekly as a ration: 1 lb of rice for each working day, given on a Saturday, some dholl, lentils, peas and butterbeans, ½lb of salt, 1 lb of flour, ½ bottle of coconut oil. This would be my labourer's salary until the age of 16.

At 16 years of age, Fernand was classed as an adult, and with it came the right to live in a thatched house, constructed by the administration. Working conditions were imposed from above, and his first job was to de-husk coconuts. It was very hard work, as he recalls:

> I had to carry a sharp machete and a basket on my head. I used the machete to spear the coconuts and place them in the basket. The basket was very heavy. Not everyone could do this work. The first time I did it my hands were raw. After a few days one got used to it. Some people could not do it and went back to Mauritius.

Significantly, notes Fernand, the quality of life of the Ilois depended very much upon the administrator and the *commandeurs*, with whom one was obliged to work. He recalls individuals who were violent with workers and sexually assaulted women and even young girls. With no police force to resolve disputes, *commandeurs* and administrators were referred to in case of arguments and had powers to imprison trouble-makers: 'Prison was hard, those incarcerated had to live on a few dry grains of rice with some salt for six days, or it could be for twelve days depending on the crime,' Fernand remembers.

The sometimes harsh realities of Ilois working lives in the 1950s are counterpoised in Fernand's narrative by his lively descriptions of local customs and celebrations. Recollections of the drudgery of labor and the dark shadow of violence that were a daily reality for islanders coexist with happy memories of a vibrant and distinctive cultural life that had been forged by the Ilois communities of the Chagos archipelago. These were difficult times for both workers and management. In May 1949, an official of the Labour Department, Mr G. Mayer visited the Chagos and this was followed up by a visit of the new Governor of Mauritius, Sir Hilary Blood, in 1951. He was accompanied by Dr Maurice Lavoipierre who wrote a depressing report on health and hygiene, especially at Diego Garcia with widespread anemia and parasitic infestations. The absence of toilets meant that intestinal diseases were widespread. As a result of this visit, a sanitary inspector was sent to the Chagos to oversee the building of latrines and drains, and to organize waste disposal.[32]

In late 1956, an investor in the Seychelles expressed an interest in purchasing the Diego Company's assets in Agalega and Chagos. Overtures were also made to London to investigate the possibility of a government buy-out of the under-performing coconut plantations, but this was rejected. In 1959, the Mauritius Director of Agriculture, Mr Maurice Lucie-Smith made a tour of the copra producing islands to assess the prospects for restoring them to profitability. At this time, Diego Ltd owned and operated the plantations on

Diego Garcia, Peros Banhos and Salomon, while Agalega Ltd owned those of Agalega. The two companies shared ownership of Diego-Agalega Shipping Ltd and also co-owned the copra-processing plant Innova Ltd. The two subsidiaries, at this time, were heavily indebted. Lucie-Smith's report highlighted the poor performance of the coconut plantations compared to Trinidad, where output was 0.29 tons of nuts per acre compared to 0.14 tons on Chagos and Agalega.[33]

By 1961, the companies were negotiating with Seychelles investor, Paul Moulinié, and with Rogers & Co of Mauritius. René Maingard, Managing Director of Rogers, visited the islands, along with Moulinié and Dr Wiehe, an agriculturalist. Wiehe's report revealed that the productivity of the Chagos plantations had shown virtually no improvement between 1939 and 1960. After the visit, René Maingard sent a telegram to the Rogers Board informing them, 'MOULINIE OF OPINION THAT REORGANISATION WOULD NOT COST EXCESSIVELY UNDER SUPERVISION EXPECT IMPROVEMENT FIVE YEARS TEN YEARS ESPECIALLY DIEGO WHOSE POTENTIALITIES ARE MUCH LARGER.' In his private diary, however, Maingard confided, 'I don't want to see another coconut in all my life or smell the rancid odour of copra ever again as long as I live.' In reply to the telegram, the Rogers Board replied,

> COPRA REPORT RECEIVED FROM LONDON VERY BAD FURTHER DECLINE LIKELY AS SUPPLIES EXCEED DEMAND AND RECORD PRODUCTION SOYA IN USA LIKELY TO REDUCE PRICE OF COCONUT OIL NO IMPROVEMENT IN THE MARKET ANTICIPATED FOR THE TIME BEING IF NOT FOR A LONG TIME STOP THIS HAS CONSIDERABLY REDUCED OUR ENTHUSIASM AND NOW FEEL WHETHER WOULD NOT BEADVISABLE KEEP OUT OF THIS BUSINESS AND CONCENTRATE ON SHIPPING SIDE ONLY.[34]

On his return to Mauritius, Maingard nevertheless recommended the purchase of a one-third share in the islands: 'I feel Diego particularly is bound to come into its own one day and with the importance the Indian Ocean is taking we should never abandon the old oil islands,' he wrote in his report.[35] A subsidiary of Rogers & Co, the Colonial Steamship Company, took a one-third share of the new company Chagos-Agalega, with Moulinié as Chairman, and he and family members taking the remaining two thirds. The transfer of ownership took effect in February 1962.[36]

The impact on the workforce of this period of uncertainty is significant. Many left for Mauritius. Between 1944 and 1962, the numbers of individuals born in the Chagos archipelago recorded as residents in Mauritius according to census data, increased from 57 to 494. Movements of contract workers to and from the archipelago can also be related to changes in management. Paul Moulinié appointed Seychellois managers to Diego Garcia, Peros Banhos and Salomon. The departing Mauritian Manager, Robert Talbot, took about 40 workers away with him when he left Diego Garcia, and on Peros Banhos Fernand Mandarin has described the difficulties for the Ilois of interacting with new managers who 'lacked manners and became violent, giving hard tasks to elderly people or putting in prison those who had not completed their tasks.' Fernand remarks that the tendency for the younger Ilois to leave in search of better opportunities intensified in this period; scores of adults had left Peros Banhos by 1964; he recalled that their empty houses were subsequently destroyed, while children were called upon to undertake adult tasks (Wenban-Smith & Carter, 2016, pp. 466–476).

The events leading to the creation of BIOT, and particularly the negotiations between Britain and Mauritius in which the excision of the Chagos was used as a bargaining tool in return for independence have –exceptionally – been carefully researched and discussed by Mauritian historians. Jocelyn Chan Low (2011) has described a meeting between Mauritian Premier Seewoosagur Ramgoolam and British Prime Minister Harold Wilson on the morning of 23 September 1965. Wilson stated that the Mauritian delegation

> could return to Mauritius either with independence or without it. On the Defence part, Diego Garcia could either be detached by Order in Council or with the agreement of the Premier and his colleagues. The best of all might be independence and detachment by agreement.

According to Chan Low (2007), 'Sir Seewoosagur Ramgoolam said that he was convinced that the question of Diego Garcia was a matter of detail. There was no difficulty in principle.' Mauritian historian Narainduth Sookhoo (2015) has asserted that Ramgoolam was 'a compromiser on Chagos' and cites the steering brief dated 22 September 1965:

> SSR is coming to see you tomorrow at 10.00. The object is to frighten him with hope that he might get independence. Fright lest he might not unless he is sensible about the detachment of the Chagos ... call him Sir Seewoosagur or Premier, his official titles. He likes to be called Prime Minister ... Getting old. Realise he must get independence soon or it will be too late for his personal career.

Sir Seewoosagur Ramgoolam later admitted before the Select Committee on the Excision of the Chagos archipelago:

> I thought that independence was much more primordial and more important than the excision of the island which is very far from here, and which we had never visited, which we could never visit .... If I had to choose between independence and the ceding of Diego Garcia, I would have done again the same thing. (De l'Estrac, 1983, p. 22)

The perspective of the Indo-Mauritian political elite in the pre-independence negotiations was summed up by Houbert (1992, p. 471) who wrote, that they 'considered that the excision of a distant archipelago, and the expulsion of some poor illiterate Creoles, was a small price to pay for state power, with British support, in decolonisation.' Crucially, the anti-independence Parti Mauricien Social Démocrate, which purported to represent 'Creole' interests, had walked out of the discussions, leaving the way clear for Ramgoolam to make his own judgement as to what terms he was prepared to accept.

While the negotiations leading to the creation of BIOT have been carefully examined by historians, the long history of the Ilois and their forebears on the archipelago has been glossed over in studies focusing on the expulsion of the population of the Chagos, and the subsequent Chagossian fight for justice. British and subsequently Mauritian arrangements for resettling the Ilois have been the subject of an extensive literature and rightly criticized and this story alongside the evolution of Ilois narratives before and after the trauma of expulsion, as they struggled to deal with life on the island of Mauritius, has been detailed by anthropologists and others (Bandjunis, 2001; Sand, 2009; Vine, 2009). Laura Jeffery (2011) offers a succinct summary of what awaited the Ilois after their removal from Chagos:

> the challenging social, economic, and political conditions that confronted the displaced islanders upon their arrival in Mauritius, the main site of relocation ... demographic constraints, economic challenges, and ethnic tensions in Mauritius during the decades each

side of independence in 1968 negatively impacted upon relocated Chagos islanders. First, Chagos islanders in Mauritius suffered from overcrowded living conditions in poor-quality houses in disadvantaged neighbourhoods with associated educational and social problems. Second, they were marginalised economically by the obsolescence of their skills in Mauritius, where they were exposed to unemployment, underemployment, and low wages. Third, they were marginalised socially through ethnic stereotypes and discrimination.

The marginalization of the Ilois in Mauritius, argues Jeffery, 'has inspired self-identification by Chagos islanders as a victimized community and has attracted external support.' This has resulted in the creation of a 'homeland discourse' whereby Chagossians recount 'standardised collective narratives that romanticised and idealised the Chagos archipelago as their homeland.' An interesting example of the dichotomous discourse that has evolved is reflected in the changing lyrical content of the sega songs of the Ilois. Those that were written while Ilois were still resident on the archipelago may be said to 'Represent' Chagos and discuss everyday sorrows as well as joys, while those written after displacement instead 'Romanticise' Chagos (Jeffery, 2011, pp. 62–64).

The institutional racism, ethnic stereotyping and nepotism in Mauritius identified by researchers, which has served to restrict opportunities for Afro-Creoles, was especially marked insofar as Chagossians were concerned. Miles (1999) has written that 'Chagos islanders … are doubly marginalized in Mauritius: primarily by race but also by origin.' Maurer (2014) explicitly states that the Ilois were 'rejected' by Mauritians, while Walker (1986) recorded examples of inhumane treatment in shared housing and discrimination at the workplace.[37] Hence Chagossians have negatively framed the cultural changes resulting from their relocation and intermarriage with Mauritians (and others) while 'cultural distinctiveness and cultural revival are framed positively.' The contrasting conceptualizations of culture, Jeffery (2011, p. 22) argues, should not be understood as contradictions but rather as 'survival strategies in the face of severe structural disadvantage.' Rosabelle Boswell (2006, p. 55) has stressed that the 'shared sense of suffering and shared territory' emphasized by Ilois have enabled them to 'reaffirm their status as a culture-possessing group, an important achievement in a society concerned with primordial ties.'

The collective, romanticized narrative framed by Chagossians has posed some problems in the legal fight for justice. In his 2003 judgement Mr Justice Ouseley ruled against the Ilois, noting that 'evidence was … given, as if at first hand, about events which the witness could not have seen or heard.' He 'dismissed several Chagossian witnesses as unreliable and inconsistent because they initially presented as first-hand eyewitness evidence stories that later appeared to have been based not on individual experience but rather on collective memory' (Jeffery, 2007, pp. 963–964). It has been observed that the legal 'processes of transcription and translation concealed the deployment in Chagossian oral traditions of rhetorical devices such as collective narrative and standardized history.' These rhetorical devices worked effectively in garnering media support but broke down in the court room where judges were expecting 'first-hand experience and recollection of specific events' (Jeffery, 2006).

Saïd (2000, pp. 177–179) has eloquently conveyed the process through which exiled communities create a 'reassembled identity' as a coping mechanism, reconstituting broken lives by re-imaginings of the 'homeland.' Chagossians, likewise, have striven to emphasize a distinct identity and at the same time, in order to demonstrate their victimhood and establish that they deserve recompense and repatriation, Chagossians must show that they have suffered cultural loss in exile, where they have both struggled to sustain their own traditions and been influenced by interaction and intermarriage with non-Chagossians (Jeffery, 2011, p. 27).

The re-creation of an idealized vision of the lost homeland can however damage diaspora communities, according to Radhakrishnan (2003, p. 123), who writes that over time, ignorance of historical realities and over-emphasis on stereotypes creates a disjuncture with the lived history of exiles and migrants.

In the case of the Chagossians, the loss of memory has been 'sacralized' and 'instrumentalized' for a cause. In so doing, engagement with the present and the future can be compromised, because the past has become frozen, objectified and sterile (Ricoeur, 2006, pp. 97–98; Todorov, 1995, pp. 51–61). Discussing her interactions with the child descendants of Chagossians, Sandra Evers (2011, p. 120) notes that their 'representations of Chagos echoed the narratives of parents and grandparents, who portrayed Chagos as a paradise.' Elsewhere she writes

> first generation Chagossians depicted Chagos as paradise, a message which resonates with their grandchildren and which they virtually all remember ... tales of harsh aspects of life in Chagos were omitted from the discursive and creative framework of these narratives, to such an extent that children fail to mention negative aspects of life in the archipelago. (Evers & Kooy, 2011, p. 262)

The taking-up of this narrative by journalists and other representatives of the Chagossians has served to mobilize support but in the long term, it may do a disservice to their cause as the over-simplifications of the re-imagined lives of the Ilois trouble readers and observers. In an illuminating critique of Mauritian journalist Shenaz Patel's (2004) fictional retelling of the Chagossians' story Antje Ziethen (2013) observes:

> In her honorable attempt to defend their cause, Patel simply mimics their discourse and ends up caricaturing Chagossians and Mauritians. The text turns the Chagossians themselves into docile Blacks [who] serve white Europeans and lead a simple but happy life on a tropical island.

If sources detailing social and racial hierarchies, exploitative working conditions and economic powerlessness are not explicitly referenced, uninformed readers of such 'mimic discourses' risk misinterpreting the narrative for the reality.

Conclusion

Ann Stoler, who describes herself as an ethnographer by training and a historian by passion, has noted how

> imperial dispositions are formed with the capacity to turn towards what one may partially know and as quickly turn away, by what it means to know and not know something at the same time. Empire has been predicated on such dispositions of dis-regard.

Equally, the gaze of the historian and the ethnographer must not 'dis-regard' the realities of the lived histories of workers on the Chagos archipelago. Stoler's own work (2010, pp. 215–219), emphasizes the importance of 'studying the shadows cast by imperial governance, in tracking the violence of social distinctions, and in attempting to discern the muted forms of managing people's lives.' In his influential work on the Haitian Revolution,

Trouillot (1995, p. 27) notes 'any historical narrative is a particular bundle of silences' which enter the process of historical production when sources, archives, and narratives are assembled. Unpicking and interrogating these 'silences' has enabled postcolonial historians to liberate themselves 'from national or imperial stories stored in childhood or learned from gatekeepers' (Hoerder, 2001, p. 874). This article speaks to the necessity of incorporating the history of labor on the Chagos archipelago into the larger corpus of writings about subaltern Indian Ocean diaspora communities who are constructing new identities against the 'detritus' of wounding and traumatizing colonial experiences (Govinden, 2009).

Disclosure statement

No potential conflict of interest was reported by the authors.

Notes

1. The term 'Chagossian' replaced the use of the term Ilois relatively recently [in the 1990s]. In this article, slave, or worker, or laborer or 'Ilois' is used wherever historical references are made; the word Chagossian is used when referring to the present day.
2. There are virtually no substantive works on Chagos written by professional historians. Previous works covering aspects of the eighteenth- and nineteenth-century history of the archipelago include Scott (1961), Edis (1993), Fry (1967), Stoddart (1971), Chelin (2012). An attempt to address this lacuna has been made by Wenban-Smith and Carter (2016). Much of the documentation in this article is derived from research undertaken for this book.
3. Archives Nationales [AN] Paris, 3JJ 358 Mémoire anonyme, 1780.
4. Royal Society of Mauritius Archives [RSA], Papiers Doyen 22/36 Despatch of Vicomte de Souillace, 31 October 1786.
5. Slaves and other non-white workers were usually ethnically categorized according to their place of birth at this time.
6. Mauritius Archives [MA] TB 3/2. The island was also said to abound in seabirds, turtles, fish and wild hens, but water was difficult to find and brackish.
7. RSA, Papiers Decaen 22/36 Despatch of Vicomte de Souillac, 31 October 1786.
8. Maharashtra State Archives, Secret & Political Diary no 33A, Bombay Government to Governor General and Council, Fort William, 18 March 1786, ditto to President and Council, Fort St George, 31 March 1786.
9. Maharashtra State Archives, Secret & Political Diary no 33A, Bombay Government to John Richmond Smyth, 27 November 1786.
10. According to the notes of Baron d'Unienville, made shortly after the British took possession of Mauritius, these de facto arrangements were not formalized because the French administration was still flirting with the idea of setting up a lazaret for lepers at Chagos, see MA TB 3/2.
11. Their fate is unknown but it is likely that the navy retained only those slaves who had maritime skills and disposed of the others in British settlements around the Indian Ocean.
12. Royal College of Physicians Archive, London, OFFIP/4000/1 and National Archives, London [NA] Colonial Office [CO] 167/107 enclosures to Governor's dispatch dated 20 May 1829 for Jones and Greville reports respectively.
13. See for example MA IG 59 No 5353 for details of 52 slaves belonging to Ozille Majastre in 1832
14. NA CO 167/182, Governor's dispatch of 16 February 1835.
15. NA CO 167/204 Mr Special Justice Anderson to Colonial Secretary 5 Sept 1838.
16. MA RA 1135 Petition of John Sanpath, Marie Orelie, Both Hyanth, Pascalle, Eloise Celina, Desire, Desire, Mozambique, and Estelle, 18 September 1851.
17. MA RA 1386 Statement of Chaccoo, 1857.

18. MA RA 1386 Statement of Chaccoo, Report of Peyton, 27th January 1857.
19. NA CO 167/412 Report, dated 14 July 1859 enclosed with Mauritius dispatch No.113
20. NA CO 167/452 Johnstone dispatch, 17 October 1863.
21. NA CO 170/93 Appendix, p. 250. In
22. NA CO 170/96 Appendix p. 1484.
23. NA CO 170/98 Report of Magistrate Ackroyd, 1878.
24. Since Eugene Genovese published his pathbreaking study *Roll Jordan roll the world the slaves made,* New York, Pantheon Books, 1974, historians have investigated ways in which subaltern groups have sought to express their humanity and contest their oppression through culture, music and religion.
25. NA CO 167/784 Governor's dispatch 11 May 1908.
26. See NA CO/167/861/10 and 865/4 for details of magistrates' reports 1927-1929.
27. Berenger report enclosed in dispatch no 481 of 19 December 1928, NA CO 167 862/8; Hanning report enclosed in dispatch of 16 Nov 1931 NA CO 167/875/12.
28. Mauritius Blue Books NA CO 172/154-9.
29. As late as 1946 it was found that some workers had been signing contracts at rates of Rs 8 per month. This was considered to have enabled managers to dock the actual earnings of non-performers. NA CO 167/912/10 Report of Rousset, 26 June 1946.
30. NA CO 167/912/10 Report of Lavoipierre, Glover & Rousset, 26 June 1946
31. See Wenban-Smith and Carter, 2016, chapter 20 which draws heavily on transcriptions of interviews conducted by Robert Furlong and additional material from interviews with Fernand recorded for the book.
32. The population of Chagos increased from 980 in 1947 to 1151 in 1952. CO 1032/132 Enclosure to Despatch of 31 Oct 1951.
33. Reports of de Broglio on Diego Ltd are held in NA CO 1036/421; Lucie-Smith's report is in NA CO 1036/502
34. Personal diary of R. H. Maingard, September 1961.
35. Maingard, R. H. 'Report on a visit to the Oil Islands', unpublished report.
36. Details of the formation of the Chagos-Agalega company and the financial background are taken from the report of Robert Newton, NA CO 2114/64.
37. The persistence of racist attitudes towards the Chagossians in Mauritius is exemplified by the comments of Sir Satcam Boolell 'Diego Garcia and the International Community', *l'Express*, 24 March 1995 and the subsequent critique of those remarks.

References

Abraham, G. (2011). Paradise claimed: Disputed sovereignty over the Chagos Archipelago. *South African Law Journal, 128,* 63–99.

Bandjunis, V. B. (2001). *Diego Garcia: Creation of the Indian Ocean base.* Lincoln: Writer's Showcase.

Boswell, R. (2006). *Le Malaise Creole: Ethnic identity in Mauritius.* New York, NY: Berghahn Books.

Carter, M. (2006). *Slavery and unfree labour in the Indian Ocean.* Oxford: History Compass.

Chan Low, J. (2007). The making of the British Indian Ocean territory: A forgotten tragedy. In S. M. Toorawa (Ed.), *The Western Indian Ocean essays* (pp. 105–126). Port Louis: Hassam Toorawa Trust.

Chan Low, J. (2011). The making of the Chagos affair: Myths and reality. In S. J. Evers & M. Kooy (Eds.), *Eviction from the Chagos Islands displacement and struggle for identity against two world powers* (pp. 61–70). Leiden: Brill.

Chelin, J. M. (2012). *Les ziles là-haut: histoire de l'archipel des Chagos.* Port Louis: Author.

De l'Estrac, J. (1983). *Report of the select committee on the excision of the Chagos Archipelago.* Port Louis.

Dubofsky, M. (2000). *Hard work: The making of labor history*. Binghamton, NY: SUNY.
Dussercle, R. (1934). *Archipel de Chagos: En mission Novembre 1933 – Janvier 1934*. Port-Louis: General Printing & Stationery.
Duyker, E. (Ed.). (1986). *Mauritian heritage: An anthology of the Lionnet, Commins and related families*. Ferntree Gully, Victoria: Australian Mauritian Research Group.
Edis, R. S. (1993). *Peak of Limuria*. London: Bellew.
Evers, S. (2011). *Not just a victim: The child as catalyst and witness of contemporary Africa*. Leiden: Brill.
Evers, S. J., & Kooy, M. (Eds.). (2011). *Eviction from the Chagos Islands displacement and struggle for identity against two world powers*. Leiden: Brill.
Fraassen, V. C., & Klapwijk, P. J. (2008). *Herinneringaaneen reis naar Oost-Indië*, Linschoten-Vereeniging.
Fry, H. T. (1967). Early British interest in the Chagos Archipelago and the Maldive Islands. *Mariners Mirror, 53*(4), 343–356.
Govinden, D. B. (2009). Healing the wounds of history: South African Indian writing. *Current Writing, 21*(1&2), 286–302.
Hebert, J. C. (1984). *Les Français sur la Côte Ouest de Madagascar au Temps de Ravahiny [1780–1812]*. Madagascar: Omaly Si Anio.
Hoerder, D. (2001). How the intimate lives of subaltern men, women, and children confound the nation's master narratives. *Journal of American History, 88*(3), 874–881.
Houbert, J. (1992). The Indian Ocean Creole Islands: Geo-politics and decolonisation. *The Journal of Modern African Studies, 30*(3), 465–484.
Hurgobin, Y., & Basu, S. (2015). Oceans without borders: Dialectics of transcolonial labor migration from the Indian Ocean World to the Atlantic Ocean World. *International Labour & Working Class History, 87*, 7–26.
Jackson, A. (2001). *War and empire in Mauritius and the Indian Ocean*. Basingstoke: Palgrave.
Jeffery, L. (2006). Historical narrative and legal evidence: Judging Chagossians' high court testimonies. *PoLAR: Political and Legal Anthropology Review, 29*, 228–253.
Jeffery, L. (2007). How a plantation became paradise: Changing representations of the homeland among displaced Chagos Islanders. *The Journal of the Royal Anthropological Institute, 13*(4), 951–968.
Jeffery, L. (2011). *Chagos islands in Mauritius and the UK. Forced displacement and onward migration*. Manchester: Manchester University Press.
Lagesse, M. (1967). *d'Un Carnet*. Port Louis: Editions Paul Mackay.
Lepelley, R. (1992). *Croisieres dans la Mer des Indes 1810–1811*. Spezet: Keltia Graphic.
Linden, M. (2003). *Transnational labour history: Explorations*. London: Routledge.
Maurer, S. (2014). Post-colonialism: The so-called malaise creole in Mauritius. *Antrocom Online Journal of Anthropology, 10*(1), 87–97.
Miles, W. (1999). The Creole Malaise in Mauritius. *African Affairs, 98*(391), 211–228.
O'Hanlon, P. (1988). Recovering the subject subaltern studies and histories of resistance in colonial South Asia. *Modern Asian Studies, 22*, 189–224.
Patel, S. (2004). *Le silence des Chagos*. Paris: Éditions de l'Olivier.
Pilger, J. (2004, October 2). Diego Garcia: Paradise Cleansed. *The Guardian*.
Radhakrishnan, R. (2003). Ethnicity in an age of diaspora. In J. Evans Braviel & A. Mannur (Eds.), *Theorizing diaspora: A reader* (pp. 119–131). Malden: Blackwell.
Richon, E. (2016). *Retour aux Chagos quand Fernand Mandarin raconte*. Port Louis: Mauritius.
Ricoeur, P. (2006). *La mémoire, l'histoire, l'oubli*. Paris: Seuil.
Saïd, E. (2000). *Reflections on exile and other essays*. Cambridge, MA: Harvard University Press.
Sand, P. H. (2009). *United States and Britain in Diego Garcia*. New York: Palgrave Macmillan.
Scott, J. C. (1985). *Weapons of the weak: Everyday forms of resistance*. New Haven, CT: Yale University Press.
Scott, J. C. (1992). *Domination and the arts of resistance: Hidden transcript*. New Haven, CT: Yale University Press.
Scott, R. (1961). *Limuria – the lesser dependencies of Mauritius*. Oxford: Oxford University Press.
Snoxell, D. (2008). Expulsion from Chagos: Regaining paradise. *The Journal of Imperial and Commonwealth History, 36*(1), 119–129.

Sookhoo, N. (2015, March 30). Independence and post-colonial Mauritius (1968–1982). *Week-End*.
Spivak, G. (1988). Can the subaltern speak? In C. Nelson & L. Grossberg (Eds.), *Marxism and the interpretation of culture* (pp. 271–313). Basingstoke: Macmillan.
Stoddart, D. R. (1971). Settlement and development of Diego Garcia. *Atoll Research Bulletin*, *149*, 209–217.
Stoler, L. (2010). Archival dis-ease: Thinking through colonial ontologies. *Communication and Critical/Cultural Studies*, *7*(2), 215–219.
Thompson, E. P. (1963). *The making of the English working class*. London: Victor Gollancz.
Todorov, T. (1995). *Abus de la mémoire*. Paris: Arléa.
Toorawa, S. (Ed.). (2007). *The Western Indian Ocean essays on islands and islanders*. Port Louis: Hassam Toorawa Trust.
Trouillot, M. (1995). *Silencing the past power and the production of history*. Boston, MA: Beacon Press.
Van Onselen, C. (1976). Randlords and Rotgut, 1886–1903: An essay on the role of alcohol in the development of European Imperialism and Southern African Capitalism, with special reference to black mineworkers in the Transvaal republic. *History Workshop*, 2.
Vine, D. (2009). *Island of shame*. Princeton: Princeton University Press.
Walker, I. (1986). *Zaffer pe sanze, ethnic identity and social change among the Ilois of Mauritius*. Vacoas: KMLI.
Wenban-Smith, N., & Carter, M. (2016). *Chagos: A history exploration, exploitation, expulsion*. London: Chagos Conservation Trust.
Zeitlyn, D. (2008). June, life-history writing and the anthropological silhouette. *Social Anthropology*, *16*(2), 154–171.
Ziethen, A. (2013). Shifting geo/graphies: Between production and reception of imagined spaces. In G. Everson (Ed.), *Perspectives on space and place* (pp. 11–16). Oxford: Interdisciplinary Press.

'Indo-Mauritians' and the Indian Ocean: literacy accounts and anthropological readings

Mathieu Claveyrolas

ABSTRACT
Starting from a broad historical overview, and focusing on the main group in the Mauritian population (the Hindu descendants of indentured laborers), this paper goes through the many and changing narratives of indenture, as a 'domesticating paradigm' promoted in both literature and identity discourses. It deals with three connected questions, each helping us understand the relations between Mauritius and the Indian Ocean. First, is the issue of the links between so-called Indo-Mauritians and India, the territories their ancestors came from: have they been severed or enhanced? Second, comes the auto-representations and status of Mauritius: is it an ideal *center-of-the-world*, or a relegated island lost in the Indian Ocean? Third are the representations Indo-Mauritians have of their original migrations, through the crossing of the Indian Ocean. A final point notes the poor inclusion of Mauritius in the Indian Ocean compared with the powerful and exclusive link between India and Mauritius.

Introduction

The Republic of Mauritius comprises several islands, out of which the Island of Mauritius is the largest one.[1] Located in the Indian Ocean some 500 miles east of Madagascar, it is densely populated, with 1.2 million inhabitants for only 787 square miles in area. Remembering Certeau's (1975) warning against the ethnocentric temptation to assimilate Western colonization with the beginning of history, we must refrain from separating Mauritius from its regional, Indian Ocean, context: well before the West played, here, a central role, the Indian Ocean had been a major passage for various maritime routes for centuries and, consequently, a place where Asia, Africa and the Muslim worlds already interacted. Arabs knew the Island of Mauritius (and the islands of Rodrigues and Reunion) well before the Europeans and the Mascarene Islands maps of Al-Idrissi of 1154 AD are a testimony to that (Kalla, 2016).

Yet, despite a brief Portuguese presence, Mauritius remained uninhabited until the seventeenth century, when it was first briefly and unsuccessfully colonized by the Dutch (1658–1710). The French then took possession of the island in 1715 and stayed for a century (up to 1810), importing slaves from Africa and Madagascar, before the

British eventually took over the island – from 1810 to its independence in 1968. After the abolition of slavery in 1835, roughly coinciding with the development of a plantation society based on sugarcane, the need for cheap labor was met through the importation of half-a-million indentured laborers, mostly Indians, from 1834 to 1907 (Carter, 1995, p. 7). This is the first, basic, and enduring fact in Mauritian history: Mauritius is a settlement colony built over less than three centuries on the meeting (whether conflictual or not) of diverse populations, all originally migrants, mainly from Europe, Africa and India (as well as China).

Indeed, as Vaughan righteously puts it: 'There is no moment in the human history of Mauritius that is prior to creolization, or "pre-Creole"' (2005, p. 22). Compared with the French Caribbean islands where creoleness was conceptualized (Bernabé, Chamoiseau, & Confiant, 1993), there is a strong specificity of Mauritian creoleness: its dialectic relation with indianness. The slave population already included Indians.[2] Then, as soon as 1861, Indians counted for two-thirds of the Mauritian population (Benedict, 1961, p. 27). And, according to the 2011 census, 48% of the Mauritian population declares Hinduism as its religion. Such a major role played by Indians in the young, local society should make us speak of an Indo-French-African-Chinese creolization process in Mauritius, contrasting with the dual White masters/Black slaves opposition classically structuring French West Indies creoleness.

Starting from such a broad historical overview, and focusing on the main group in the Mauritian population (the descendants of indentured laborers), this paper deals with three connected questions, each helping us understand the relations between Mauritius and the Indian Ocean. First, is the issue of the links between so-called Indo-Mauritians and India, the territories their ancestors came from: have they been severed or enhanced? Second, comes the auto-representations and status of Mauritius: is it an ideal *center-of-the-world*, or a relegated island lost in the Indian Ocean? Third are the representations Indo-Mauritians have of their original migrations, through the crossing of the Indian Ocean.

Changing links above the Indian Ocean

Mauritius has sometimes been called 'Little India.' Whether political, economic, diplomatic or religious, the various links between India and Mauritius have been abundantly developed in the last two decades. But this should not hide the, sometimes dramatically, changing relations between the two countries along the years, nor the role played by internal, Mauritian, identity stakes in the evolution of such relations.

As often, ambiguities are already visible, or rooted, in terminology. The official 'Indo-Mauritian' category is indeed very misleading from the point of view of the analyst. What kind of links between India and Mauritius does it stand for? After all, such a designation of a Mauritian from Indian origins also works for an individual who enjoys both nationalities. Furthermore, local categories being based on religion, 'Indo-Mauritians' are in fact Hindus, even if Mauritian Muslims and Mauritian Tamil Catholics also come from India and should thus be considered 'Indo-Mauritians.'[3] Let us also note that the 'Indo-Mauritian' category misleadingly refers to a homogeneous community – an image seriously undermined by a quick look at internal scissions according to regional origins, languages or castes (Claveyrolas, 2015). Such divisions are sometimes imported from India, but others have been developed in the specifically Mauritian context. Thus,

Mauritian Tamils (from South India) claim a 'Tamil religion' distinct from 'Hinduism' (Trouillet, 2014), an affiliation then reserved for Mauritian Bhojpuris (from North India – locally called 'Hindus') – a division largely unknown in India.

The history of most Mauritian Indian communities is often, and rightfully, labeled as a success story. In less than 150 years, they passed from a quasi-enslaved minority to a majority group leading the battle for independence and controlling the political power ever since. I insist (Claveyrolas, 2017) that the main reasons behind such collective success lie first and foremost in the Mauritian history of sugar and plantation, and not back in India, or in some Indian cultural genius as it is often argued locally.[4] However, the links with India have indeed been instrumentalized by Indo-Mauritian elites to galvanize, or legitimize, the historical rise to power.

Symbols were used to signify a brotherhood above the Indian Ocean, such as the day chosen to celebrate the Mauritian national Independence: 12 March, i.e. the very day of Gandhi's Salt March. But concrete networks of relations also played a major role in bonding the two countries together. As soon as the early twentieth century, the new Indo-Mauritian elites gathered with Indian nationalists. Gandhi himself had stopped in Mauritius when coming from South Africa to India, and met with local elites before sending his emissary, Manilal Doctor, to represent them in Court and promote their empowerment. Even Hindu reformist movements such as the Arya Samaj, founded in India in 1875, were implanted in Mauritius as soon as the beginning of the twentieth century, and have had a major influence in Mauritian religious and political life, jointly promoting religious reform and a revival of indianness. Studying the Indian diaspora, Carsignol (2011) shows how the indentured laborers or their descendants were a major lever for the nationalist movement in India. It was a matter of solidarity between colonized victims of the British, grounded on the ability of indentured laborers to focus nationalist protest against these sons and daughters being abandoned and ill-treated.

Among influential political individuals in Mauritius and specifically among the Indo-Mauritians, some were born in India (Manilal or Gandhi), others in Mauritius (the Bissoondoyal brothers – Basdeo having been influenced by a trip in India) and some (like Ramgoolam, the 'Father of Independence') met with Indian elites while studying in London. Beyond individuals, Indian institutions (whether religious such as the Arya Samaj reformists, or political such as the young Indian Congress Party) were deeply involved in the Mauritian situation. When the centenary of indenture was celebrated in 1935, for instance, such Indian elites helped their Indo-Mauritian counterparts to organize an odd staging of their history culminating in the erection of an obelisk (precisely in the courtyard of the Mauritian Arya Samaj building) commemorating, according to the written text, the first hundred years of 'Indian colonization' (Carsignol, 2011, pp. 211sq).

Yet, the relations between India and Mauritius loosened during the following decades (1950–1970). On the one hand, Indo-Mauritians had to secure their place in the Mauritian society and prove their loyalty towards this new nation they were bound to run. On the other hand, Nehru, governing recently independent India, did not want to interfere into the fate of new nations to come, nor to abandon his vision of India as a nation state defined by its territory which could not include Mauritius.

In the context of the evolving link with India, the Indo-Mauritian elites present themselves as leaders and conquerors of the island, but also as objective allies of the British who will eventually yield them the political power. Consequently, the only 'fight' for independence was an internal one, opposing pro-independence Indo-Mauritians to anti-independence Creoles and Franco-Mauritians (descendants of planters), who feared that a democratic Mauritius would become fully indianized. Such fears (to be obliged to speak Hindi, wear the sari, convert to Hinduism or being annexed by India) are illustrated by the novelist Amal Sewtohul from the Sino-Mauritian point of view:

> Uncle Lee Song Hui kept harping us on terrible stories of Hindus who would soon turn the island into Little Calcutta, with sacred cows wandering everywhere on the streets of Port-Louis, among cadaverous beggars squatting in gutters to defecate. (2012, p. 106)[5]

I argued elsewhere that, from the Indo-Mauritian point of view, growing political hegemony went hand in hand with the first temptations to break away from the creoleness they used to share with other Mauritians, most of all the descendants of slaves (Claveyrolas, 2012), and turn towards a re-invented indianness.

In the 1970s, interethnic rivalries calmed down thanks to the consensual personality of Seewoosagur Ramgoolam, the first independent Mauritius Prime Minister, more eager to turn to Britain than to India, and because of the general social improvement brought by the welfare state policy, emphasizing class rather than ethnic identities (Chan Low, 2008). However, at the end of the 1980s, with the death of class struggle and the rapid industrial development of the country through ultraliberal policies, the competition for social advantages hardened, and communalism blossomed again. Only in the 1990s did the links with India flourish again, culturally, politically and economically. This was most of all the result of a reciprocal instrumentalization: India was discovering again, and enhancing the assets of its worldwide diaspora (in terms of financial flows and of diplomatic 'soft power') while Indo-Mauritians strengthened their political legitimacy and their perception to belong to a civilization all the more prestigious that it was recently booming as a worldwide political and economic power (Carsignol, 2011, pp. 203sq).

During the same period (from the 1990s on), we note an ever-growing institutionalization of Mauritian Hinduism (Claveyrolas, 2014), going together with a reinforcement of the links with India. National temple federations, partly financed by the Mauritian secular state as 'socio-cultural associations,' have monitored the institutionalization of such bridges above the Indian Ocean. Symbolic bridges, first, when Mauritian Hindu Federations joined in 1989 the Hindutva[6] worldwide campaign sending consecrated bricks to India to rebuild god Rama's temple in Ayodhya, supposedly destroyed and replaced by a mosque, following the Hindutva agenda as 'provider of [nationalistic] values for overseas Hindus' (Eisenlohr, 2006, p. 37). But also very concrete bridges when, all over the island, Hindu temples are built, or renovated, highlighting the Indian origins of Hinduism (Claveyrolas, 2010). Such 'renovations' in fact lead to a sanskriticization of temples and practices, erasing the Mauritian plantation, popular, uninstitutionnalized Hinduism long prevailing locally. Doing so, Mauritian Hindu Federations have set-up a network of Indian priests, architects and craftsmen, but also ritual statues, they bring to Mauritius in a dense linkage with India.

In the above section, we argued how India–Mauritius bilateral relations above the Indian Ocean must be contextualized within the Mauritian issue of creoleness/indianness. I now turn to the way Mauritius is represented within the Indian Ocean region, and beyond.

Mauritius, an Island in the Indian Ocean

Many founding narratives can be studied in Mauritius, telling us about the representations of the local territories, identities and communal claims.

Such narratives often present Mauritius as the very center of the world. This could be pointed as the main leitmotiv of the Mauritian identity discourse: an island standing at the crossroads of the entire world. The Mauritian writer Alain Gordon-Gentil gives a humorous example of this in the preface of his novel *Quartiers de Pamplemousses*:

> If you look attentively at a map of the world, you will be surprised to notice that Mauritius is not put in its centre. How annoying! Yet, every Mauritian will tell you: we are the centre of the world. (1999, p. 11)[7]

This leitmotiv must be linked with Creole aspirations to a *metissage* anticipating the future of humanity at large, and building new identities as proclaimed in the opening sentence of the Caribbean manifesto, *In Praise of Creoleness*: 'Neither Europeans, nor Africans, nor Asians, we proclaim ourselves Creoles' (Bernabé et al., 1993, p. 75). Concluding their chapter on the economic and geopolitical history of Mauritius, Grégoire and Lemoine precisely use the same formula: 'In spite of African, Asian and European imprints, Mauritius is not an African, or Asian or European country' (2011, p. 68).[8]

This status of Mauritius as crossroads of the three continents cannot be denied: it is illustrated by the many languages, religions and cultures still alive in Mauritius. Such ability to link the continents, or to represent all of them, is also visible in the many affiliations of Mauritius to varied worldwide cultural, economic or political spaces. Mauritius is a member of numerous African organizations, whether economic (such as the COMESA, *Common Market for Eastern and Southern Africa*) or political (such as the OUA, *Organisation de l'unité africaine*, now the African Union, whose 1976 Summit was organized in Mauritius and presided by the Mauritian Prime Minister), even representing Africa at the United Nations Security Council in 2001–2002. Mauritius is also a leader of the ACP countries (Africa–Caribbean–Pacific). As far as Europe is concerned, it is one of the rare members of both the *Organisation internationale de la Francophonie* and the Commonwealth. Turning to the Indian subcontinent, Mauritius also enjoys an 'observer' status in the SAARC (*South Asian Association for Regional Cooperation*). Last but not least, Mauritius hosts many institutions linked to Indian Hindu nationalist movements (Eisenlohr, 2006, p. 36), and it is a very active player in GOPIO (General Organization of People of Indian Origin) – a kind of the institutional link between India and its 'diaspora.'

Though Mauritius is definitely a node in transnational networks, it is worth noting that most links point to Europe, Africa and India (but also, more and more, China). Conversely, the Island of Mauritius is not so well integrated in the immediate Indian Ocean world (the Mascarenes or Madagascar for instance), despite recent efforts to favor Indian Ocean networks rather than networks turned towards the *ex-metropole* or territories of origins (OSIO Conference, 2015).

In fact, focusing on the center-of-the-world image is not enough. We should also explore Mauritius as an isolated territory where identities remain very unstable. Remember that the first decades of settlement in this small island of Mauritius lost in the middle of the Indian Ocean were particularly uncertain. Meghan Vaughan quotes visitors describing Mauritius as 'a place from which everyone [...] desired to escape. Everyone was in some sense marooned here' (2005, p. 9). Contradicting the center-of-the-world image is not specific to the Dutch period. In his *Voyage à Rodrigues*, the French and Mauritian writer Le Clézio also speaks of Mauritius as a territory for temporary migrations only, a 'land of no belonging'[9] (1986, p. 125). In another context, the Mauritian writer Amal Sewtohul draws similar conclusions. Laval, the Mauritian hero of his novel, was born of Chinese parents in a container only *transiting* through Mauritius, an island the hero himself leaves for Australia. Laval describes the container as 'both my womb and my world'[10] (2012, p. 109), and the writer makes of this container-parable for transit the very base of the platform supporting the Mauritian independence ceremony.

Indeed, the reference to a Mauritian diaspora is part and parcel of the local daily life. Mauritius remains a land of migration far from the Indian Ocean, to Europe, North America, India, South Africa and Australia. In 1976, eight years after the new nation was born, half the respondents answered to a questionnaire that 'if they had the opportunity they would be tempted to leave Mauritius and live in another country,' and 75% 'said that they would advise their children to work in another country' (Simmons, 1982, p. 197). The general context of migration following Independence is often described in Mauritian literature. Shenaz Patel writes:

> That ship … was sailing farther and farther, to Australia – *Lostrali? Ki été sa?* She had never heard of it. He had explained to her. At least what he could himself understand. It was a new eldorado where some Mauritians who were afraid of independence went to try their luck.[11] (2005, p. 73; see also Sewtohul, 2012, pp. 106, 170)

Alain Gordon-Gentil confirms:

> The news in the daily press was about Mauritians who were leaving the country, selling their houses and all their furniture. The Whites were leaving for South Africa or Rhodesia. They were the only inhabitants of the island to be able to get the residents' pass in those countries where apartheid reigned supreme. They felt good and they could express freely feelings that were more and more difficult to evoke in a country where the Hindus had taken the political power. The mixed Creoles were leaving for Australia. They, too, felt good there. As for the Chinese, they were interested in Canada, a country that welcomed them with open arms.[12] (2009, p. 106)

Alongside literature, popular songs bear witness of such 'acceleration of migratory patterns' as an 'endless recommencement of exile and separation' (Servan-Schreiber, 2010, p. 286). Nowadays, one of the main reasons for leaving Mauritius has to be found in the very competitive educational system aiming at studying abroad, again far from the Indian Ocean (Day-Hookoomsing, 2011, p. 276).

After this brief review of the representations of Mauritius as center-of-the-world and as lost-in-the-ocean, we can even go one step forward, viewing the Indian Ocean island as a relegated territory.

Mauritius has indeed been systematically used throughout history as a halt on the route to India, or for geopolitical purposes – all insisting the island was not interesting *by itself*. Arab and Portuguese sailors stopped in Mauritius for supplies. The Dutch even left Mauritius, preferring other places on their route to India. As for the French, the main motive for possessing the island was to prevent the British from settling here and attacking next-door Bourbon Island. Mauritius, notes Vaughan, never had the prestige of French Caribbean colonies, nor did it ever represent a similar source of wealth (2005, p. 35). Figures easily confirm that the colonization process was long kept to its minimum: according to the first official census, in 1706 (more than a century after the first Dutch landed), the colony counted 236 individuals, of whom 67 are slaves (L'estrac, 2007, p. 48). Thirty years later, when Governor Mahé de la Bourdonnais reached Mauritius, the census counted 648 slaves and only 190 colonists (L'estrac, 2007, p. 76). Even under La Bourdonnais' rule (1734–1746), the French *Compagnie des Indes* insisted that the capital-city Port-Louis 'was to be a mere *escale* (stopover), not a town' (Vaughan, 2005, p. 38), a warehouse for 'passing ships' (Teelock, 1998, p. 39). And in 1764, only 4% of the lands conceded to the colonists were cultivated (Teelock, 1998, p. 35). Eventually, though Mauritius was meant to provide water and food for halting boats, until the beginning of the nineteenth century, it all worked the other way round; Mauritius depending on these boats for its own supply of provisions (Teelock, 1998, p. 41).

The British also took over the island for geostrategic reasons only, trying to prevent privateers to attack their own boats. The decision to let the French colonists rule the local economy speaks for itself as to the lack of potential the British saw in Mauritius per se. And, by 1900, for a governor, being appointed in Mauritius sounded like relegation (Simmons, 1982, p. 18). Such lack of interest remained the rule until the end, with the British very poorly contesting Mauritian independence. Sewtohul (2012, p. 189) describes the anger and humiliation of his hero reading the *Time Magazine* title on 22 March 1968: 'Independence – with relief,' naming Mauritius 'Britain's unlikeliest colony.' Finally, the negotiation consisting in yielding the Chagos archipelago to the British (who would rent it to the Americans to install there a military base) again illustrates this representation of Mauritius as only worthy of interest for its strategic geographic position.

The Mauritian economic history also confirms this representation of an un-interesting island. Halt on the route to India, sugar single-crop farming meant for export, as well as more recent sectors such as textile, offshore finance or tourism all focus on networks and interests far away from Mauritius, and poorly connected to the Indian Ocean.

Sure, one could argue such hesitation between Mauritius as the perfect node in transnational networks, or Mauritius as a small islands' nation unable to develop for itself is a typical dialectical issue in globalized times. And indeed, Mauritius has always been (more still than other countries) embedded in globalized logics. Let us think about naval battles between European nations for the control of the route to India. Let us remember the slave trade. But my point, here, will focus on another episode: the indenture crossing of the Indian Ocean, from India to Mauritius, of half-a-million individuals from one region of the British Empire to another.

The indenture crossing: deadly rupture or sacred link?

From the point of view of the Mauritian Hindu communities, we have to pay particular attention to the changing nature of the Indian Ocean. The very association of the Indian Ocean with indenture and the original crossing from India to Mauritius allows changing narratives to insist on the ocean standing for either the enduring link between the two countries, or the place where the links were severed. Was the crossing a traumatic transgression of the Hindu taboo of leaving the sacred Indian land, leaving the Indentureds no other choice than to join ex-slaves in creoleness? Or was it a pilgrimage-like experience leading to the successful rooting of Hinduism and indianness in Mauritius?

On the one hand, one of the most pervasive *cliché* about Hinduism refers to its consubstantiality with the Indian territory, alleging Hindus have been historically both unwilling to migrate, and unable to transfer their religion into far-away lands. According to Crooke (1897), Hindus just do not have any 'migratory instinct.' Of course, this is a very misleading assertion. First, many intense and sometimes long-distance circulations among Indian peasants, soldiers, merchants or religious groups have been documented well before indenture (Markovitz, Pouchepadass, & Subrahmaniam, 2003). Then the many million Hindus' successful emplacement in ex-sugar colonies, in North America and all over the world clearly contradicts the idea that a 'Hindu diaspora' would be an oxymoron.

On the other hand, in Mauritius, as in most societies based on slavery, the ocean is closely related with the original trauma of the crossing following the up-rooting. In many narratives, crossing the Indian Ocean for the Indian indentured gets pretty close to the slaves' Middle-Passage experience. It can also be embedded in competing victimization strategies between contemporary communities of descendants of the two groups.

Let us have a look at a couple of narratives of the indenture crossing as they appear in contemporary literature, most of all *Les Rochers de Poudre d'Or* by the Mauritian novelist Appanah (2003), and *Sea of Poppies*, by the Indian writer Ghosh (2008). Both books focus on the experience of indenture, from the description of the recruitment conditions in India to the crossing of the Indian Ocean and the landing in Mauritius.

Appanah's narrative is particularly underpinned by the comparison between indenture and slavery – even if in a nuanced way. Both Appanah and Ghosh describe very diverse and sometimes hard conditions in India (quite close to slavery, in fact) for the candidates to indenture: leaving the motherland is not abduction, nor a unilateral rupture. But the crossing clearly evokes the experience of slave ships: segregation between migrants and sailors, promiscuity, dysentery, sexual abuse of women, suicides, rats or dead bodies thrown into the sea without cremation or ceremony are all leitmotiv of such narratives.

But the Middle-Passage paradigm soon gives way to a more specifically Hindu paradigm: the trauma of crossing the *kalapani* ('dark waters'). Leaving the Indian territory and crossing the Ocean would have added a cultural trauma to the harsh conditions of the experience. Appanah (2003) describes the tearing apart of Hindu cultural markers on the boat where socializing is not only forced (separation, suffering, humiliation) but also transgressive vis-à-vis Hindu ideology. Packed in the boat and cut from their village society organized according to Hindu ritual purity requirements (endogamy, avoidance of contact and commensality), the indentured laborers were directly exposed to a dangerous anonymity incompatible with caste identity.

Clémentin-Ojha (2016) precisely explains what is at stake behind the idea of *kalapani*, and the crossing conditions, at least for nineteenth-century orthodox Hindus. Even if it seems highly doubtful that lower (or even middle) caste indentured ever shared such a taboo, the Mauritian literature constantly uses the loss of caste as symbol for the experience of indenture (Claveyrolas, 2015).

Putting forward the *kalapani* paradigm as Marina Carter does in her book's title *Across the kalapani: The Bihari presence in Mauritius* (2000) still means exploring the experience of the Indian Ocean crossing as a trauma, bringing indenture somehow closer to slave trade, and leaving open the possibilities for a creole future born out of a shared up-rooting experience. But, at the same time, from Middle-Passage to *kalapani*, the representation of the Indian Ocean turns from the comparison with slaves to the specifically Hindu experience of the crossing. Such a change in paradigm parallels the historical rise to power of the Hindu communities in Mauritius, eager to break away from the shared experience of creoleness rooted in the boat and in the plantation.

At this point, it comes as no surprise that contemporary narratives do not stop here. Once the Indian territory left behind, the ocean crossing has been re-read as a rite of passage, with its three classical phases (separation, liminality, aggregation) and its ritualized context. As a rite of passage, the indenture crossing of the Indian Ocean is thus assimilated to a threshold. Indeed, such tearing apart of cultural markers focuses on the (at least, theoretical) impossibility to go back to the previous status. Another Mauritian novelist, Ananda Devi, describes the indentured as truly dead to their kin: 'They had all crossed "Kala pâni", the ocean's dark waters, and they knew that they were already dead to those of their caste who stayed in India, that the ritual for the dead had been celebrated in their name' (1993, p. 47). Add to that, the fact that the impossible cremation of those dead during the crossing prevents the Hindus from their dearest hope of being born again in India.

However, as a rite of passage, the crossing of the Indian Ocean also entails a re-birth to a new status. Many literary narratives share the idea of the experience of the crossing ruled by *communitas,* a spirit of temporary solidarity among an egalitarian community (Turner, 1979). Quite logically, such positive vision of the Indian Ocean turned to comparing the crossing with the ideal reference for *communitas*: pilgrimage. Writers repeatedly use the comparison of indentured boats with these other boats leading the pilgrims to the Jagannath temple – one of the most famous Hindu pilgrimage site. Onboard, the indentured are united as Hindu pilgrims are supposed to be and, just as during pilgrimage, socio-religious categories are supposed to be no longer relevant.

Let us listen to Amitav Ghosh's use of such comparison. When his Indian employee volunteers to supervise a ship to Mauritius, the British employer is amazed: 'Are you not afraid of losing caste? Won't your Gentoo brethren ban you from their midst for crossing the Black Water?' But the Indian employee answers: 'Oh no, sir, […] Nowadays all are going for pilgrimage by ship. Pilgrims cannot lose caste – this can also be like that. Why not?' (2008, p. 226). Later on, Paulette, a young woman whose father is French, dressed as an Indian laborer, offers the perfect argument to her shipmates:

> But aren't you afraid [asks an indentured woman to Paulette] of losing caste? Of crossing the Black Water, and being on a ship with so many sorts of people?
>
> Not at all, the girl replied, in a tone of unalloyed certainty. On a boat of pilgrims, no one can lose caste and everyone is the same: it's like taking a boat to the temple of Jagannath, in Puri. From then on, and forever afterwards, we will all be ship-siblings – *jahazbhais* and *jahazbahens* – to each other. There'll be no differences between us. (Ghosh, 2008, p. 372)

In Ghosh and Appanah's narratives, the liminal phase of the Indian Ocean crossing opens to a re-birth, a hope which may well be emphasized as the main difference with the African slaves' experience. Ananda Devi insists:

> Together they suffered hardships and rites of passage. That gave them the same wrinkles and the same eyes, and made them closer to each other still, tightly knit by their common experience, like children united by fear. They did not know any other friendship or any other loyalty

any longer. They would get together in the evenings and would re-live what had become a true obsession for them: the crossing.[13] (1993, p. 47)

Indeed, the social links created in the depot or onboard between individuals sharing their fears, humiliations and hopes, will not disappear once Mauritius is reached. Just like for initiation groups, the links between 'brothers of the ship' (*jahajibhai*) will grow and shipmates will even engage in marrying their respective children together (Benoist, 1989). This is a very strong symbol of the replacement, in Mauritius, of Indian criteria of yesterday (caste endogamy) by new, Mauritian, categories.

Amitav Ghosh goes on and develops the same parable of the crossing as a womb for the new society to come. Deeti, a woman running away from her status as a widow in India, signed for indenture with Kalua, an Untouchable man who helped her. During the Indian Ocean crossing, they learn Deeti is pregnant. Ghosh assimilates the ocean to the maternal womb, the foetus to the ship, and the crossing to the pregnancy. When Deeti invites Kalua to touch her belly and feel the baby's moves, Kalua answers:

Yes, yes, it's the little one, kicking.

No, she said, not kicking – rolling, like the ship.

How strange it was to feel the presence of a body inside her, lurching in time to her own movements: it was as if her belly were the sea, and the child a vessel, sailing towards its own destiny.

Deeti turned to Kalua and whispered: Tonight it's like we too are being married again. (2008, p. 528)

Far from the image of quasi-slaves torn away from their motherland, appears the representation of Mauritius as a promised land for Indian indentureds. This meets Appanah's title, *Les Rochers de Poudre d'Or*, in reference to those rocks the laborers would just have to lift to find gold – or so said the recruiters. With Poudre d'Or village, many other Mauritian toponyms (such as L'Espérance-Trébuchet) bear witness of this hope for a better future. Well after having landed in Mauritius, descendants of indentured re-invented their *success story* on the same utopian bases. Dookhee Gungah (1867–1944), a rich planter and promoter of Hinduism and education among his community, claims he became rich the day he discovered a treasure in a sugarcane field after having been revealed the precise spot in a dream (*Indradhanush*, 2004).

Just as for African slaves, the rupture with India is traumatic for the indentureds, but it is also regenerative (Carter & Torabully, 2002), like a promise for new individual and collective possibilities. The Mauritian poet Khal Torabully thus speaks of the liminal Indian Ocean as a 'mother's womb' and a 'box full of ancestors' dreams'[14] (1995, p. 28). In another poem, Torabully evokes the arrival in the Mauritian depot, and clearly associates the ocean with a door open towards a rooting process:

Delighted after crossing the black waters, they blessed the water
At the end of the voyage. The sea is rest and risk.
To live here, at last, in the land to be cultivated ...
Before digging in the bowels of that fertile earth
Silence and waiting will be our next getting together:
We must hope between the walls of the depot.[15] (in Carter, 2000, p. 63)

The passage from the Indian Ocean crossing as Middle-Passage to the Indian Ocean as *kalapani* symbolized and paralleled the rise of Mauritian Hindus to political hegemony and the consequent denial of a fate their ancestors would have shared with slaves. This new vision of indenture as an experience or hope and re-birth de-focuses on the traumatic up-rooting from India (with the Indian Ocean as tombstone), and opens on a possible rooting in Mauritius (with the Indian Ocean as womb). This could well be the major difference with the slaves' history: 'Mauritius is, first, a settlement colony where migrants – excepted slaves – have come seeking wealth'[16] (Day-Hookoomsing, 2011, p. 253).

Whether you focus on the Indian Ocean as a traumatic rupture, or on the possibilities following the crossing, the descendants of Indian indentured laborers soon and lastingly turned their back to the Indian Ocean. As noted by Hookoomsing, out of the three main life-size statues on Port-Louis' seafront, only the French Governor La Bourdonnais faces the sea. Seewoosagur Ramgoolam and Basdeo Bissoondoyal, heroes of the 'Indo-Mauritian' community, both look the other way '« In order to clearly notify their status as sons of the land, and not as sons of migrants anymore'[17] (2011, p. 226). I analyzed elsewhere (Claveyrolas, 2012) how patrimonialization issues have backed the idea of indenture as a positive rooting process (through the successful application of the Aapravasi Ghat to the UNESCO's World Heritage Site list).

Enslaved and forever lost to Hinduism according to the first narratives, the Indian indentureds are now immigrants, ready to seize any opportunity, including taking the lead of the new Mauritian nation's destiny. But after trauma and rite of passage, let us focus on the last paradigm through which the crossing of the Indian Ocean has been read: discovery and conquest.

If Mauritius has been thought of as a center-of-the-world, it is also so in the very first sense of the phrase. Many narratives indeed present Mauritius as nothing less than the secret spot of the origins of the universe and of humanity. Mauritius would then stand for the only remains of Lemuria, this original continent supposedly disappeared in an unknown cataclysm. The Mauritian writer Malcolm de Chazal contributed to anchor such myth with his cosmogonic novel, *Petrusmok* (2004/1951), tracking in the Mauritian landscape the signs and evidence of the myth of Lemuria.

It should be noted that Lemuria meets Indian mythologies. South-Indian Tamils, for instance, refer to such a 'spatial fabulation' known as Kumari Kandam or Kumari Nadu, and founding an imaginary geography invented by the elite literate classes during the colonial period to express the feeling of a lost Tamil territory (Ramaswamy, 2000). More generally, the ocean is, in Sanskrit texts, the typical cosmogonic place. According to the Vedas, the Earth was born from the Ocean, and the *Mahabharata* narrates the famous myth of the Ocean churning creating various elements (poison and nectar) and beings.

As a kind of echo to this Lemuria, we read another association between Mauritius and geological cataclysms in the famous *Lal Pasina* novel (1977) by the Hindi-speaking Mauritian writer Abhimanyu Unnuth. The prologue of the book starts with the description of two Indian monks gone on a boat in order to discover unknown territories, sometime since the '1st millennium before JC.' The monks die off the coasts of Mauritius in a volcanic eruption, evoking a quasi-geological creation of the island.

Indo-Mauritian elites legitimized their rise to power after the 1930s through a fierce rejection of any comparison between Indian indentured and African slaves. As the (often racist) arguments go, the collective success story of the indentureds is only explained by the merits of the antique Indian civilization – a *cliché* also encompassing being hard-working and sober, i.e. everything those descending of African slaves are supposed to be deprived of.

The ideological ambiguity can indeed go very far, as with Hazareesingh who was the author of one of the first synthetic history of Indo-Mauritians, published in 1950. In the 1973 French edition, Hazareesingh defends an idealized vision of indenture. Refusing to 'believe that poverty alone could make people migrate massively and, in many cases, persuade all the inhabitants of many villages to abandon their motherland and go settle in a foreign land'[18] (1973, p. 16), Hazareesingh favors the image of the voluntary immigrant, and even introduces a 'revisionist theory' (Carter, 1995, p. 6) of indenture as conquest and colonization.

The 'spirit of conquest' idea is backed by the historical participation of Indian soldiers in the British army which conquered Mauritius in 1810. Even colonized, Indians approached Mauritius as winners. And Hazareesingh changes the uprooted laborers in saviors of the Empire:

> Not only did India help our island by sending an abundant workforce to develop its then endangered agriculture but it also showed the heroic worth of its sons by sharing with the English, the glory and the merit of having successfully fought during the takeover of the island [from the French].[19] (Hazareesingh, 1973, p. 23)

Yet, Hazareesingh could not reduce the Indians to soldiers serving the British. He argues the indentureds were drawn by nothing less than the will to extend the territory of the Indian civilization through colonizing Mauritius:

> The concept of a greater India germinated in some people's minds and, in the middle of revolutionary fervour [in India], a migratory movement happened that evoked clearly the wake up of the Indian colonizing genius that took place in the Vedic times, when the sons of the Great Peninsula took the torch of national culture to the farthest countries.[20] (Hazareesingh, 1973, p. 18)

The author refers here to the idea of 'Greater India,' a representation of the Indian territory fantasized by Hindu nationalists, assimilating an 'eternal India' to a geography of India expanded to the whole hinduized Asia (Claveyrolas, 2008). In such a context, indenture grows as a mythological saga, as proposed in Vijay Mishra's title for his book on Indian indenture in the Fiji: *Rama's banishment* (1979). Unnuth also stages indentured prisoners who named their watchmen after Mahabharata's anti-heroes (2001/1977, p. 40).

The dangerous Indian Ocean, the taboo crossing of *kalapani* becomes for Hazareesingh and others the playground of India which extends its territory in a kind of proselyte mission presupposed by the well-named *Indian* Ocean. The Indian Ocean network of exchanges and influences then refer to the most prestigious dimensions of Hinduism: the Hindu pilgrimage site of Grand Bassin in Mauritius is compared to the Javanese temple of Borobudur (Hazareesingh, 1973, p. 19)! And one should no longer read Dina Robin (first designation of Mauritius) on the old maps of the Arab sailors and geographer, but *Diva* Robin, of course coming from *dvipa*, sanskrit for 'island.'

Conclusion

It proves highly relevant for anthropologists to study Mauritian literature. In Mauritius (Jean-François & Ravi, 2014) as in the French West Indies (Lesne, 2013), writers play a crucial role in the construction of 'national' identities, and in the simultaneous putting together of founding narratives.[21]

Reading the highly contextual narratives of the Indian Ocean and its crossing from the Indo-Mauritian point of view echoes the various phases of the community's history. In a sense, everything was a matter of 'domestication.' Leaving the motherland was domesticated as a pilgrimage. The promiscuity onboard the ships was domesticated as a time of exception (*apad-dharma*) when survival was what really mattered – not withstanding successful attempts to negotiate better conditions with the authorities. The uneasy arrival in an unfamiliar land was domesticated as an opportunity for success, or even as conquest.

Now that the descendants of those who crossed the Indian Ocean are successfully rooted in the Mauritius land, the Indian Ocean appears to develop as a place for crossing back to India. Mauritian Hindu temples and practices are indianized, Mauritian descendants of indentured laborers use the archives for tracing their roots back to their ancestors' village, and the ashes of the dead are ritually poured into the Indian Ocean to reach the Indian motherland again.

As a final conclusion, let us insist that the Indian Ocean is both crucial to the Mauritian (Creole) history and peripheral in the sense that the whole region is increasingly overshadowed by Indian issues and the bilateral links above the Ocean between Mauritius and India.

Notes

1. As a nation, Mauritius includes the island of Mauritius (the main island), the small island of Rodrigues and other smaller islands. This paper essentially refers to the island of Mauritius.
2. In 1823, 5% of plantation slaves were Indians (Ly-Tio-Fane, 1992).
3. As was the case for Muslims until the introduction of the 'Best Loser System' in 1967.
4. See Hazareesingh (1973, p. 18) or Le Clézio in the preface of Unnuth's novel (2001, p. 10). In quite the same way, Benoist refers to a specifically Indian 'cultural capital' (1994, p. 135)
5. « L'oncle Lee Song Hui nous rebattait les oreilles d'affreuses histoires, nous disant que bientôt les hindous allaient tourner l'île en petit Calcutta, il y aurait des vaches sacrées partout errant dans les rues de Port-Louis, parmi les mendiants cadavériques s'accroupissant dans les caniveaux pour déféquer. » All translations are mine.
6. Hindutva is a political and aggressive claim to Hindu-ness as opposed to all other possible Indian identities.
7. « Si vous regardez attentivement une carte du monde, vous serez étonné de noter que l'île Maurice n'est pas placée au centre. Cela est très contrariant. Pourtant, tout Mauricien vous le dira : Nous sommes le centre du monde. »
8. « Marqué à la fois d'empreintes africaines, asiatiques et européennes, Maurice n'est ni un pays africain, ni asiatique, ni européen. »
9. Une « terre d'inappartenance».
10. « Ma matrice et mon monde tout à la fois ».
11. « Ce bateau-là … allait plutôt vers le bas, plus loin, vers l'Australie. – Lostrali? Ki été sa? Elle n'en avait jamais entendu parler. Il lui avait expliqué. Du moins ce qu'il avait compris lui-même. C'était un nouvel Eldorado où partaient tenter leur chance un certain nombre de Mauriciens, que l'indépendance effrayait. »
12. « On pouvait lire quotidiennement dans les journaux des informations concernant les Mauriciens qui quittaient le pays, vendaient leur maison et tout leur mobilier. Les Blancs partaient pour l'Afrique du Sud ou la Rhodésie. Ils étaient les seuls habitants de l'île à pouvoir obtenir les permis de résidence dans ces pays où l'apartheid faisait rage. Ils s'y sentaient à l'aise, pouvant exprimer en toute tranquillité des sentiments de plus en plus difficiles à évoquer dans un pays

13. « Ils [*jahajibhai*] traversèrent ensemble de nombreuses épreuves et des rites de passage. Ils en acquirent les mêmes rides et les mêmes regards, plus étroitement unis encore, soudés par leur expérience commune comme des enfants unis par la peur. Ils ne connurent plus d'autre amitié ni d'autre loyauté. Ils se réunissaient le soir et revivaient ce qui était devenu pour eux une véritable obsession : Le voyage. »
14. "Matrice de mère" et "boîte des rêves des ancêtres."
15. « Ravis d'avoir traversé l'eau noire, ils bénirent l'eau / Au bout du voyage. La mer est repos et péril ! / Vivre enfin ici, au pays à cultiver … / Avant de creuser son ventre de terre fertile / Silence et attente seront nos proches assemblées : /Il nous faut espérer entre les murs du dépôt ! »
16. « l'île Maurice est à l'origine un pays de peuplement où les immigrants, à l'exception des esclaves, sont venus chercher fortune. »
17. « pour bien signifier leur statut de fils du sol, non plus de fils d'immigrants. »
18. « croire que seule la pauvreté pouvait pousser un peuple à émigrer en masse et, dans bien des cas, inciter la totalité des habitants de nombreux villages à abandonner leur patrie pour aller s'établir en terre étrangère. »
19. « l'Inde a non seulement aidé notre île en lui envoyant une abondante main-d'œuvre pour développer son agriculture, alors menacée d'extinction, mais […] elle a aussi fait la preuve de la valeur héroïque de ses fils en partageant avec les Anglais la gloire et le mérite d'avoir combattu avec succès lors de la prise de l'île [aux Français]. »
20. « Le concept d'une plus grande Inde germa alors dans le cerveau de certains, et en pleine ferveur révolutionnaire [en Inde] se produisit un mouvement migratoire rappelant beaucoup le sursaut du génie colonisateur indien qui eut lieu dans les temps védiques, lorsque des fils de la Grande Péninsule allèrent porter la torche de la culture nationale jusque dans les contrées les plus lointaines. »
21. Note that the frontier between anthropology and literature in Creole worlds is, again, blurred by the constant dialogues between Glissant and Leiris or Balandier, by the confusion between Chamoiseau's characters and anthropologists, but also by the fact that Ananda Devi herself, for instance, engaged in a Ph.D. in anthropology.

Disclosure statement

No potential conflict of interest was reported by the authors.

References

Appanah, N. (2003). *Les Rochers de Poudre d'Or*. Paris: Gallimard.
Benedict, B. (1961). *Indians in a plural society: A report on Mauritius*. London: HM's Stationery Office.
Benoist, J. (1989). De l'Inde à Maurice et de Maurice à l'Inde, ou la réincarnation d'une société. In G. L'Étang (Ed.), *L'inde en nous. Des Caraïbes aux Mascareignes* (pp. 185–201). Fort de France: Carbet.
Benoist, J. (1994). Présences indiennes dans le monde. In G. L'Étang (Ed.), *Présences de l'Inde dans le monde* (pp. 121–136). Paris: Presses universitaires créoles-L'Harmattan.
Bernabé, J., Chamoiseau, P., & Confiant, R. (1993). *Éloge de la Créolité* [In praise of Creoleness]. Paris: Gallimard.

Carsignol, A. (2011). *L'Inde et sa diaspora. Influences et intérêts croisés à l'île Maurice et au Canada*. Paris: PUF.
Carter, M. (1995). *Servants, Sirdars and Settlers: Indians in Mauritius, 1834–1874*. Delhi: Oxford University Press.
Carter, M. (2000). *Across the Kalapani: The Bihari presence in Mauritius*. Port-Louis: Centre for Research on Indian Ocean Studies.
Carter, M. & Torabully, K. (2002). *Coolitude: An anthology of the Indian labour diaspora*. London: Anthem Press.
Certeau, M. (de) (1975). *L'écriture de l'histoire*. Paris: Gallimard.
Chan Low, L.-J. (2008). Une perspective historique du processus de construction identitaire à l'île Maurice. *Interethnicité et Interculturalité à l'île Maurice, Kabaro, 4*, 13–26.
Chazal, M. (de) (1951/2004, The standard printing Est). *Petrusmok*. Paris: Éditions Léo Scheer.
Claveyrolas, M. (2008). Les temples de Mère Inde, musées de la nation. *Gradhiva, 7*, 84–99.
Claveyrolas, M. (2010). L'ancrage de l'hindouisme dans le paysage mauricien: Transfert et appropriation. In S. Bava & S. Capone (Eds.), *Migrations et transformations des paysages religieux* (pp. 17–38). Paris: IRD-Presses de Sciences Po (coll. « Autrepart » 56).
Claveyrolas, M. (2012). With or without roots: The compared and conflicting memories of slavery and indenture in the Mauritian public space. In A.-L. Araujo (Ed.), *Politics of memory: Making slavery visible in the public space* (pp. 54–70). London: Routledge.
Claveyrolas, M. (2014). Un prêtre tamoul dans le chantier de l'hindouisme mauricien. Orthodoxies et autorité religieuse. In C. Servan-Schreiber (Ed.), *Indianité et créolité à l'île Maurice* (pp. 139–168). Paris: Éditions de l'EHESS (Purusartha n° 32).
Claveyrolas, M. (2015). *The 'Land of the Vaish'? Caste, Structure and Ideology in Mauritius, Samaj*. Retrieved from http://samaj.revues.org/3886.
Claveyrolas, M. (2017). *Quand l'hindouisme est créole. Plantation et indianité à l'île Maurice*. Paris: éditions de l'EHESS.
Clémentin-Ojha, C. (2016). Kālāpānī ou les limites à ne pas franchir. Le voyage en Angleterre du maharaja de Jaipur (1902). In M. Claveyrolas & R. Delage (Eds.), *Territoires du Religieux dans les mondes indiens. Parcourir, mettre en scène, franchir* (pp. 251–274). Paris: Éditions de l'EHESS (Purusartha n° 34).
Crooke, W. (1897). *The north-western provinces of India: Their history, ethnology and administration*. London: Methuen.
Day-Hookoomsing, P. (2011). Aspects institutionnels et sociaux de l'éducation à Maurice. In E. Grégoire, V. Hookoomsing, & G. Lemoine (Eds.), *Maurice: De l'île sucrière à l'île des savoirs* (pp. 253–311). Vacoas: Éditions le Printemps.
Devi, A. (1993). *Le voile de Draupadi*. Paris: L'Harmattan.
Eisenlohr, P. (2006). *Little India. Diaspora, time, and ethnolinguistic belonging in Hindu Mauritius*. Berkeley: University of California Press.
Ghosh, A. (2008). *Sea of poppies*. London: John Murray.
Gordon-Gentil, A. (1999). *Quartiers de pamplemousses*. Paris: Julliard.
Gordon-Gentil, A. (2009). *Légère approche de la haine*. Pamplemousses: Pamplemousses productions.
Grégoire, E., & Lemoine, G. (2011). Une île ouverte sur le monde. In E. Grégoire, V. Hookoomsing, & G. Lemoine (Eds.), *Maurice : De l'île sucrière à l'île des savoirs* (pp. 27–72). Vacoas: Éditions le Printemps.
Hazareesingh, K. (1973). *Histoire des Indiens à l'Île Maurice*. Paris: Adrien Maisonneuve.
Hookoomsing, V. (2011). Développement économique, mutations sociopolitiques et le legs de l'histoire. In E. Grégoire, V. Hookoomsing, & G. Lemoine (Eds.), *Maurice : De l'île sucrière à l'île des savoirs* (pp. 225–247). Vacoas: Éditions le Printemps.
Indradanush (2004). « Dookhee Gungah: The Unforgettable Philanthropist of Mauritius », *Dookhee Gungah special issue*.
Jean-François, E.-B., & Ravi, S. (2014). Ethnicité, sexualité et mythologie. Ananda Devi et l'indo-mauricianité. In C. Servan-Schreiber (Ed.), *Indianité et créolité à l'île Maurice* (pp. 239–266). Paris: Éditions de l'EHESS (Purusartha n°32).
Kalla, A. Cader (2016). *The primary school Atlas of Mauritius* (4th ed.). Mauritius: Osman.
L'estrac, J.-C. (de). (2007). *Mauriciens, enfants de mille races. Au temps de l'île de France*. Vacoas: Éditions le Printemps.

Le Clézio, J.-M.-G. (1986). *Voyage à Rodrigues*. Paris: Gallimard.
Lesne, A. (2013). S'écrire aux Antilles, écrire les Antilles. Écrivains et anthropologues en dialogue. In J.-L. Bonniol (Ed.), *Un miracle créole ?, L'Homme 207-208* (pp. 17–36). Paris: éditions de l'EHESS.
Ly-Tio-Fane, H. (1992). Les esclaves 'de plantation' de l'île Maurice à la veille de l'abolition, d'après le recensement de 1823. In *Histoires d'outre-mer : Mélanges en l'honneur de Jean-Louis Miège* (Vol. II, pp. 635-655). Aix-en-Provence.
Markovitz, C., Pouchepadass, J., & Subrahmaniam, S. (2003). *Society and circulation: Mobile people and itinerant cultures in south Asia, 1750–1950*. Delhi: Permanent Black.
Mishra, V. (Ed.) (1979). *Rama's banishment: A centenary tribute to the Fiji Indians, 1879–1979*. Auckland: Heinemann.
OSIO Conference (2015, November 5–6). *Dire l'océan Indien*. Observatoire des sociétés de l'océan Indien, Université de la Réunion.
Patel, S. (2005). *Le silence des chagos*. Paris: Éditions de l'Olivier.
Ramaswamy, S. (2000). History at land's end: Lemuria in Tamil spatial fables. *The Journal of Asian Studies*, *59*, 575–602.
Servan-Schreiber, C. (2010). *Histoire d'une musique métisse à l'île Maurice. Chutney indien et séga Bollywood*. Paris: Riveneuve éditions.
Sewtohul, A. (2012). *Made in Mauritius*. Paris: Gallimard.
Simmons, A. (1982). *Modern Mauritius: The politics of decolonization*. Bloomington: Indiana University Press.
Teelock, V. (1998). *Bitter sugar. Sugar and slavery in 19th century Mauritius*. Moka: Mahatma Gandhi Institute.
Torabully, K. (1995). *Kot sa parol làRôde Parole*. Vacoas: Éditions Le Printemps.
Trouillet, P.-Y. (2014). Les lances de Muruga à Maurice : Trajectoires d'un hindouisme tamoul. In C. Servan-Schreiber (Ed.), *Indianité et créolité à l'île Maurice* (pp. 169–198). Paris: Éditions de l'EHESS (Purusartha n° 32).
Turner, V. (1979). *Process, performance and pilgrimage*. New Delhi: Concept.
Unnuth, A. (1977/2001, Lal Pasina). *Sueurs de sang*. Paris: Stock.
Vaughan, M. (2005). *Creating the creole island: Slavery in eighteenth-century Mauritius*. Durham: Duke University Press.

Small islands' understanding of maritime security: the cases of Mauritius and Seychelles

James A. Malcolm and Linganaden Murday

ABSTRACT
The inclusion of a Sustainable Development Goal (No. 14) on the oceans by the United Nations (UN) provides formal and global recognition that the effective management of the blue economy is a key component of global development efforts. For island states, the importance of the maritime domain is unquestionable with many having responsibility for, and access to, vast areas of ocean. In the Indian Ocean region, island states have increasingly recognized this situation by placing greater emphasis on ocean policy and the opportunities the maritime domain offers. However, island states inevitably face challenges as their smaller size often means they lack the capacity to enhance their maritime domain awareness and effectively respond to insecurity. This paper seeks to shed further light on the maritime security considerations – their characteristics and influencing factors – of island states in the Indian Ocean. The paper contains a content analysis of key documents to examine the way in which maritime security challenges have been publicly communicated by island states in the region. It then utilizes additional documents and interview material to elaborate the way in which two specific states – Mauritius and Seychelles – have approached their maritime security in maritime piracy for Seychelles and drug trafficking in Mauritius. In doing this, the paper provides valuable insights into the way in which policy-makers in Indian Ocean island states understand the sustainable development–maritime security relationship.

Our Exclusive Economic Zone and territorial waters, our surrounding islands, national interests and security imperatives, regional commitments and an extremely dynamic geo-strategic environment are giving rise to many challenges. The maritime realm is vulnerable to a wide array of threats, including illegal, unreported, and unregulated fishing, environmental degradation, smuggling, drug trafficking, piracy, proliferation of weapons of mass destruction and dreadful acts, including terrorism. Sir Aneerood Jugnauth, Prime Minister of Mauritius (Week-End, 2016)
Maritime security is a central component of the blue economy and Seychelles and the whole region of East and Southern Africa and the Indian Ocean should make maritime security, which is combating all forms of maritime threats, including piracy, a core component of its national and regional security. Ralph Agrippine, Seychelles Ministry of Foreign Affairs (Athanase & Uranie, 2016)

Introduction

The Indian Ocean is a vast space of approximately 73.4 million square kilometers, making up approximately 20% of the world's total ocean area. The sheer size of the Ocean, its strategic location between the Atlantic and Pacific Oceans, alongside the vast array of states with some claim on it, has ensured that the Indian Ocean's significance for geopolitics, global trade and as a source of natural resources is considerable. As such, insecurity in the Indian Ocean has the propensity to have negative implications for state and human security, and well beyond the coastal states and island communities associated with the Ocean itself. More specifically, Somali piracy illustrated the challenges posed when maritime insecurity negatively impinged on global sea routes, clear evidence of how instability on land, here in Somalia, can play out into criminality in the maritime domain (Guilfoyle, 2013; Kellerman, 2011; Percy & Shortland, 2013; Treves, 2009).

For Seychelles and Mauritius, arguably the two most politically stable and economically prosperous island states in the Indian Ocean, Somali piracy highlighted the negative consequences that a lack of good governance and effective law enforcement associated with the maritime domain could have. Both countries, for example, also undertook the burden of stepping in to facilitate the prosecution and jailing of pirates with Somalia's judicial system inadequate to the task (Denselow, 2013; Reuters, 2012). Yet beyond piracy, the consequences of insecurity at sea and the need to effectively respond to it, has been increasingly acknowledged by both countries at the highest level of government, as illustrated in the quotations laid out at the beginning of this article.

Both quotations represent public articulations illustrating the way in which the state thinks about maritime security in these two small island states. More generally, for small island states' globally, their national security is inextricably wrapped up in maritime security, yet these states also often face challenges when seeking to enhance maritime security as limited resources can mean they lack the capacity to improve their maritime domain awareness and effectively respond to insecurity. Moreover, smaller states often have complex relationships with larger, external actors to manage that can shape policy and practice (Ingrebritsen, Neumann, Gstohl, & Beyer, 2006; Reiter & Gartner, 2001). The need for maritime security is thus self-evident, but the means of attaining, enhancing and sustaining maritime security can be less clear cut.

By recognizing and exploring the above, and focussing on developments since the turn of the decade, this article seeks to answer the following question, 'What are the maritime security considerations of Seychelles and Mauritius?' Seychelles' population is one of the smallest in the world at approximately 87,400. Its total land area is just 451 km^2, yet it is responsible for an Exclusive Economic Zone (EEZ) of approximately 1.3 million km^2 (Republic of Seychelles, 2013, p. 6). Economically, the country is reliant on tourism with this industry's total contribution of 56.9% to the gross domestic product (GDP) in 2014 (World Travel and Tourism Council, 2015, p. 1). The Republic of Mauritius meanwhile has a population of approximately 1.3 million people and a total land area of 2040 km^2 (Republic of Mauritius, 2013, p. 5). Its EEZ covers 1.9 million km^2 and has a 396,000 km^2 extended continental shelf area co-managed with the Seychelles (Board of Investment, n.d., p. 5). The overall objective of this paper is to elaborate how these two small island states have managed their maritime security responsibilities and to provide a clearer picture of maritime security in the Western Indian Ocean.

The article argues that overall for these two island states maritime security thinking and activity has been wrapped up in sustainable development efforts, and specifically the growth and exploitation of the blue economy. In short, sustainability is understood as a central route to maritime security and vice versa. Beyond concern about the negative implications of climate change, both states have highlighted and sought to respond to a range of maritime security challenges. The threat of armed violence associated with the maritime domain, specifically Somali piracy, was the most prominent concern in the late 2000s, yet as multi-national efforts to respond to this challenge significantly suppressed pirate activity; the damage caused by wider illicit activities such as drug trafficking by sea or illegal fishing has gained greater recognition.

Seychelles and Mauritius have responded to this maritime security context, with a series of responses that encapsulate a combination of the development and implementation of new strategies, the establishment or reform of departmental and security structures, embracing multi-national partnerships, alongside the implementation of a variety of new working practices. The article concludes that both states clearly recognize the importance of maritime security to their wider development efforts, each has demonstrated a combination of proactivity and reactivity in the area, and both still have maritime security capacity-building needs. Finally, the article posits, a further and even deeper examination of the way in which small island states in general, and these two cases in particular have navigated their maritime security challenges could provide a useful additional case study to better understand the role and interactions of small states in International Relations as a whole.

Methodology

The article utilizes the case study approach in order to shed light on the maritime security considerations of Seychelles and Mauritius. The cases are taken and discussed with the same framework of analysis applied to both cases. More specifically, the article sheds light on how each country has publicly articulated the importance of its maritime domain, the threats associated with that domain, and maps out the main contours of the institutional and policy responses instigated by each state over the last decade in response to maritime insecurity. This provides a good basis for undertaking comparative analysis and drawing conclusions. Given the limitation of space, the article's case studies are exploratory in nature and should be considered as a pilot study in to how island states in the Indian Ocean approach maritime security. The article's focus is limited to highlighting key trends in how the state in both cases articulates their thoughts on maritime security, whilst examining the more detailed response to two of these presented threats – piracy and drugs trafficking by sea. Moreover, the article focuses on the eight-year period since the turn of the decade (2009–2016) recognizing the way in which concern over Somali piracy and national efforts to develop the blue economy have placed maritime security higher on the agenda of both countries in this time and the need for an up-to-date security picture.

The article also draws upon multiple sources of evidence to deepen the case study. Data collection principally focuses on documentary analysis with strategy and policy papers alongside ministerial speeches on the ocean economy and maritime security issues examined. For Seychelles, we examined documents from the State House and the Office of the

President of the Republic of Seychelles, with all speeches at the latter, from June 2010 read. For Mauritius, the Government Information Service which appears on the Ministries websites, particularly the Prime Minister's Office, was the principal source of documents. Alongside, we examined documents from the Ministry of Ocean Economy, Marine Resources, Fisheries and Shipping and the Mauritius Police Force, particularly its section on the National Coastguard.

Supplementing these documents were articles from the local press in both countries published during 2015 and 2016. These helped to bring the case study up to date, highlighted the general mood around maritime security and directed us to additional official documents and speeches of relevance. More specifically, for the Seychelles, the online versions of both the *Seychelles News Agency* and *Seychelles Nation* were consulted. In the case of Mauritius the *L'Express* and *Le Mauricien* daily newspapers were utilized with hard copy archives accessed via the National Library. In addition to documentary analysis, insights were gained from a series of informal discussions and semi-structured interviews with policy and security personnel in both Seychelles and Mauritius, all of which clarified our thinking. Interviews in Mauritius were conducted during a scoping research visit by one author in August 2015, with informal discussions with individuals from both islands conducted by the other author in 2016 and 2017 as the article was drafted.

We do not claim that the response to either specific maritime security threat is necessarily duplicated in relation to other threats, nor do we argue that every small island state has embarked on the same specific pathway in relation to maritime security. We do, however, conclude that there may be valuable insights that can be taken from this case study for those interested in how small states approach global affairs, but argue more widespread research is required. Ultimately, we share the view held by Wellington and Szcerbinski (2007, p. 84) that 'people reading case studies can often relate to them, even if they cannot always generalize from them,' and therefore hope the insights provided shed some light on this topic and provoke interest and further research.

Sustainability as maritime security

Seychelles and Mauritius are both members of the international Small Island Developing States (SIDS) community. For this group of islands, a significant emphasis on the international policy stage has been to highlight the very real, and in certain cases, existential threat posed by climate change. The 'Agenda 21, Rio Declaration on Development and Environment,' had at its heart, a claim by the international community that, 'humanity stands at a defining moment in history' (UN, 1992, para. 1.1), with a series of challenges including the 'continuing deterioration of the ecosystems on which we depend for our well-being' prominent (UN, 1992, para. 1.1). The Agenda 21 document also highlighted the wider implications of these challenges noting that,

> integration of environment and development concerns and greater attention to them will lead to the fulfilment of basic needs, improved living standards for all, better protected and managed ecosystems and a safer, more prosperous future. (UN, 1992, para. 1.1)

This explicit connection between the environment, development and human wellbeing captured a wider effort within the United Nations' structures to publicly conceptualize security in more comprehensive terms. Indeed in 1994, the UN Development Programme introduced the concept of 'human security' in to popular terminology seeking, in their own words, to equate 'security with people rather than territories, with development rather than arms' (UNDP, 1994). SIDS were themselves formally recognized as ' ... a special case both for environment and development' (UN, 1992) at the Rio Summit. Against this backdrop, SIDS have met collectively on a periodic basis to discuss their sustainable development needs. The first such international conference took place in Barbados in 1994; the second took place in Mauritius in 2005, whilst the third took place in Samoa in 2014. The importance of the oceans and seas have been recognized in discussions across this near 25-year period with the Samoa 2014 conference outcome document having a specific section on the maritime domain. More specifically the document noted that:

> Healthy, productive and resilient oceans and coasts are critical for, inter alia, poverty eradication, access to sufficient, safe and nutritious food, livelihoods, economic development and essential ecosystem services, including carbon sequestration, and represent an important element of identity and culture for the people of small island developing States. Sustainable fisheries and aquaculture, coastal tourism, the possible use of seabed resources and potential sources of renewable energy are among the main building blocks of a sustainable ocean-based economy in small island developing States. (UN, 2014, para. 13)

The goal of growing and sustaining a viable ocean-based economy – the blue economy – recognizes that SIDS often have access to and rights over vast swathes of oceans and seas. Today, the oceans are the principle focus of the 14th goal for Sustainable Development committed to by the international community in 2015 as a successor regime to the Millennium Development Goals (UN, n.d.), whist there is arguably a maritime dimension to other goals too (Chapsos, 2017). The inevitable challenge for SIDS, however, is that the vast swathe of waters needs managing, and they often have limited resources and overall capacity to do this effectively. These governance challenges also open up opportunities for the maritime domain to be exploited by those with ill intent. This can have real, negative implications for SIDS and their populations as we witness the diminishing of state and human security (Chapsos & Malcolm, 2017).

By taking a closer look at the outcome documents from the SIDS conferences and their associated periodic reviews, we can further clarify the mutual relationship between sustainable development and maritime security for island states like Seychelles and Mauritius. Organized violence, environmental threats beyond climate change and maritime crime have all been highlighted by SIDS with illegal fishing a crime particularly noted (Malcolm, 2017). The 1999 Barbados + 5 review document for example emphasized that Illegal, Unregulated and Unreported fishing must be addressed ' ... to ensure essential sources of food supplies for island populations and economic development' (UN, 1999). At a regional level, the 'Atlantic, Indian Ocean, Mediterranean and South China Sea' (AIMS) grouping of SIDS that Seychelles and Mauritius are part, have for example emphasized the negative consequences of piracy.[1] In the regional synthesis document, published in 2010 as part of the five-year review of the Mauritius Conference, the Executive Summary notes,

> Piracy in the Western Indian Ocean is a major security concern for AIMS countries in the region. Limited initially in the region off Somalia, it has now extended south of the equator. In Seychelles, fishing activities alone are reported to have declined by 54% from January to August 2009 due to the risk of piracy. (AIMS, 2010, p. 2)

In a similar vein and more recently, in September 2015, Premdut Koonjoo, Mauritian Minister of Ocean Economy, Fisheries, Shipping and Outer Islands, flagged maritime security as a challenge to 'the sustainability of our economic development agenda' at an Indian Ocean Rim Association (IORA) conference (Koonjoo, 2015). The Minister emphasized how the region had to deal with 'the persistent scourge of piracy off [the] coast of Somalia and the challenges it posed to private sector development, regional and international trade, economic integration and development' (Koonjoo, 2015). Furthermore, in the Seychelles' national report to the 2014 Samoa UN SIDS Conference, the country explicitly noted that 'the Seychelles continues to see peace and security as one of the most important enablers for sustainable development' (Republic of Seychelles, 2013, p. 17). Indeed, speaking to the UN General Assembly in September 2015, Seychelles President James Michel noted,

> For oceanic nations the sea is our lifeblood and the Blue Economy is the catalyst upon which we learn to thrive. But we cannot thrive in an environment of insecurity. Maritime security is of the utmost importance to the vast majority of SIDS and to coastal states. (Republic of Seychelles, 2015, p. 3)[2]

These direct references to, and reflections about, maritime security have grown in recent years in policy circles, just as they have within the academic community. Regional blocs such as the African Union and European Union, alongside individual states like the United Kingdom have published strategies reflecting on the security dimension of the maritime domain (African Union, 2014; European Union, 2014; United Kingdom, 2014). Each strategy firmly highlights the importance of the maritime domain economically, politically, environmentally and culturally, and as such notes more diverse threats associated with that domain. Intellectually, the emergence of maritime security represents a broadening of the conceptualization of security in the maritime domain beyond naval power towards non-traditional threats and the role of non-state actors (Bueger, 2015; Chapsos & Malcolm, 2017). This more comprehensive understanding of maritime security is captured well in the 2008 UN Secretary-General's Report on the Oceans and the Law of the Sea where terrorist acts against ships and offshore installations, piracy and armed robbery against ships, illicit traffic in narcotic drugs and psychotropic substances, alongside the smuggling of people by sea, were all highlighted and discussed (UN, 2008).

Securing the maritime domain in Seychelles and Mauritius

In recognizing that for small island states like Seychelles and Mauritius, maritime security considerations are inextricably wrapped up in sustainable development efforts, and by noting the diversity of possible threats to the maritime domain; we have the backdrop against which the maritime security considerations of both countries are played out. Transitioning to the case studies, it is important to outline the broad policy and institutional structures associated with maritime security in each country.

The Seychelles' principle sustainable development mechanism is the Seychelles Sustainable Development Strategy 2012–2020 (SSDS 2012–2020), a document that organizes activity around 13 thematic areas including 'Fisheries and Marine Resources.' The strategy emphasizes that the Seychelles are 'economically dependent upon its fishery resources,' noting that 'maritime security and enforcement of illegal and unreported fisheries will remain a major challenge' to the country (Republic of Seychelles, 2012, p. 11).

The Republic of Mauritius meanwhile adopted, in 2008, the *Maurice Ile Durable* project for a sustainable vision to national development (Republic of Mauritius, 2013, p. 11). This sits alongside an 'Economic and Social Transformation Plan' for the country (Republic of Mauritius, 2013, p. 5) and is now replaced by the country's 2030 vision which also embraces the idea of sustainable development. Launched in 2015, the 2030 vision aims to bring about a second economic miracle and reduce the increasing level of unemployment in Mauritius. More specifically, the Ocean Economy sector is central for realizing this 'miracle' which, according to governmental estimates, will create 25,000 jobs between 2015 and 2020 (Jugnauth, 2015, p. 17). Policy-makers in Mauritius are conscious that there are several challenges to the ocean economy project, one of which is the various maritime security threats. Former Prime Minister Anerood Jugnauth recognized that 'a safe and secure maritime environment is a prerequisite for the achievement of a Second Economic Miracle' (Government Information Service, 2016a).

Drawing upon the documentary analysis conducted, supplemented with insights from informal discussions and semi-structured interviews, we can begin to map which threats to the maritime domain have been publicly articulated by the state over the past decade. Ultimately, the two states have highlighted a similar range of maritime security threats with piracy, drug trafficking, oil spills, climate change and Illegal, Unreported and Unregulated (IUU) fishing particularly prominent. Differences in geographical position and contexts have also meant that the extent to which both islands are affected by the threats can vary. For instance, even though both Mauritius and Seychelles were affected by piracy off the coast of Somalia, Seychelles was more affected because of its geographical position and stronger reliance on the seas for its economic wellbeing. The specific prioritization of threats has also been dictated by events which, once solved, have tended to recede as a maritime security issue without ever fully disappearing from the picture. For example, Somali piracy has receded as a prominent threat with drug trafficking emerging as a new priority in both Seychelles and Mauritius. However, policy-makers are aware that the piracy threat will not disappear as long as Somalia remains unstable (Michel, 2011).

The responsibility for maritime security at the state-level in each country is shared between a range of political and security actors. These governance structures remain a work in progress, while it is notable that neither country has an overarching maritime security strategy yet.

In the Seychelles (Figure 1), the main institution dealing with piracy is the Seychelles People's Defence Forces (SPDF). Within the SPDF, there are several branches involved in the fight against piracy. The most obvious one is the Seychelles Coast Guard (SCG) but it is helped in the task of providing maritime security by the air force and the army. Within the army, a special elite antipiracy unit called Tazar Unit was created in 2009 and was instrumental in engaging pirates and freeing hostages at the height of the piracy threat (Seychelles Nation, 2009). It is worth noting that the overall institutional structure is overseen by the President who is also the Commander-in-Chief of the SPDF. The Ministry of Foreign Affairs (now, Department of Foreign Affairs) also plays a role because it represents the country in forums for coordinating actions against piracy (e.g. in the Contact Group on Piracy off the Coast of Somalia, or CGPCS). Furthermore, it oversees the Seychelles Maritime Safety Administration (SMSA) which was created in 2004 and

Figure 1. Seychelles key anti-piracy governance structure.

which the new president – Danny Faure – now wants to transform into an independent institution regulating maritime activities (Faure, 2016). There is also the Marine Police Investigation Unit, created in 2014, whose task includes maritime safety issues as well as security issues like piracy and drug trafficking (Nicette, 2014). Finally, the judiciary plays an important role, previously ending the impunity for those involved in piracy.

In the case of Mauritius (Figure 2), the major agency dealing with drug trafficking is the Anti-Drug and Smuggling Unit (ADSU) which has among its main functions the detection and prevention of smuggling (The Mauritius Police Force, n.d.). In dealing with that task in the maritime realm, it needs the assistance of the National Coast Guard (NCG) and as such both organizations must coordinate their efforts. The NCG has several units that help establish its presence in Mauritian waters and to undertake surveillance missions which are important for disrupting drug trafficking networks. These include the Maritime Air Squadron and the Patrol Vessel Squadron. The Marine Special Force was created in

Figure 2. Mauritius key anti-drugs trafficking governance structure.

2009 to combat piracy but they are also trained to deal with complex security situations like hostage taking and other maritime security threats (Tuyau, 2010). The other institutions mentioned in the figure are involved if smugglers try to use the port and airport to smuggle drugs. In these situations the Mauritius Revenue Authority (MRA) plays an important role together with ADSU. In the cases discussed in this article, the criminals generally avoided the port and sought to exploit the unguarded coastline instead. The current institutional architecture in both Mauritius and Seychelles remains imperfect but are constantly adapted to emerging maritime security threats. There is a willingness to learn and improve accordingly in order to deal with increasingly complex security situations.

Seychelles' response to piracy

Piracy was a turning point in the maritime security field for Seychelles because it led to practices, institutions and the acquirement of capabilities that are now being appropriated to deal with a wider range of maritime security threats. Given its geographical position, the Seychelles was directly concerned by the rise of piracy off the coast of Somalia in the mid-2000s and unsurprisingly, it was right within the high-risk area delimitation. Its economy, essentially based on the export of fish and tourism, was directly impacted by the rise of Somali piracy (Independent, 2010; Malbrook & Uranie, 2015). The following extract from the presidential speech at a symposium on piracy aptly captures the depth of the impact:

> In 2009, our conservative estimates indicate a loss of 4% of our GDP due to piracy. Insurance costs have ballooned by 50%. Port and fisheries receipts have dropped by 30%. And we are spending over 2.3 million Euros per year on our anti-piracy patrols and surveillance. (Michel, 2010a)

President Michel expressed even more pronounced grief at the human consequences of piracy:

> In the last few days, there have been 3 attacks in and around our Exclusive Economic Zone, with an additional 8 in the Indian Ocean. In one of the attacks, 7 of our sea cucumber fishermen were taken hostage and were being ferried back to Somalia. Our forces intervened, and through decisive action we were able to prevent 7 of our brothers from being dragged away from their homes, their families and their livelihoods.

> This is not the first time we have lived through such torment. 10 of our compatriots have already endured more than we could expect of any seafarer after being held in Somalia for over 6 months. My government did its utmost to ensure their release, and by the grace of God, we were able to welcome them home. Earlier this year our forces also rescued another 7 Seychellois and 21 Iranians being held on a captured dhow, after disabling the vessel while it was under the control of pirates. (Michel, 2010b)

It is unsurprising with this negative impact that the threat from Somali piracy became a national priority for Seychelles. This coincided with international concern about the insecurity at sea, which in large part stemmed from the global importance of the Indian Ocean Sea Lines of Communication (SLOC). This is illustrated by the several resolutions passed by the United Nations Security Council to provide the necessary authorization and encourage international cooperation in combating the threat both through forceful means and prosecution (UNSC, 2016). While Seychelles, like the international society as a whole, was caught unprepared to deal with the threat posed, the country was soon among the leaders in the response; an interesting development bearing in mind it does not possess a navy.

Indeed despite its limited means, the Seychelles' Coast Guard (SCG) has been involved in several counter piracy operations against Somali pirates. In 2009, for example, the SCG responded to a luxury cruise ship's (MSC Melody) call for help and arrested nine suspected pirates (USA Today, 2009). In April 2011, the SCG rescued four local fishermen from Somali pirates (The Maritime Executive, 2011). Whilst probably the most famous case was the action of 30 March 2010 when the SCG vessel *Topaz* exchanged fire with Somali pirates and rescued several Seychellois and Iranians hostages from Somali pirates without causing any death (France 24, 2010). These events helped affirm the image of the

Seychelles as a maritime security provider in the region. It also showed that it was a worthwhile enterprise to help the SCG acquire new capabilities.

When tackling suspected cases of piracy, many countries have been reluctant to prosecute pirates arrested by their navies because of legal complexities inherent in the prosecution of pirates and fear that these individuals will become eligible for asylum (BBC, 2011). However, prosecution is important because of its deterrent effect. Seychelles played a vital role in ending impunity for piracy acts with other states such as Kenya and Mauritius also contributing to the task. Following a High Court judgement in Kenya that the country could not judge crimes that happened outside its territory and refusal of the Kenyan government to try more pirates (Achieng, 2010; BBC, 2010a, 2010b), the international community was in dire need of states that could take responsibility to prosecute pirates. With the support of international organizations like the United Nations Office on Drugs and Crime (UNODC) and the European Union (EU) alongside, individual state partners (e.g. in terms of building new court facilities and jails), Seychelles accepted that responsibility and began to prosecute pirates in March 2010 (Onyiego, 2010). This was despite Seychelles' own very limited prison capacity.

By 2012, Seychelles 'held over 100 pirate prisoners and had conducted more piracy trials than any other country (some 140-150)' (House of Lords, 2012, p. 16). The last remaining pirates were sentenced to 12 years by the Seychelles Supreme Court in June 2016 (CGPCS, 2016, p. 4). Given the long sentences handed down, Seychelles' limited prison capacity meant it became increasingly difficult for pirates to remain in the country. As a result, an agreement with the Transitional Federal Government of Somalia was reached whereby Seychelles can transfer the prisoners to Somalia where they will serve their sentences (Malbrook & Uranie, 2015; Seychelles Nation, 2011). Seychelles' way of combating piracy has been described as the 'prosecution model' and has been deemed so effective that it is now sharing its experience with states like Togo and Ghana (Malbrook & Uranie, 2015) – leadership through the sharing of best practice.

Alongside interdiction at sea and the prosecution of suspected pirates, Seychelles has played a very active role in the 'Contact Group on Piracy off the Coast of Somalia' (CGPCS). This governing instrument has played a central role in combating Somali piracy and is credited with considerable success in responding to the threat. It was created in New York in 2009 pursuant to UN Security Council Resolution 1851 (December 2008). It called for the creation of:

> an international cooperation mechanism to act as a common point of contact between and among states, regional and international organizations on all aspects of combating piracy and armed robbery at sea off Somalia's coasts. (UNSC, 2008)

Even if it is not unprecedented, the CGPCS is an innovative security governance mechanism because of its informal and flexible characteristics (Tardy, 2014). It does not have a formal membership and consists of states and non-states actors, including international and regional inter-governmental organizations, NGOs and actors evolving in the maritime realm (CGPCS, 2014, p. 4). The CGPCS has several working groups (WG) that are created and modified according to the evolution of the security situation. There are currently three main WG in the CGPCS: capacity building, coordination at sea and the third one aims at disrupting the financial networks supporting piracy and the prosecution of piracy kingpins. Initial assessment of the CGPCS shows that the contact group has been generally successful despite its imperfections (Swarttouw & Hopkins, 2014, pp. 11–18).

The Seychelles was very active within the WG of the CGPCS. For example, it was co-chair of the WG 3 on coordination with the industry in 2014 and participated in drafting best management practices. Moreover, Seychelles chaired the CGPCS in 2016 following on from the EU and its mandate was renewed for another year. This renewal is testimony that the role played by Seychelles is highly appreciated and recognition that despite its status as a SIDS and its limited capacities, it can be a reliable security partner. As former UN Secretary-General Ban Ki Moon observed during a visit to Seychelles in 2016, 'The United Nations also appreciates Seychelles' leadership on the problem of piracy as Chair of the Contact Group on piracy off the coast of Somalia' (Ban Ki-moon, 2016).

The incoming Seychellois Chairman of the CGPCS, Joel Morgan (also Seychelles' Minister of Foreign Affairs), made it clear that the Seychelles' agenda as Chair would reflect the agenda of the region (CGPCS, 2015, p. 3). While the CGPCS was meant to be an ad hoc mechanism, at the 19th Plenary Session of the Group in Seychelles, it was decided that the institution would be maintained despite the declining threat of piracy. One reason for maintaining the CGPCS is because the root cause of piracy –instability in Somalia – is still present, yet there has also been acknowledgement that the success of the contact group can be replicated to dealing with other threats. The contact group's mandate is broadening with The Djibouti Declaration (15 May 2016) calling for the expansion of the CGPCS mandate to include other maritime security issues. The Seychelles has used its chairmanship of the CGPCS to push this agenda of consolidating this instrument into a durable one.

This direction of travel makes sense for a small island like Seychelles because the CGPCS focussed the attention of the international community on the maritime security of the Indian Ocean. Maintaining the CGPCS is a way to keep that attention. This is important because as the Chairman Joel Morgan explained,

> The region has already started to take its share of responsibility but we still need the International Community to maintain its effort until we attain a much higher level of maritime capability. (CGPCS, 2016, p. 1)

Here the theme chosen for the 19th Plenary Session of the CGPCS was 'From the Region to the Region: Creating a Lasting Legacy' (Seychelles Nation, 2016a). With the multilateral nature of the CGPCS, small islands and regional states have a stronger voice in decision making in comparison to global institutions such as the UN Security Council. They can use this forum as a tool to acquire capabilities that will make them providers of security instead of just receivers. The emphasis on capacity building is one that has been seized by Seychelles as an important way forward with regards to enhancing maritime security. As Joel Morgan has argued,

> Since 2008, we fought this scourge and have emerged victorious. We must, however, not become complacent as maritime insecurity takes on a different form today and evolves. The continued reporting in the news of terrorist attacks and other related maritime threats such as drugs and weapons trafficking, has proven how vulnerable the world and in particular especially our region can be if these dangers are not dealt with swiftly and in a systematic manner. The CGPCS community cannot remain indifferent to these problems, and we should continue to promote international mobilization and find tangible solutions together

for our common long-term security, even as we work to achieve our own objectives. (Morgan, 2016)

That need to keep that international mobilization going is thus a way that small islands respond to the context where they have vast responsibilities in the maritime realm but limited capacity. Despite their willingness and regional leadership, small islands remain reliant on sustainable and concerted international efforts to promote maritime security.

The piracy threat also showed the importance of having an integrated security system for policing the Western Indian Ocean. With the help of the Indian Ocean Commission (IOC), an inter-governmental organization composed of the Comoros, Madagascar, Mauritius, France for La Réunion and Seychelles, two regional centers have been set up: The Regional Maritime Centre for Fusion of Maritime Information (RMIFC) which is based in Madagascar, and the Regional Maritime Centre for Operational Coordination (RMCOC) in Seychelles. The RMIFC is currently in a 'soft opening' phase while the RMCOC is on 'pre-operational mode' (CGPCS, 2016, p. 8). The RMCOC is set up by the Anti-Piracy Unit (APU) of the IOC but will cater for range of maritime security threats affecting the Western Indian Ocean (Seychelles Nation, 2016b). These include piracy and armed robbery, trafficking of persons, drug trafficking, oil spills as well as natural calamities like cyclone and tsunami (Seychelles Nation, 2016b). The RMIFC will feed the RMCOC with maritime information and in turn have the task of coordinating regional operations (Morgan, 2016). After receiving intelligence from Madagascar, the RMCOC will mount a regional response involving the resources (e.g. coast guard vessels and planes) of all member countries (Seychelles Nation, 2016b). In other words, the RMCOC will coordinate the pooling of resources among states in the region.

The RMCOC has the potential to transform Seychelles into a security hub and further contribute towards affirming the intention of the region to take responsibility for its own maritime security. As the Director of the APU, R. Agrippine, observed, Seychelles has been chosen because of its strategic position in the Indian Ocean and its experience in dealing with maritime security threats (Seychelles Nation, 2016b). In fact, its active role to combat piracy has given Seychelles the legitimacy to host this center. According to the Chief of Staff of the SPDF, 'our region's capacity to deal with the increasing threats of wider maritime crimes will be greatly enhanced' (Athanase & Bonnelame, 2016). In the same vein, President Faure has portrayed the RMCOC as 'the response mechanism for the East and Southern Africa and the Indian Ocean Region under the Maritime Security Programme which targets all forms of maritime threats' (Seychelles Nation, 2017). Yet the centers will continue to need the support of the international community to work properly (Department of Foreign Affairs, 2016), especially given ongoing capacity-building needs. Only time will tell whether these regional mechanisms will be successful.

Mauritius' response to drug trafficking by sea

The decline of the piracy threat left states more space to devote attention to the trafficking of drugs by sea. Drug abuse is a major social problem plaguing Mauritius with the 'World Drug Report' regularly expressing concerns. For example, the 2008 report highlighted that Mauritius had the highest rate of use of opiates (mostly heroin) in Africa with 2% of the population affected (UNODC, 2008, p. 57). The 2012 report confirmed this problem noting that,

In Africa, the increasing use of heroin and drug injecting is also emerging as an alarming trend, particularly in Kenya, Libya, Mauritius, Seychelles and the United Republic of Tanzania. (UNODC, 2012, p. 18)

Indeed, the longstanding challenge posed by the use of illegal drugs in Mauritius was noted by security personnel in an interview conducted by one of the authors (Interview No. 9, 2015). In a speech to mark the occasion of the commissioning ceremony of the Mauritian Coastguard vessel *Victory*, the Prime Minister underlined the need to enhance the maritime safety and security of the country against threats like drug trafficking and other maritime crimes (Government Information Service, 2016d). For many years, the main points of entry were the port and more particularly the airport with several spectacular seizures of drugs. However, there is now mounting evidence that a porous coastline is a major entry point for a vast amount of drugs. Recently there have been cases that suggest that the problem is closely linked to a lack of surveillance in the maritime realm in the region. This section documents some of these cases which reveal the need for collective and concerted action both within Mauritius and among states in the region.

A recently declassified 1986 United States' Central Intelligence Agency (CIA) document highlights that concern over the security of the Mauritian coastline, and its use as an entry point for illegal drugs, is longstanding (CIA, 1986). The CIA found that drugs illegally entering Mauritius were destined both for local consumption and, in the case of Mandrax (methaqualone) and heroin specifically, were transited through Mauritius to South Africa (CIA, 1986, p. 14). Consequently the report predicted that,

> [o]ver the longer term, the inability of the authorities to control the borders may encourage international smugglers to use Mauritius as a regional transship point for narcotics destined for other markets. (CIA, 1986, p. 14)

Nevertheless, the report acknowledged that the drug smuggled in Mauritius was mainly destined for local consumption (CIA, 1986, p. 11). It was believed that the drugs originated mainly from three countries: India, Pakistan and South Africa and was introduced in Mauritius through 'private yachts and cruise ships or through the VIP lounge at the country's single airport' (CIA, 1986, p. 11). The declassified document also revealed the existence of a politically connected drug smuggling network between Mauritius and Reunion Island (CIA, 1986, pp. 11–13). Interestingly, the CIA noted that the 'the three police patrol craft cannot adequately patrol the approximately 100-mile-long coastline' (CIA, 1986, p. 11). Furthermore, it pointed out that 'checks of private yachts in the local harbor are rare' (CIA, 1986, p. 11). While the local and international context has changed, the report provides evidence that there is a potential challenge to Mauritius and one that has a maritime dimension. The cases explained below show that most of those findings remain valid today even if the means available to deal with these kinds of issues have increased.

Indeed in 2012, the issue of drugs trafficking by sea came to prominence in the island of Mauritius. More specifically, a steward (H.M.) of the *Mauritius Trochetia* – a passenger and general cargo ship owned by the Mauritian Government – admitted to being involved in the trafficking of drugs after the confessions of one of the traffickers. The steward is now a star witness in the drug case before the Mauritian court and benefits from round-the-clock police protection. He described the whole mode of operation as child play because the maritime realm is vast and it is easy to avoid getting caught (Olitte, 2015). The drug was bought from Madagascar by the steward while working on the *Mauritius Trochetia*. He pointed out that laxity and corruption in Madagascar meant that it was easy to escape the control posts at the port (Olitte, 2015). To escape control at Port Louis in Mauritius, the steward would, once the vessel had reached close to the west coast of Mauritius, call an accomplice who took a motor boat to reach the vicinity of the *Mauritius Trochetia* (Olitte, 2015). From there, the drugs would be dropped to the sea with a floater. He admitted to have carried out this kind of operation at least six times for three major drug dealers (Olitte, 2015).

In 2016, the Reunionese police force intercepted a speed boat in Sainte Rose (Reunion Island) and arrested three Mauritian smugglers with 42.3 kg of heroin while they were loading drugs on a speedboat destined for the Mauritian market (Le Mauricien, 2016a; Le Mauricien, 2016b). This was the first time that such a huge amount of heroin has been seized in the South West Indian Ocean and estimates suggest that the stock would have been sufficient to supply the Mauritian market for a period of 15–24 months (Le Mauricien, 2016c). The traffickers used a yacht by the name of *Ilot Gabriel* that was registered in Mauritius with the intention of transporting the drugs from Madagascar to Mauritius. However, they had to stop at Reunion Island due to engine problems. The drug was kept in a safe place in Reunion Island for a period of time before they then used a speedboat by the name of *Sweet Love Mama* (also registered in Mauritius) to transport the drugs from Reunion to Mauritius. Reunion Island authorities arrested the Reunionese accomplices of the traffickers while they were transferring the drug on to the speedboat. The traffickers sought to align the speedboat's arrival in Mauritius with the weekend in the belief that it would be easier to avoid the NCG inspection due to usual increased vessel movements during weekends (Le Mauricien, 2016a; Le Mauricien, 2016b). Those caught by the Reunion Island authorities admitted that they carried out a similar operation at the beginning of 2016 (Abel & Denmamode, 2016; Le Mauricien, 2016a, 2016b).

More recently, on 9 March 2017, a joint operation by ADSU and MRA enabled the seizure of 135 kg of heroin (worth two billion rupees), concealed in imported gas cylinders for compressors, on board the *MSC Ivana* from South Africa (Le Mauricien, 2017a, 2017b; Week-End, 2017). Given that massive amount of heroin and the relative smallness of the population of drug addicts in Mauritius, there are doubts that the drug was destined only to the Mauritian market. The lead that the 135 kg of drug was destined to Europe and Australia with Mauritius as a tranship point is thus being investigated (Abel, 2017).

Collectively, these cases suggest a threat exists and that there remain questions over the extent of maritime surveillance. Unsurprisingly, the Mauritian government discourse links the fight against drug trafficking with arming the NCG with better equipment to undertake surveillance in the maritime domain (Government Information Service, 2016a). As the Mauritian Prime Minister pointed out in 2016:

> [T]he surveillance systems is being reinforced by equipping the Police with state-of-the-art equipment and technology to counter the attempt to introduce drugs in Mauritius. The recent acquisition of Fast Interceptor Boats and patrol vessels are just a few examples. (Parliamentary Debates, 2016b, p. 147)

At the same time, the cases suggest that there is a need for a regional strategy to deal with the drug trafficking problem. As Captain G. Colpitts of US Africa Command, who supervised the Cutlass Express Maritime Exercise in 2017 puts it, 'there is a need for greater collaboration among countries in the region to combat drug trafficking' (Le Defi, 2017), with better information sharing a priority. Here the evidence of cooperation in the region is patchy at best. In the case of the *Sweet Love Mama* for example, the French authorities in Reunion Island were slow to collaborate with the Mauritian ADSU (Le Mauricien, 2016a, 2016b). Reunion Island authorities insisted that any request for international cooperation should go through the French Ministry of Foreign Affairs (Le Mauricien, 2016c). Furthermore, the request should come from the French authorities rather than those of Mauritius (Le Mauricien, 2016c).

The latest Mauritian Government strategies to combat the drug problem take into account the need for regional cooperation. In 2016, the now former Prime Minister announced the elaboration of a National Master Plan with the help of the UNODC (Le Mauricien, 2016d). In line with its 2015–19 program, the Mauritian Government has set up a Commission of Inquiry on Drug Trafficking (Cabinet Decision, 2015). The terms of reference of the Commission (chaired by a former judge of the Supreme Court) includes investigating the sources and routes of illicit drugs, the effectiveness of local agencies involved in drug trafficking and the need to coordinate actions among local, regional and international agencies working to combat drug trafficking (Cabinet Decision, 2015). Similarly, the Strategic Policing Plan 2015–18 underlines the need to 'strengthen local, regional and international cooperation and intelligence network' (The Mauritius Police Force, 2016, pp. 31–32). The NCG is also becoming increasingly involved in the fight against drug trafficking.

Dealing with the maritime security aspect of the drug problem seems to be a task with new prioritization for the NCG. In the 2013 NCG leaflet, the word 'drug' does not appear in its list of objectives which were geared towards combating IUU fishing and reducing drowning cases (National Coast Guard, 2013). In contrast, the NCG's 2015–16 Action Plan leaflet recognized the problem of drug trafficking in the maritime realm. The NCG has amongst its five objectives to increase joint operations at sea with the ADSU (National Coast Guard, 2015, p. 2). Undeniably, the NCG has sought to develop its capacities to address the problem of a lack of surveillance of the coastline. Between 2009 and 2016, a sum of 4.1 billion Mauritian Rupees (MUR) was spent on acquiring equipment for the NCG and the Police Helicopter Squadron (Parliamentary Debates, 2016a, p. 115). More than half of this sum, 2.1 billion, was invested between January 2015 and June 2016 (Parliamentary Debates, 2016a, p. 115). The new equipment was acquired with multiple threats in mind. For instance, 10 fast interceptor boats equipped with machine guns enhanced NCG capabilities in terms of 'coastal patrol, effective surveillance, anti-smuggling, anti-poaching activities, search, rescue and fisheries protection amongst others' (Government Information Service, 2016a). Another important addition to the capabilities of the NCG was the *CGS Barracuda* at the cost of US$58 million (Government Information Service, 2016c). It is used to patrol Mauritian waters to deal with pirates, boats and vessels indulging in IUU fishing and drug trafficking (L'Express, 2015). The Barracuda has long endurance capabilities and is also capable of carrying helicopters (Interviewee No. 4, 2015). Similarly, the Dornier aircraft, acquired in 2016, is equipped with technologies such as a maritime patrol radar and infrared camera, all of which should enhance the NCG's capabilities to deal with threats such as drugs trafficking by sea (Government Information Service, 2016b).

Despite this investment however, there are still potential gaps that could hinder Mauritius' capacity to tackle the supply side of the drug problem. The NCG still lacks equipment and personnel for the effective control of the Mauritian coastline (Carrim & Jaulim, 2016). The western coastline is especially vulnerable to drug trafficking but the NCG faces a lack of personnel and equipment for the effective surveillance and control of boat movements in that area (Carrim & Jaulim, 2016). More specifically, it has been reported that the NCG only have two (sometimes three) fast interceptor boats for the surveillance of the western coastline (Carrim & Jaulim, 2016). A look at the map of NCG posts around Mauritius also shows that many resources have been devoted to the northern and eastern part of the island whereas the western and southern coasts boast only six NCG posts (National Coast Guard, 2013, 2015). While the south coast is very difficult to navigate because of rough seas, the west coast has very calm water making it suitable for navigation and potentially increasing the risk of exploitation. Nevertheless, the NCG does make use of radar systems for monitoring vessels with the Automatic Identification System for large vessels and the Coastal Ready Surveillance System for fishing vessels and boats (Maugueret, 2016). The NCG is working on a way to install transponders on board pleasure crafts to facilitate their monitoring (Maugueret, 2016).

Collectively, this situation underlines the need for continued capacity building and strategies to combat drug trafficking by sea in Mauritius. It also shows that given the regional characteristics of drugs trafficking, it will be extremely difficult to win the battle alone. The United States has funded capacity-building exercises for Coast Guard officers from Mauritius and other states in the Indian Ocean and Eastern Africa. One such instance is the annual Cutlass Express exercise which Mauritius hosted in 2017. The aim of the exercise was to develop participants' capabilities in 'controlling the waters around their countries, exercise law enforcement, reduce piracy, illicit trafficking, and promote commerce and trade' (US Navy, 2017). In the same vein, the EU Critical Maritime Routes Law Enforcement Agencies (CRIMLEA) projects that includes CRIMLEA I (2010–2014) and CRIMLEA II (2014–2017) has up to January 2017, organized 65 capacity-building training events for Western Indian Ocean states to deal with maritime crimes (CRIMLEA, 2017). These exercises are also important because they help the various coast guards and navies of the region to learn how to work as a team. India has also been a key actor in conditioning the way that Mauritius interprets maritime security. India has the largest navy amongst Indian Ocean states and has been keen to help Mauritius in capacity building. The acquisition of the *CGS Barracuda* was, for example, financed by India.[3] Indeed, the Indian High Commissioner to Mauritius has also affirmed that India is ready to respond all Mauritian maritime security demands (Groëme-Harmon, 2015). While there are long-standing and intense cultural relations between Mauritius and India, undoubtedly Mauritius is also benefitting from a favorable geopolitical context in which an increased Chinese presence in the Indian Ocean is pushing India to win influence in the region.

Conclusion

In recent years, both Seychelles and Mauritius have, at state level, articulated more publicly recognition of the importance of their maritime domains for sustainable development efforts. In doing this, there has been a parallel increased emphasis on the way in which insecurity in these domains can undermine their development efforts threatening both state and human security, with a push to enhance maritime security. Through these two exploratory case studies, the ways in which both islands states have presented and responded to specific threats have been explored. Undoubtedly, Somali piracy forced countries in the Western Indian Ocean to take note of the negative implications of insecurity at sea; yet as the focus on Seychelles' response to this piracy illustrated, there has been a willingness on the part of Seychelles and the broader region to institutionalize best practice and look at the transferability of responses for other maritime threats. This situation emphasizes that while countries often react to security challenges after they have emerged, there has also been recognition of the importance of being proactive in enhancing maritime security capacity.

Indeed, across both cases there has been a clear leap forward in maritime security capabilities since the start of the decade. New strategies and action plans with a relevance to the maritime domain have been introduced, departmental and security governance structures have been reformed, multi-national partnerships have been embraced and new working practices implemented. Seychelles has played a significant leadership role in the CGPCS, whilst Mauritius has sought support to develop an action plan from organizations such as the UNODC and embraced its partnership with countries such as India. The basis of an integrated maritime security system in the region is emerging but there remain capacity-building needs in both countries. Moreover, it remains too early to claim success on the part of new initiatives such as the RMCOC. Ultimately, it will require continued political will and sustained investment in assets and training to see this maritime security system thrive. Yet as international attention on the Western Indian Ocean reduces in the midst of reduced piracy incidents, it will be interesting to see how the regional states sustain activity in the maritime security field.

This recognition that external actors matter when considering the maritime security of island states such as Seychelles and Mauritius, highlights that for small states, capacity is a particular structural constraint on enhancing capabilities. Whilst it is not possible to make definitive claims from this case study for the way SIDS as a whole approach their maritime security, this seems a conservative and fair conclusion. The case studies and comparative analysis of Seychelles and Mauritius also suggests that small states can play an active, leading role in regional security policy. Both Seychelles and Mauritius have begun to reframe themselves as 'large ocean states' (Poonoosamy, 2013, p. 3; Jumeau, 2013), whilst there is a clear acknowledge that maritime security is not a zero sum game with increased capacity in one island state understood as benefiting the region as a whole. Going forward, additional case studies of the way in which SIDS have approached maritime security could offer important insights in to the way in which small states as a whole can sustainably develop and positively interact in the global arena.

Notes

1. It is worth noting that there are currently no Mediterranean members of the grouping as Malta is represented through the European Union. AIMS has no standing secretariat nor formal structures.
2. The former President of the Republic of Seychelles, James Michel, has also published a book titled, 'Rethinking the oceans – Towards the blue economy.'
3. The Barracuda cost $58.5 Million. $10 million came from the Indian authorities and $48.5 million from a loan from EXIM Bank India.

Disclosure statement

No potential conflict of interest was reported by the authors.

References

Abel, V. (2017, March 30). Maurice au Coeur du Trafic de Drogue Dans la Région? *L'Express* [online]. Retrieved April 22, 2017, from https://www.lexpress.mu/article/303475/maurice-au-coeur-trafic-drogue-dans-region

Abel, V., & Denmamode, Y. (2016, November 15). Saisie De Drogue A la Réunion : Le trafic Raconté par un Skipper. *L'Express*.

Achieng, C. (2010, November 9). Kenya Court orders release of Somali piracy suspects. *Reuters* [online]. Retrieved May 2, 2017, from http://www.reuters.com/article/somalia-piracy-kenya-idUSLDE6A81SI20101109

African Union. (2014). *2050 Africa's integrated maritime (AIM) Strategy* [online] Retrieved August 15, 2016 from http://pages.au.int/maritime/documents/2050-aim-strategy-0

AIMS. (2010). *Regional synthesis report* [online] Retrieved February 10, 2017, from https://sustainabledevelopment.un.org/content/documents/11787AIMS_Regional_Synthesis-MSI5-Final.pdf

Athanase, P., & Bonnelame, B. (2016, September 4). Soon in Seychelles: Regional coordination centre to battle maritime crimes. *Seychelles News Agency* [online]. Retrieved January 19, 2017, from http://www.seychellesnewsagency.com/articles/5843/Soon+in+Seychelles+Regional+coordination+centre+to+battle+maritime+crimes

Athanase, P., & Uranie, S. (2016, December 14). *NATO ends anti-piracy operation; Seychelles to continue to monitor sea threats*. *Seychelles News Agency* [online]. Retrieved January 15, 2017, from http://www.seychellesnewsagency.com/articles/6434/NATO+ends+anti-piracy+operation%3B+Seychelles+to+continue+to+monitor+sea+threats#sthash.lMIRJ0oX.dpuf

Ban Ki-moon. (2016, May 7). *UN Secretary-General Ban Ki-moon's statement to the media following bilateral talks with President Michel, State House* [online]. Retrieved January 18, 2017, from http://www.statehouse.gov.sc/speeches.php?news_id=3042

BBC. (2010a, April 1). Kenya ends trials of Somali pirates in it courts. *BBC World* [online]. Retrieved May 2, 2017, from http://news.bbc.co.uk/2/hi/africa/8599347.stm

BBC. (2010b, October 1). Kenya ends co-operation in hosting Somali pirate trials. *BBC World* [online]. Retrieved May 2, 2017, from http://www.bbc.com/news/world-africa-11454762

BBC. (2011, January 25). Q&A: What do you do with a captured pirate?. *BBC World* [online]. Retrieved May 2, 2017, from http://www.bbc.co.uk/news/mobile/world-africa-11813168

Board of Investment. (n.d.). *Mauritius: Your investment and business hub: The marine industry* [online], Port Louis: Mauritius. Retrieved April 25, 2017, from www.investmauritius.com/Seafood/document.pdf

Bueger, C. (2015). What is maritime security? *Marine Policy*, 53(2015), 159–164.

Cabinet Decision. (2015). 10 July 2015 [online]. Retrieved January 20, 2017, from http://pmo.govmu.org/English/Documents/Cabinet%20Decisions%202015/Cabinet%20Decisions%2010%20July%202015.pdf

Carrim, Y., & Jaulim, F. (2016, November 14). L'Ouest Veritable Passoire Pour les Trafiquants. *L'Express*.

Central Intelligence Agency. (1986, August). Directorate of Intelligence, *Narcotics Review* [online]. Retrieved February 3, 2017, from https://www.cia.gov/library/readingroom/docs/CIA-RDP87T00685R000100010001-7.pdf

CGPCS. (2014). *CGPCS Newsletter*, Contact group on piracy off the coast of Somalia March 2014.

CGPCS. (2015). *CGPCS Newsletter*, Contact group on piracy off the coast of Somalia October 2015.

CGPCS. (2016). *CGPCS Newsletter*, Contact group on piracy off the coast of Somalia October 2016.

Chapsos, I. (2017). Maritime security and the UN sustainable development goals. *Centre for Trust, Peace and Social Relations Maritime Security Briefings* [online] Retrieved February 13, 2017, from http://www.coventry.ac.uk/research/areas-of-research/trust-peace-social-relations/our-research/Armed_violence_illicit_activities/maritime-security-briefings/

Chapsos, I., & Malcolm, J. A. (2017). Maritime security in Indonesia: Towards a comprehensive agenda? *Marine Policy*, 76, 178–184.

CRIMLEA. (2017). Law enforcement capacity building in East Africa 2010/2017 [online]. Retrieved April 25, 2017, from https://criticalmaritimeroutes.eu/projects/crimlea/

Denselow, A. (2013, May 19). *Seychelles cells: The Somali pirates 'jailed in paradise'*. BBC [online]. Retrieved January 15, 2017, from http://www.bbc.co.uk/news/magazine-22556030

Department of Foreign Affairs. (2016, May 19). Seychelles highlights scope of CGPCS in Djibouti at 3rd Eastern Southern African and Indian Ocean Region Ministerial Meeting. *The Republic of Seychelles* [online]. Retrieved January 5, 2017, from http://www.mfa.gov.sc/static.php?content_id=18&news_id=1257

European Union. (2014). *European Union maritime security strategy* [online] Retrieved August 15, 2016, from http://register.consilium.europa.eu/doc/srv?L=EN & f=ST%2011205%202014%20INIT

Faure, D. (2016, Octoeber 18). *Speech by President Danny Faure before the national assembly*, [online]. Retrieved February 5, 2017, from http://www.statehouse.gov.sc/speeches.php?news_id=3197

France 24. (2010, March 29). Seychelles coastguard vessel rescues fishermen from Somali pirates. *France 24* [online]. Retrieved January 1, 2017, from http://www.france24.com/en/20100329-seychelles-coastguard-vessel-rescues-fisherman-somali-pirates-indian-ocean-piracy

Government Information Service. (2016a, March 14). Maritime security: Induction of ten fast interceptor boats. *Government information service* [online], Mauritius. Retrieved January 5, 2017, from http://www.govmu.org/English/News/Pages/Maritime-Security-Induction-of-ten-Fast-Interceptor-Boats.aspx

Government Information Service. (2016b, July 14). Maritime surveillance: National coast guard equipped with new Dornier aircraft. *Government Information Service* [online], Mauritius. Retrieved January 8, 2017, from http://www.govmu.org/English/News/Pages/Maritime-Surveillance-National-Coast-Guard-equipped-with-new-Dornier-aircraft.aspx

Government Information Service. (2016c, September 21). Sécurité Maritime: Mission de Surveillance Dans la ZEE de Maurice Par le CGS Barracuda. *Government Information Service* [online], Mauritius. Retrieved January 8, 2017, from http://www.govmu.org/French/News/Pages/S%C3%A9curit%C3%A9-maritime-Mission-de-surveillance-dans-la-ZEE-de-Maurice-par-le-CGS-Barracuda-.aspx

Government Information Service. (2016d). *Newsletter*, December, Mauritius.

Groëme-Harmon, A. (2015, August 15). Anup Kumar Mudgal, Haut-Commissaire de L'Inde: 'le Traité de Non Double Imposition Sera Bénéfique Aux Deux Parties'. *L'Express*.

Guilfoyle, D. (2013). *Modern piracy legal challenges and responses*. Cheltenham: Edward Elgar.

House of Lords. (2012, August 21). European Union committee, 3rd report of session 2012–13, *Turning the tide on piracy, building Somalia's future: Follow-up report on the EU's Operation Atalanta and beyond*.

Independent. (2010, February 8). How the Seychelles became a Pirates' Paradise. *Independent* [online]. Retrieved July 11, 2016, from http://www.independent.co.uk/news/world/africa/how-the-seychelles-became-a-pirates-paradise-1892279.html

Ingrebritsen, C., Neumann, I., Gstohl, S., & Beyer, J. (2006). *Small states in international relations*. Seattle, WA: University of Washington Press; Reykjavik: University of Iceland Press.

Interviewee No. 4. (2015). Author interview conducted in Mauritius.

Interviewee No. 9. (2015). Author interview conducted in Mauritius.

Jugnauth, A. (2015, August 22). Prime minister of the Republic of Mauritius, speech at the launch of the *high powered committee on achieving the second economic miracle and vision 2030*.

Jumeau, R. (2013). 'Small island developing states, large ocean states', speech of Seychelles Ambassador for climate change and SIDS issues at the expert group meeting on oceans, seas and sustainable development: Implementation and follow-up to Rio+20 [online], United Nations Headquarters 18–19 April. Retrieved May 2, 2017, from https://sustainabledevelopment.un.org/content/documents/1772Ambassador%20Jumeau_EGM%20Oceans%20FINAL.pdf

Kellerman, M. G. (2011). Somali piracy: Causes and consequences. *Inquiries Journal* 3 (9) [online]. Retrieved January 21, 2017, from https://www.inquiriesjournal.com/articles/579/somali-piracy-causes-and-consequences

Koonjoo, P. (2015, September 3). Speech by Honourable Premdut Koonjoo, Minister of ocean economy, marine resources, fisheries, shipping and outer islands [Online] at the *Inaugural ceremony of IORA – Blue Economy Conference (BEC)*. Retrieved April 25, 2017, from www.iora.net/media/158007/address_by_the_hon_premdut_koonjoo__mauritius.pdf

Le Defi. (2017, February 8). Capitaine Geoffrey Colpitts : Il faut une meilleure collaboration des pays de la région pour combattre le trafic de drogue. *Le Defi* [online]. Retrieved February 10, 2017, from http://defimedia.info/capitaine-geoffrey-colpitts-il-faut-une-meilleure-collaboration-des-pays-de-la-region-pour-combattre-le-trafic-de-drogue

Le Mauricien. (2016a, November 12). Des Mauriciens Arrêtes Avec 40 Kg D'heroine. *Le Mauricien*.

Le Mauricien. (2016b, November 14). Drogue: Démantèlement D'un Réseau Régional Rodé. *Le Mauricien*.

Le Mauricien. (2016c, November 19). Enquête: Trafic de Drogue Dans L'OI: 42.6 KG D'Héroïne: Le Lead a L'ICAC. *Le Mauricien*.

Le Mauricien. (2016d, November 30). UN National Drug Control Master Pan Annoncé. *Le Mauricien*.

Le Mauricien. (2017a, March 10). Saisie Record de 135 kg d'Héroïne D'une Valeur de Rs 2 Milliards. *Le Mauricien*.

Le Mauricien. (2017b, March 21). Saisie Record de 135 Kg D'Heroine : Zenfant Lacaz : « Mo Pa Konn Nanye Ladan ». *Le Mauricien*.

L'Express. (2015, March 3). Le CGS Barracuda Est Enfin Arrivé. *L'Express*.

Malbrook, J., & Uranie, S. (2015, October 23). The Seychelles anti-piracy model. *Maritime Security Review* [online]. Retrieved January 15, 2017, from http://www.marsecreview.com/2015/10/the-seychelles-anti-piracy-model/

Malcolm, J. A. (2017). Sustainability as maritime security: A small island developing state perspective? *Global Policy*, 8(2), 237–245.

Maugueret, X. (2016, November 21). Questions Au Chef Inspecteur Isurey, National Coast Guard: 'La NCG s'équipe constamment'. *L'Express*.

Michel, J. A. (2010a, July 12). *Speech by President James A. Michel of the occasion of the opening of the International Symposium on Piracy, Le Meridien Barbarons* [online], Mahe, Seychelles. Retrieved January 15, 2017, from http://www.statehouse.gov.sc/speeches.php?news_id=2229

Michel, J. A. (2010b, November 23). *Opening speech by President James Michel on the occasion of the 2nd ACP Fisheries Ministers Meeting* [online], ICCS, Victoria. Retrieved January 15, 2017, from http://www.statehouse.gov.sc/speeches.php?news_id=2238

Michel, J. A. (2011, February 25). *State of the nation address by president* [online]. Retrieved November 28, 2016, from http://www.statehouse.gov.sc/speeches.php?news_id=2255

Morgan, J. (2016, May 31). *Speech of Minister Joël Morgan for the CGPCS 19th plenary session* [online], Seychelles, Retrieved January 28, 2017, from http://www.mfa.gov.sc/static.php?content_id=20&news_id=292

National Coast Guard. (2013). *National coast guard annual policing plan 2013* [online]. Retrieved January 25, 2017, from http://police.govmu.org/English/Publication/Documents/NCG2013.pdf.

National Coast Guard. (2015). *National coast guard, action plan 2015–16: Quality service with pride and care* [online]. Retrieved January 25, 2017, from http://police.govmu.org/English/Documents/action%20plan%202015/NCG.pdf.

Nicette, J. (2014, May 23). New Seychelles marine police investigations unit to be set up soon. *Seychelles News Agency* [online]. Retrieved November 5, 2016, from http://www.seychellesnews

agency.com/articles/553/New+Seychelles+marine+police+investigations+unit+to+be+set+up+soon

Olitte, I. (2015, September 6-12). Le Star Witness Dans L'Affaire Gro Derek Se Confie: Hayeshan Maudarbaccus: 'Le Trafic de Drogue Par la Mer ne S'arrêtera Jamais'. *Le Dimanche/ L'Hebdo*.

Onyiego, M. (2010, May 5). Seychelles to establish regional court to prosecute pirates. *Voice of America* [online]. Retrieved December 10, 2016, from http://www.voanews.com/a/seychelles-to-establish-regional-court-to-prosecute-pirates-92969969/117142.html

Parliamentary Debates. (2016a, June 28). Hansard, sixth national assembly, first session, Tuesday.

Parliamentary Debates. (2016b, November 29). Hansard, sixth national assembly, first session, Tuesday.

Percy, S., & Shortland, A. (2013). The business of piracy in Somalia. *Journal of Strategic Studies*, 36(4), 541–578. DOI:10.1080/01402390.2012.750242

Poonoosamy, K. (2013). 'Editorial' *Board of Investment Mauritius E-Newsletter* [online] issue No. 56 July. Retrieved May 2, 2017, from http://www.investmauritius.com/ezine_July13/

Reiter, E., & Gartner, H. (2001). *Small states and alliances*. Heidelberg; New York: Physica-Verlag.

Republic of Mauritius. (2013). *National report of the Republic of Mauritius to the Third International Conference on Small Island Developing States* [online] Retrieved February 10, 2017, from http://www.sids2014.org/content/documents/215Mauritius%20National%20Report.pdf

Republic of Seychelles. (2012). *Seychelles sustainable development strategy 2012–2020 vol. 1* [online] Retrieved February 13, 2017, from http://www.egov.sc/edoc/pubs/frmpubdetail.aspx?pubId=26

Republic of Seychelles. (2013). *National report to Fiji summit* [online]. Retrieved February 10, 2017, from http://www.sids2014.org/content/documents/232SIDS_National%20report_6.06.13.pdf.

Republic of Seychelles. (2015). *Statement by Mr James Alix Michel, President of the Republic of Seychelles at the 70th session of the United Nations general assembly* [online]. Retrieved February 10, 2017, from https://gadebate.un.org/sites/default/files/gastatements/70/29_SC_en.pdf

Reuters. (2012, May 19). Mauritius, Somalia in deal to prosecute pirates. *Reuters* [online]. Retrieved January 15, 2017, from http://www.reuters.com/article/ozatp-mauritius-pirates-idAFJOE84I00Q20120519

Seychelles Nation. (2009, November 26). Special defence force unit set up to combat piracy. *Seychelles Weekly* [online]. Retrieved November 30, 2016, from http://www.seychellesweekly.com/November%2029,%202009/p09_defense_piracy.html

Seychelles Nation. (2011, December 2). Seychelles signs historic accord on transfer of jailed Somali pirates. *Seychelles Weekly* [online]. Retrieved January 4, 2016, from http://www.seychellesweekly.com/February%2021,%202011/pol1_seychelles_signs.html

Seychelles Nation. (2016a, June 1). 19th plenary session of the contact group on piracy off the Coast of Somalia (CGPCS): Delegates meet to discuss the group's future. *Seychelles Nation* [online]. Retrieved April 25, 2017, from http://www.nation.sc/article.html?id=249638

Seychelles Nation. (2016b, Octoeber 21). Seychelles to host new centre to respond to maritime threats in the region. *Seychelles Nation* [online]. Retrieved November 20, 2016, from http://www.nation.sc/article.html?id=251518

Seychelles Nation. (2017, February 2). 28th AU summit – President Faure welcomes Lusaka master roadmap. *Seychelles Nation* [online]. Retrieved February 10, 2017, from http://nation.sc/article.html?id=252756

Swarttouw, H., & Hopkins, D. (2014). The contact group on piracy off the coast of Somalia: Genesis, rationale and objectives. In Thierry Tardy (Ed.), *Fighting piracy OFF the coast of Somalia: Lessons learned from the contact group* (pp. 11–18). Paris: EU Institute for Security Studies.

Tardy, T. (2014). *Fighting piracy OFF the coast of Somalia: Lessons learned from the contact group*. Paris: EU Institute for Security Studies.

The Maritime Executive. (2011, April 20). Seychelles coast guard rescues fishermen from pirates. *The maritime executive* [online]. Retrieved January 28, 2017, from http://maritime-executive.com/article/seychelles-coast-guard-rescues-fishermen-from-pirates

The Mauritius Police Force. (2016). *Police Magazine 2016*.

The Mauritius Police Force. (n.d.). Anti-drug and smuggling unit [online], Retrieved January 31, 2017, from police.govmu.org/English/Organisation/Branches/Pages/Anti-Drug-and-Smuggling-Unit-.aspx

Treves, T. (2009). Piracy, law of the sea, and use of force: Developments off the coast of Somalia. *European Journal of International Law*, *20*(2), 399–414. doi:10.1093/ejil/chp027.

Tuyau, J. (2010, June 3). La National Coast Guard Cree Un Commando pour Lutter Contre La Piraterie. *L'Express* [online]. Retrieved November 15, 2016, from https://www.lexpress.mu/article/la-national-coast-guard-cr%C3%A9e-un-commando-pour-lutter-contre-la-piraterie

UNDP. (1994). *Human development report 1994* [online] New York, NY: Oxford University Press. Retrieved January 18, 2017, from http://hdr.undp.org/en/content/human-development-report-1994

United Kingdom. (2014). *The UK national strategy for maritime security*. London: H.M Government.

United Nations. (1992). Agenda 21. *Proceedings of the conference on environment and development* [online] Retrieved October, 2016, from https://sustainabledevelopment.un.org/content/documents/Agenda21.pdf

United Nations. (1999). Report. *Proceedings of the ad hoc committee of the whole of the twenty-second special session of the general assembly,* held in New York, [27–28 September 1999].

United Nations. (2008). *Report of the Secretary-general on the oceans and the law of the sea* [online] Retrieved January 18, 2017, from https://documents-dds-ny.un.org/doc/UNDOC/GEN/N08/266/26/PDF/N0826626.pdf?OpenElement

United Nations. (2014). Report. *Proceedings of the third international conference on small island developing states held in Samoa*, [1–4 September 2014]. A/CONF.223/10.

United Nations. (n.d.). *Sustainable development goals* [online] Retrieved January 18, 2017, from http://www.un.org/sustainabledevelopment/sustainable-development-goals/

UNODC. (2008). *World drug report 2008*, Vienna: United Nations Publication.

UNODC. (2012). *World drug report 2012*, New York, NY: United Nations.

UNSC. (2008, December 16). *Resolution 1851*, Adopted at its 6046 meeting.

UNSC. (2016, November 9). Security Council unanimously adopts Resolution 2316 (2016), renewing authorization for international naval forces to combat piracy off Somali Coast [online]. Retrieved April 24, 2017, from https://www.un.org/press/en/2016/sc12582.doc.htm

US Navy. (2017, February 1). Exercise Cutlass Express 2017 begins. *DefenceWeb* [online]. Retrieved February 10, 2017, from http://www.defenceweb.co.za/index.php?option=com_content&view=article&id=46653:exercise-cutlass-express-2017-begins&catid=108:maritime-security&Itemid=233

USA Today. (2009, April 28). Seychelles coast guard arrests 9 suspected pirates. *USA Today* [online]. Retrieved January 25, 2017, from http://usatoday30.usatoday.com/news/world/2009-04-28-pirates_N.htm

Week-End. (2016, December 11). *OCÉAN INDIEN: Au cœur des grandes manœuvres*. *Week-End* [online]. Retrieved January 15, 2017, from http://www.lemauricien.com/article/ocean-indien-au-coeur-des-grandes-manoeuvres

Week-End. (2017, March 26). Lutte Contre La Drogue- Saisies En Série. *Week-End*.

Wellington, J., & Szcerbinski, M. (2007). *Research methods for the social sciences*. London: Continuum.

World Travel and Tourism Council. (2015). *Travel and tourism: Economic impact 2015 Seychelles* [ONLINE]. Retrieved April 23, 2017, from https://www.wttc.org/-/media/files/reports/economic%20impact%20research/countries%202015/seychelles2015.pdf

The European Union and the Indian Ocean Islands: identifying opportunities for developing a more ambitious and comprehensive strategy

Erwan Lannon

ABSTRACT

The aim of this paper is to analyze, from a geostrategic, geo-economical and cooperation perspective, the relationships established by the European Union with the Indian Ocean Islands: Comoros, Madagascar, Maldives, Mauritius, Seychelles and Sri Lanka. The analysis also takes into consideration the cases of Mayotte, La Réunion, the Scattered Islands and the Chagos Archipelago. At strategic level, the EU has developed its actions in the Indian Ocean since the launching of the naval operation EU NAVFOR-ATALANTA in 2008, in response to the rising levels of piracy in the region. At geo-economic level, the implementation of the interim Economic Partnership Agreement with Madagascar, Mauritius, the Seychelles, and Zimbabwe is a major step, but other (potential) trade agreements, notably with Indonesia and India, have to be taken into consideration. At cooperation level, different EU's (sub-)regional and bilateral actions are analyzed, including new specific programs and projects combining external and internal financial instruments in the region. The analysis of this complex network of relationships is the basis for identifying opportunities for developing a more ambitious and comprehensive strategy of the European Union vis-à-vis the Indian Ocean islands.

1. Introduction

The aim of this paper is to analyze, from a geostrategic, geo-economical and cooperation perspective, the relationships established by the European Union (EU) with the Indian Ocean (IO) Islands: Comoros, Madagascar, Maldives, Mauritius, Seychelles and Sri Lanka. Indonesia, being the world's largest island state, cannot be compared to the other Indian Ocean islands. However, this country is, from an EU perspective, a key partner in the region (Member of the G20, ASEAN and most populous Muslim-majority country) and is taken into consideration in the EU's 'Wider Indian Ocean' approach. The analysis also addresses the cases of La Réunion, Mayotte, the Scattered Islands and the Chagos Archipelago, given their respective specific statuses under the Lisbon Treaty.

From an historical perspective, relations between European Economic Community (EEC) and its Member States and the African Indian Ocean islands dates back to the

1957 Treaty of Rome that included a part IV on the 'association of overseas countries and territories,' including the 'Comoro Archipelago' and 'Madagascar and dependencies,' for the purpose of promoting their 'economic and social development' and in order to establish 'close economic relations between them and the Community as a whole' (Article 131 and annex IV of the EEC Treaty). In 1963, the first formal Convention between the EEC and a group of 18 francophone developing countries, the 'Associated African and Malgache Countries' was signed in Yaoundé and renewed in 1969 (Yaoundé II). The Yaoundé II Convention expired in January 1975 and in February; the first Lomé Convention was signed by the 'Head of state and of government of the Malagasy Republic' and 'Her Majesty the Queen of Mauritius.' Then, the 'Federal Islamic Republic of the Comoros' and the 'Republic of Seychelles' joined the 1979 Lomé II convention. This convention was revised several times (1984: Lomé III; 1990: Lomé IV; 1995: Lomé IV rev.) and finally replaced, in 2000, by the Cotonou Agreement (revised in 2005 and 2010) that is today the main legal basis for sub-Saharan African countries' relations with the EU. For their part, the Maldives and Sri Lanka relations with the EU are more recent and also much weaker from a legal and political point of view. In fact, EEC–Asia relationships were developed in the 1970s, notably after UK's accession in 1973, and became more strategic from 1994 onwards with the adoption of the EU 'New Asia strategy.' The creation of strategic partnerships (China – 2003, India – 2004, Japan – 2011) as well as the launching of a number of trade negotiations are clear indicators of the upgrade of EU–(South and South-East) Asia relations. However, until now, the Maldives and Sri Lanka relations with the EU have remained comparatively less developed.

Today, from an EU policy perspective, the countries and islands in and around the Indian Ocean are still scattered into different EU administrative silos, but other layers of regional, sub-regional and bilateral frameworks have to be considered.

The first one is the EU–Africa policy framework. EU–Africa relationships have been for many years tackled through two main frameworks: the Euro–Mediterranean track (Algeria, Morocco, Tunisia and Egypt) and the EU–African Caribbean Pacific (ACP) track through the Cotonou agreement that includes provisions for concluding Economic Partnership Agreements (EPAs). In December 2007, the creation of an Africa–EU Strategic Partnership and of a 'continental approach' including a new relationship between the EU and the African Union (AU) changed the perspectives. The development of EU sub-regional strategies, like the one for the Horn of Africa, and the EPAs with African regional organizations constitute the EU–Africa sub-regional levels of strategic and trade cooperation. This Africa–EU multidimensional policy framework covers the Comoros, Madagascar, Mauritius and the Seychelles.

The second external policy framework is the EU–Asia framework. At the sub-regional level, the EU–SAARC (South Asian Association for Regional Co-operation) is of specific interest for the Maldives and Sri Lanka, the EU having the observer status in this organization since 2006. The EU–ASEAN (Association of Southeast Asian Nations) Partnership is also to be kept in mind for Indonesia. The Maldives and Sri Lanka are, like Indonesia, eligible to the funds of the Development Cooperation Instrument (DCI).

The third policy framework is very specific, due to the existence two EU Outermost Regions (ORs): La Réunion and Mayotte, and of two Overseas Countries and Territories (OCTs): the Scattered Islands (which constitutes one of the five districts of the French

Southern and Antarctic Territories since 2007) and the British Indian Ocean Territory (BIOT; Chagos Archipelago).

Different actors, competences and policies of specific nature, enshrined into the Lisbon Treaty, have also to be taken into consideration. These issues will be introduced in the three consecutive parts of this article, namely: the strategic level: the EU Common Security and Defence Policy (CSDP) missions and operations in the Indian Ocean (1), the geo-economic level: the progressive creation of a network of Free Trade Agreements (FTAs) between the EU and the Indian Ocean islands (2), and the EU–Indian Ocean islands main frameworks for cooperation (3).

2. The strategic level: the EU CSDP missions and operations in the Indian Ocean

The Indian Ocean is strategic for the EU, as it 'represents the world's third largest ocean, carrying out around 70% of all oil shipments' and because the 'threats on the maritime routes remain significant' (European Commission, 2 July 2015). According to Brahma Chellaney, this Ocean is a 'bridge between Asia and Europe'; however, there is a 'very real danger of this critical region becoming the hub of global geopolitical rivalry' (Chellaney, 2015). The perception of the Indian Ocean as being part of an arc of crisis is not new as, for example, Zbigniew Brzezinski referred already in 1979 to the existence of a 'crescent of crisis' stretching 'along the shores of the Indian Ocean' (Brzezinski, 1979). The 2008 French White Paper on Security and Defence also mentioned an 'arc of crisis from the Atlantic to the Indian Ocean' (Présidence de la République Française, 2008, p. 43).

The Common Foreign and Security Policy and CSDP (formerly ESDP) differ compared to the EU trade or development cooperation policies, in that they are governed by specific inter-governmental legal basis and procedures. The European Council, the EU Council and the High Representative/Vice President of the European Commission and thus the European External Action Service (EEAS), including EU special Representatives, are key actors in this inter-governmental policy framework. The design of sub-regional strategies like for the Horn of Africa implies an important input from these actors.

2.1. The 2005–2006 Aceh Monitoring Mission: the first ESDP Mission in the Eastern Indian Ocean

The 2005 Aceh Monitoring Mission (AMM) was the first so-called EU civilian ESDP mission conducted in the Indian Ocean Region. This mission was designed to 'monitor the implementation of various aspects of the peace agreement' set out in the Memorandum of Understanding signed by the Indonesian Government and the Free Aceh Movement (GAM) in August 2005. It became operational in September 2005 with the 'decommissioning of GAM armaments and the relocation of non-organic military and policy forces' and ended in December 2006 following local elections held in Aceh (EU Council, 15 December 2006).

It should be underlined that, at this occasion, the EU received an 'official invitation by the Indonesian Government (endorsed by the GAM leadership)' that 'expressed its preference for the EU and for a regional context.' This mission was 'EU-led' and conducted 'with five ASEAN countries (Brunei, Malaysia, Philippines, Singapore and Thailand) with contributions from Norway and Switzerland.' The mission included 'decommissioning,' 'demobilization' and 'reintegration of former combatants' and played, according to the EU Council, a 'critical confidence-building role' (EU Council, 15 December 2006). AMM is thus a first landmark EU ESDP civilian mission in the Indian Ocean.

2.2. The 2008–2018 CSDP Naval operation EU NAVFOR-ATALANTA

The CSDP's Naval operation EU NAVFOR-ATALANTA was launched in December 2008 in response to the rising levels of piracy, from the South of the Red Sea and the Gulf of Aden to the Western Indian Ocean, including the Seychelles (see Helly, June 2011). Its main objectives are to protect the vessels of the World Food Programme and the shipping of the AU Mission in Somalia, to deter, prevent and repress acts of piracy, and to protect vulnerable shipping while monitoring fishing activities off the Somali coast. Combat vessels and military aircrafts were deployed and hundreds of suspected pirates were arrested and transferred for prosecution, thus implying international cooperation at police and judicial levels. The EEAS stated, in May 2016, that 'over 1,200 suspects' were being 'prosecuted in 21 countries, including EU Member States' and that, in this regard, the EU has signed transfer agreements with the Seychelles in 2009 and Mauritius in 2011 (EEAS, 3 May 2016). In November 2016, the EU Council extended the mandate of the operation until 31 December 2018.

2.3. The 2009 'Djibouti Code of Conduct,' the MARSIC and CRIMLEA projects on Maritime Security and the launching of the EU Critical Maritime Routes program

The 'Djibouti Code of Conduct' was adopted, in January 2009, under the auspices of the International Maritime Organization (IMO) by the representatives of Djibouti, Ethiopia, Kenya, Madagascar, Maldives, Seychelles, Somalia, the United Republic of Tanzania and Yemen. It became effective from the date of signature and promotes the implementation of the aspects of UN Security Council resolutions falling within the competence of the IMO. France attended the Djibouti meeting as one of the 'participating delegations,' whereas the European Commission participated as an 'observer.' Since then, they have been joined by: the Comoros, Egypt, Eritrea, Jordan, Mauritius, Mozambique, Oman, Saudi Arabia, South Africa, Sudan and the United Arab Emirates (International Maritime Organisation, 2016).

In 2010, the EU decided to support the implementation this Code of Conduct using the Critical Maritime Routes program (CMR, see also Section 1.6). A project entitled MARSIC (Enhancing Maritime Security and Safety through Information Sharing and Capacity Building), funded by the EU Instrument contributing to Stability and Peace, promoted the implementation of the Code of Conduct. The project focused on 'capacity building and training of maritime administration staff, officials and coast guards' (EEAS, 23 December 2013, p. 5). MARSIC lasted between 2010 and 2015 and supported the creation of 'four operational centres for information sharing and training (in Kenya, Tanzania, Yemen and Djibouti) established under the Djibouti Code of Conduct' and 'led to the signature of the Mombasa Protocol between Djibouti, Kenya, Tanzania and Yemen, to increase cooperation on maritime security' (European Commission, 2 July 2015). Another project of the CMR program: CRIMLEA I (2010–2014) (Law enforcement capacity building in East Africa) was implemented by Interpol between 2010 and 2014 and concentrated on training activities involving seven countries: Djibouti, Kenya, Mauritius, Seychelles, Somalia, Tanzania and Yemen. CRIMLEA II (2014–2017) currently covers Djibouti, Kenya, Mauritius, Seychelles, Tanzania, Yemen, Somalia, Madagascar and Comoros (http://criticalmaritimeroutes.eu/projects/crimlea/). It is thus noticeable that MARSIC and CRIMLEA I were the first projects launched under the EU CMR program whose main objective is to 'contribute to create trans-regional synergies and increase maritime security and safety of critical maritime routes' (http://criticalmaritimeroutes.eu/mission/#who).

2.4. The 2010 Regional Strategy of the Eastern and Southern Africa-Indian Ocean Region (ESA-IO) for the Fight against Piracy and the Promotion of Maritime Security

The Regional Strategy for the Fight against Piracy and the Promotion of Maritime Security was adopted during the second regional Ministerial conference held in Mauritius in 2010. According to the Communiqué (EU Council, 7 October 2010):

> The ESA-IO Ministers and Representatives of the Republic of Comoros, the Republic of Djibouti, the Republic of Kenya, the Republic of Mauritius, the Republic of Seychelles, the Somali Republic, the Republic of South Africa, the United Republic of Tanzania, and the EU High Representative and Vice President of the European Commission Baroness Catherine Ashton meet at Grand Bay, Mauritius on the 7th October 2010. Republic of France/Réunion also attended the meeting as a member of IOC.

This excerpt is a clear indicator of the specificities of EU's and France implication as well as to the potential offered by this ESA-IO configuration that is reinforced by the fact that COMESA, EAC, IGAD, IOC and SADC attended the meeting in 'addition to the Minister of the Republic of Maldives.' Representatives of the 'People's Republic of China, India, Pakistan, Russian Federation and the US, UN, AU, INTERPOL, IONS' were also present.

At this occasion, the participants adopted a regional strategy providing a 'regional framework to prevent and combat piracy, and promote maritime security.' This 'ESA-IO configuration,' which includes Member States and Regional Economic Communities of the AU, is to be used as 'Regional Coordination Mechanism' for the implementation and follow-up of the strategy and action plan. Being complementary to the AU African Maritime Transport Charter, this strengthened cooperation with international partners such as the UN in 'political dialogue and collaboration in the fight against piracy and for maritime security' (EU Council, 7 October 2010).

During the third Regional Ministerial Meeting, held in Djibouti in May 2016, a Declaration on Maritime Safety and Security was adopted to support the extension of the Djibouti Code of Conduct mandate (Djibouti Declaration, 15 May 2016). The last point (16) states that the partners will move towards a 'new comprehensive and integrated ESA-IO strategy for Maritime Safety and Security that focus on technical capacity building' (see the MASE Project funded by the EDF at Section 3.1).

What is important is that the Djibouti Code of Conduct, signed under the auspices of the IMO, and the Regional Strategy and Action Plan of the ESA-IO region are used to ensure the 'regional ownership of the EU's actions' (EEAS, 23 December 2013).

2.5. The 2012–2017 EUCAP Nestor mission: enhancing the maritime capacities of Djibouti, Kenya, Somalia, Seychelles and Tanzania

EUCAP Nestor was an EU 'civilian maritime capacity building mission' with the initial objective to operate in five states across the Horn of Africa and the Western Indian Ocean: Djibouti, Somalia, Seychelles, Kenya and Tanzania. It was launched in July 2012 to assist the development of a 'self-sustainable capacity' for maritime security 'including counter-piracy, and maritime governance' (EU Council, 16 July 2012). The main objective of the mission was to complement ATALANTA and EUTM Somalia and to be part of the more comprehensive EU Strategy for the Horn of Africa (Chevalier-Govers, 2015).

However, after an evaluation, it was decided, in 2014, that EUCAP Nestor will have 'primary focus on Somalia, and a secondary focus on Djibouti, the Seychelles and Tanzania' (EU Council, 22 July 2014). The result was the relocation of the Mission Headquarters to Mogadishu (EEAS, October 2015). In other words, the regional dimension of the mission, renamed 'EUCAP Somalia' in March 2017 (and extended to the end of 2018), is now less relevant for the Indian Ocean islands compared to the more recent EU Maritime Security Strategy (EUMSS).

2.6. The 2014 EUMSS and the 2015–2019 CRIMARIO project of the CMR program in the 'Wider Indian Ocean'

The 2014 EUMSS takes 'particular regard of each of the European sea and subsea basins, namely the Baltic Sea, the Black Sea, the Mediterranean and the North Sea, as well as of the Arctic waters, the Atlantic Ocean and the outermost regions' (EU Council, 24 June 2014, p. 4). In the framework of the 2014 EUMSS Action Plan, the AU and sub-regional African organizations, but also the 'Union for the Mediterranean, the Gulf Cooperation Council' and the ASEAN have been identified as being regional *fora* with which the EU is 'seeking improved partnerships in the field of maritime security.' Of specific importance is the fact that the EU supports two specific aspects of the EUMSS in the 'Red Sea – Western Indian Ocean' region:

(i) The 'coherent implementation of regional maritime security strategies (AU, ECCAS, SADC, etc.), inter alia, as elaborated in the context of the Djibouti and Yaoundé Codes of Conduct';
(ii) The establishment of 'maritime information sharing environment and information fusion centres in zones of strategic interest for the EU and its Member States' (EU Council, 16 December 2014, p. 3).

Launched in 2015 within the CMR program, the CRIMARIO project (2015–2019) aims at enhancing the 'maritime security and safety in the Wider Indian Ocean' and is funded by the EU Instrument contributing to Stability and Peace. CRIMARIO builds on the first MARSIC project (see Section 1.3 and European Commission, 22 June 2016, p. 4). In other words, the project 'aims to link up the Western Indian Ocean with South East Asia in terms of Maritime Situational Awareness' (European Commission, 2 July 2015). The reference to the 'Wider Indian Ocean' is of importance, as it establishes a link, in the EU's strategy, between the African and Asian Indian Ocean islands. This implies also reinforced cooperation with

India and other internal/external actors. In this regard, the 2016 recommendations of the Observer Research Foundation (an Indian think tank) proposed that the EU and India 'should establish a regular high-level, official dialogue on maritime security within the Strategic Partnership' and improve 'maritime security in the Indian Ocean.' The report suggested that regional organization, with the IORA (Indian Ocean Rim Association) being 'at the forefront, should include discussions on maritime security in view of building such a regime in the future' and that given its 'experience, sustained interest, presence, and involvement in the Indian Ocean, the EU could become a valuable Dialogue Partner of IORA' (Observer Research Foundation, 2016, p. 8).

2.7. The June 2016 Global Strategy for the EU's Foreign and Security Policy and the Indian Ocean

The June 2016 Global Strategy for the EU's Foreign and Security Policy (EEAS, June 2016) that 'nurtures the ambition of strategic autonomy' for the EU states that:

> Connected to the EU's interest in an open and fair economic system is the need for global maritime growth and security, ensuring open and protected ocean and sea routes critical for trade and access to natural resources. The EU will contribute to global maritime security, building on its experience in the Indian Ocean and the Mediterranean, and exploring possibilities in the Gulf of Guinea, the South China Sea and the Straits of Malacca. As a global maritime security provider, the EU will seek to further universalise and implement the UN Convention on the Law of the Sea, including its dispute settlement mechanisms. We will also promote the conservation and sustainable use of marine resources and biological diversity and the growth of the blue economy by working to fill legal gaps and enhancing ocean knowledge and awareness.

In other words, the experiences in the Indian Ocean are still laboratories for the development of EU maritime initiatives. The reference to the South China Sea and the Straits of Malacca is of crucial importance for the Indian Ocean sea routes. Last but not least, the EU profiles itself as a 'global maritime security provider.' This is certainly ambitious but its initiatives in the Wider Indian Ocean can be considered as being an asset. One might, however, argue that the EU, with the exception of the AMM, has less experience in the Eastern Indian Ocean and beyond.

2.8. The limits of the EU's strategic role in the region and the issues of the Scattered Islands and the BIOT (Chagos Archipelago)

Despite a clear political will to become a strategic actor in the region, the EU is limited by its very nature: A *sui generis* organization based on a complex mix of supranationalism and intergovernmentalism approaches resulting sometimes in a lack of visibility, efficiency and consistency. For instance, a 2014 research note of the IRSEM on EU's strategy in the Horn of Africa identified a number of issues such as the proliferation of EU actors in the region ('two Special Representatives, six Heads of Delegations, three CSDP Heads of Mission or Operation, a Special Envoy and several offices in the region') resulting sometimes in 'overlapping of responsibilities' (IRSEM, 2014).

Another important element to be taken into consideration, at strategic and geopolitical levels, is that, next to the EU, two Member States, France and the UK, develop military activities in the region on their own, notably in the areas of the Scattered Islands and the BIOT (Chagos Archipelago). These islands are considered by the EU as being 'OCTs'), to which the provisions of part four ('Association of the overseas countries and territories') of the Treaty on the Functioning of the European Union (TFEU) apply. Annex II of the TFEU lists the territories covered by these provisions including the 'French Southern and Antarctic Territories' ('FSAT,' hereinafter, we refer to as the 'FSAL' (for 'Lands') as it is the official French translation, see http://www.taaf.fr/The-French-Southern-and-Antarctic-Lands) and the 'BIOT' (that in geographical terms refers to the Chagos Archipelago, see http://biot.gov.io/about/). According to Article 198 TFEU, the Member States agree to 'associate' with the EU the 'non-European countries and territories which have special relations with Denmark, France, the Netherlands and the United Kingdom.' The objective of this association is to promote their 'economic and social development' and to 'establish close economic relations between them and the Union as a whole.' This association is supposed to be primarily designed to 'further the interests and prosperity of the inhabitants of these countries and territories in order to lead them to the economic, social and cultural development to which they aspire.' The 2013 Council Decision on the association of the OCTs with the EU (EU Council, 25 November 2013) confirmed the principle that the TFEU and its secondary legislation 'do not automatically apply to the OCTs, with the exception of a number of provisions which explicitly provide for the contrary.' Although 'not third countries, the OCTs do not form part of the single market and must comply with the obligations imposed on third countries' and this regarding 'trade, particularly rules of origin, health and plant health standards and safeguard measures.' The difference with the ORs (La Réunion, Mayotte) is thus important. Last but not least, this Decision introduces provisions on 'Regional cooperation, regional integration and cooperation with other partners,' including ORs.

The FSAL includes islands, atolls and archipelagos located in the Southern Indian Ocean: Kerguelen, St. Paul and Amsterdam, Crozet and the Adélie Land on the Antarctica continent and, since February 2007 (Cointat, 17 February 2010), the Scattered Islands located around Madagascar (Bassas da India, Europa, Glorieuses, Juan de Nova and Tromelin). However, France's sovereignty over these territories is disputed (see Antrim, 2012; Bouchard & Crumplin, 2013, 2011; and CIA, 2017 for the USA perception). The debate held at the French National Assembly in January 2017 on issue of the co-management of Tromelin with Mauritius shed again the light on one of these Scattered Islands (see Gaymard, 2013; Osman, 2012). The ratification process of the agreement was finally delayed, thus reflecting the sensitivity of this issue.

Located between Eastern Africa and Indonesia, the BIOT comprises the atolls of the Chagos Archipelago, Diego Garcia being of strategic importance as it is the site of a joint military facility of the UK and the USA (currently hosting US militaries as the US Naval Support Facility Diego Garcia, but available to UK militaries if needed). The territorial dispute between Mauritius (who claim the islands) and the United Kingdom is complex given the fact that this archipelago was inhabited and because the Chagos Islanders were compulsorily removed from their homeland. Last but not least, the BREXIT means that the BIOT could, in a couple of years, disappear from the Lisbon Treaty OCTs' list. It is not possible to detail all the aspects of the disputes (see Raoof, 2014) but one should mention that an Award, delivered on 18 March 2015 in the case brought by Mauritius against the UK under the UN Convention on the Law of the Sea, stated that: 'in establishing the MPA' (Marine Protected Area) 'surrounding the Chagos Archipelago the United

Kingdom breached its obligations under Articles 2(3), 56(2), and 194(4) of the Convention' (Arbitral Tribunal, March 2015). The Mauritius Government reiterated at this occasion that 'it does not recognise the legality of the actions that the UK is taking in respect of the Chagos Archipelago as they are in breach of international law' adding that this includes 'the unilateral decisions purportedly taken by the UK Government with regard to resettlement in the Chagos Archipelago' as well as the 'continuation of the UK–US agreement in respect of the Chagos Archipelago until 2036' (Republic of Mauritius, 18 November 2016). Given the BREXIT context but also because of the result of the USA presidential election, the Diego Garcia military base could become of even greater strategic importance, having in mind that the Indian Ocean is also 'where the rivalry between the United States and China in the Pacific interlocks with the regional rivalry between China and India' and with USA 'fight against Islamic terrorism in the Middle East' (Kaplan, 2011). Despite the BREXIT, the military cooperation between France and UK should be preserved given the existing agreements (2010 Lancaster House treaties), current interdependence (e.g. missile technology) and mutual interests (see Keohane, 2017), but the USA/NATO factor is to be taken into consideration.

3. The geo-economic level: the progressive creation of a network of FTAs between the EU and the Indian Ocean Islands

At geo-economic level, the EU is currently negotiating a regional EPA with partners including Comoros, Mauritius, Madagascar and the Seychelles while an interim EPA was already signed, in 2009, with Mauritius, Madagascar, Seychelles and Zimbabwe. A comprehensive Cooperation Agreement, which came into force in 1995, governs EU–Sri Lanka relations, while EU–Maldives relations have not been yet formalized in any kind of agreement.

In fact, since the 1990s, the EU has considerably developed its network of FTAs all around the world. We will concentrate on the Indian Ocean islands but it is worth to provide first some elements of the wider regional picture. In Africa, bilateral FTAs have been concluded with Algeria, Egypt, Morocco and Tunisia between 1995 and 2004, whereas the first interim EPA was signed in 2009 with the ESA group. Another EPA of importance for this analysis is the one signed in June 2016 with the SADC group that includes: Botswana, Lesotho, Mozambique, Namibia, South Africa and Swaziland (European Commission, April 2017).

In Asia, negotiations for a FTA with India were launched in June 2007, frozen in 2013 but discussions resumed in 2016. For the ASEAN, negotiations for a regional FTA started in 2007 but, in 2009, negotiations were pursued in a bilateral format. Negotiations for a bilateral FTA with Indonesia were launched in July 2016. If the effective implementation of all these new agreements should be considered as a medium-term perspective, it is however important to anticipate the potential impacts and interactions of these FTAs as a whole.

3.1. The 2012 interim EPA with Madagascar, Mauritius, the Seychelles, and Zimbabwe and current regional negotiations

Among the so-called seven ACP regions, 'East Africa' covers the Eastern and Southern Africa (ESA) including Comoros, Djibouti, Eritrea, Ethiopia, Madagascar, Malawi, Mauritius, Seychelles, Sudan, Zambia and Zimbabwe. The first 'interim' EPA (Interim Agreement, 13

July 2009) was signed with Madagascar, Mauritius, the Seychelles and Zimbabwe in 2009. It has been provisionally applied since 14 May 2012 and, in December 2016, the parties agreed to 'jointly define the scope and objectives of' its 'possible deepening' (European Commission, January 2017). The interim EPA eliminates 'duties and quotas for imports from these countries to the EU as well as a gradual liberalization of EU exports' and covers 'rules of origin, fisheries, trade defense, development cooperation provisions and mechanisms for settling disputes' (European Commission, March 2012). Although the Comoros initialed the interim EPA they did not signed it yet. Therefore, exports to the EU are, for the time being, governed by the Generalised System of Preferences and more especially the 'Everything But Arms' (EBA) treatment (duty-free and quota-free access except for arms) as the Comoros, like Madagascar, are considered by the UNCTAD as Least Developing Countries (LDCs). The ongoing negotiations for a regional EPA include 'services and investment, sustainable development and competition, and trade facilitation' as well as 'co-operation on technical barriers to trade' (European Commission, 29 April 2016). One should stress that, from the start of the negotiations, ESA countries identified 'various outstanding issues,' including 'export taxes, agricultural safeguards and rules of origin' as well as trade coverage (European Commission, January 2012). ESA States thus decided to negotiate their own schedules and coverage to liberalize trade, liberalization of EU imports representing 98% for the Seychelles; 96% for Mauritius; 81% for the Comoros and Madagascar and 80% for Zambia and Zimbabwe, meaning that a number of products have been excluded from the liberalization process (see European Commission, January 2012).

3.2. The asymmetrical EU–ESA trade relationship and the potential impact of the foreseen FTAs and of the BREXIT

At geo-economic level, it is important to take stock of the deep asymmetry of relationships existing between the EU 28 and the IO islands. In most cases, the EU 28 is an important trade partner for the IO islands, whereas the latter are not. Taking into consideration their respective positions in the 2016 ranking of 'Client and Supplier Countries of the EU 28 in Merchandise Trade', the result is the following: Sri Lanka: 63, Mauritius: 86, Madagascar: 95, Seychelles: 126, Maldives: 152, Comoros: 171. Comparatively, Indonesia and India hold respectively the 29th and 9th positions. Moreover, in 2010, before the conclusion of the interim EPA, total EU imports from the ESA countries were reaching only '0.2% of all EU imports, including mainly processed tuna, coffee, cane sugar, textiles, tobacco, cut flowers and ferro-alloys.' Also worth noting is that 'imports from the ESA countries that initialled the interim EPA represented around 70% of the EU imports from the ESA region' as a whole (European Commission, January 2012). However, one should not underestimate the interest of some EU Member States regarding fisheries, energy and raw material resources of the region.

On the other hand, the importance of the EU-28 as top trade partner for the IO islands is also to be stressed. In 2015, the top three main trade partners of the IO islands were the following:

- Madagascar: EU 28 (26.5%); China (18.2%) and USA (5.7%);
- Mauritius: EU 28 (28.1%), India (12.6%) and China (12%);

- Seychelles: EU 28 (31.5%); Singapore (5.7%); Mauritius (3.9%);
- Maldives: United Arab Emirates (16.2%); EU 28 (13.6%); Singapore (12.2%);
- Sri Lanka: India (19.8%); EU 28 (18.9%); USA (13.2%).

(No data are currently available for the Comoros).

It is also worth comparing the IO islands to the whole ESA group, the result being for 2016: USA (17.6%); China (14.9%); and Switzerland (7.6%) (European Commission, 16 February 2017). The EU is thus comparatively more important for African IO islands than for the other ESA members and ESA as a whole. The implementation of the interim EPA should, until the BREXIT, reinforce this trend. For the Asian IO islands, the situation is a bit different as the EU is a less important for them, but the trade development potential with Sri Lanka is quite important (see Section 2.3).

The huge differences in terms of development levels of the ESA countries (from LDCs to high-income country) will certainly generate differentiated impacts despite the adoption of differentiated preferential treatment. Potential positive effects of EPAs include, in theory and in the long run, the promotion of regional integration that should in turn, in principle, stimulate investments and improve competitiveness. Potential negative effects include, by definition, tariff reduction and thus less fiscal revenues, important adjustment and social costs, risks in terms of market access and the potential loss of local and regional market shares, due to the competition of EU products. However, transitory measures, safeguard clauses and special preferential treatment minimize these potential negative impacts. The EU's partners should obviously use them at their optimum level. The 'Aid for Trade' assistance can, for instance, help them to 'take advantage of opportunities created by unilateral, bilateral or multilateral trade openings' (http://ec.europa.eu/trade/policy/countries-and-regions/development/aid-for-trade/).

The potential impact of the BREXIT at economic level is of importance as in certain cases UK is among the first trade partners of IO islands like Mauritius or Sri Lanka (as export market). The BREXIT will imply the negotiation of new trade agreements between all countries of the region and the UK. In 2019, it will be, in principle, time to reassess the situation in the light of an effective BREXIT and of the impact of the interim EPA implementation to identify if there is a new balance in the EU–IO islands trade relationship. In this regard, results of the current negotiations for a bilateral FTA between China and Sri Lanka and prospect for another one with Mauritius are also to be taken into consideration.

3.3. The 1995 EU–Sri Lanka Cooperation Agreement, the impact of the suspension of the 'GSP plus' and the ban on fisheries

The 'Cooperation Agreement between the European Community and the Democratic Socialist Republic of Sri Lanka on partnership and development' (Cooperation agreement, 19 April 1995), signed in March 1995, governs the current EU–Sri Lanka relations. It is a rather short agreement with provisions covering trade and investment aspects, technical assistance, environmental and regional cooperation. However, the implementation of the agreement 'came to a standstill' as the Joint Commission, ensuring the implementation of the agreement, 'did not meet since 2008' and, in February 2010, the EU Council decided to withdraw the preferential tariffs Sri Lanka benefitted from the Special Incentive Arrangement for Sustainable Development and Good Governance ('GSP+') due to shortcomings in

Sri Lanka's implementation of three UN human rights conventions: the International Covenant on Civil and Political Rights, the Convention against Torture and the Convention on the Rights of the Child (EU Council, 15 February 2010). The resumption of formal dialogue in December 2013 'proved timely for discussing the future priorities of EU assistance to Sri Lanka' (EEAS, 2014), but relations were affected in 2014 when the EU imposed a ban on Sri Lankan fish imports after it was 'red flagged' for engaging into 'illegal, unreported and unregulated fishing' (IUU). The EU Council removed Sri Lanka from the list of 'non-cooperating third countries' in June 2016, after Sri Lanka 'implemented its international law obligations' and adopted an 'adequate legal framework for fighting IUU fishing' (EU Council, 7 June 2016).

Meanwhile, in December 2015, the EU Council had welcomed the 'significant advances made by the government' to restore 'democratic governance, initiate a process of national reconciliation and re-engage with the international community,' underlining the positive assessment made by the EU Election Observation Mission regarding the parliamentary elections (EU Council, 17 November 2015). Therefore, the European Commission proposed, in January 2017, to amend the list of GSP+ beneficiary countries and to add Sri Lanka. The Commission stressed that the proposal 'should be adopted as soon as possible to allow Sri Lanka to benefit from GSP+ at the earliest possible time' (European Commission, 11 January 2017). This is indeed of importance as economic consequences of the sanctions included notably, according to Saman Kelegama: '2000 jobs of direct employment lost due to closure of two factories alone' and a 'declining competitiveness' of Sri Lanka exports in South Asia (Kelegama, 2016). According to the same author, the EU should develop a more 'flexible approach' based on 'incentivizing democracy building as opposed to the punitive approach currently being followed' and on a 'constructive engagement, political dialogue and capacity building in the region' instead of using 'punitive sanctions which are neither consistently applied nor very effective in democracy building' (Kelegama, 2010).

4. The EU–Indian Ocean Islands main frameworks for cooperation

For the EU–Indian Ocean islands frameworks for cooperation, many EU institutional actors and policies have to be taken into consideration. The direct implication of Member States is quite important at that level, given the specificities of the European Development Fund and due to existence of EU ORs and OCTs in the same region. Shared EU–Member States competences in the field of development cooperation and humanitarian aid, the later being important for countries like Madagascar, Maldives or Sri Lanka, are also to be considered. As it is not possible to detail every single program, we will concentrate on those having a specific interest for the Indian Ocean islands and on initiatives supporting regional integration.

4.1. The European Development Fund: the Comoros, Madagascar, Mauritius and the Seychelles

The Regional Indicative Programme (RIP), adopted within the framework of 11th European Development Fund (EDF), an entitled 'RIP for Eastern Africa, Southern Africa and the Indian Ocean (EA-SA-IO) 2014–2020' (European Commission, 2015), includes all Western Indian

Ocean islands into a regional perspective. It is designed for the benefit of five regional organizations: the Common Market for Eastern and Southern Africa (COMESA), the East African Community (EAC), the Inter-Governmental Authority for Development (IGAD), the Indian Ocean Commission (IOC) and the Southern African Development Community (SADC), representing 29 African countries. Therefore, it covers Comoros, Madagascar, Mauritius, Seychelles and La Réunion (officially France for La Réunion in the case of the IOC). The latter is not eligible to the EDF but to the European Regional Development Fund (ERDF). However, synergies exist between the two funds. The three priorities identified in the RIP are to:

(i) Foster peace, security and regional stability, help to prevent and manage conflict, and address security threats in a region of key strategic importance for Europe;
(ii) Promote regional economic integration and trade facilitation, by integrating markets, promoting investment and improving production capacities;
(iii) Support sustainable natural resource management at the regional level, improving resilience and biodiversity conservation.

For the multi-annual financial framework 2014–2020, a total amount of 1.3 billion euros has been earmarked. At the signature ceremony, Commissioner Mimica commented: 'the regional organisations are very important partners for the EU in our cooperation with Africa' while underlining that EU funding to EA-SA-IO 'more than doubled since the last financing' (European Commission, 4 June 2015).

If is not possible to mention every single project implemented at regional level, a few of them are worth to be referred to. First of all, a 'Start up Project to Promote Regional Maritime Security (Start-up MASE),' funded under the 10th EDF in 2012–2013 (2 million euros) and implemented by the IOC Anti-Piracy Unit supported immediate actions to implement the Regional Strategy against Piracy and for Promoting Maritime Security (see Section 1.4). A new MASE program (2013–2018, 37.5 million euros) to promote regional maritime security is now implemented, on the basis of this pilot project, by the IOC, COMESA, EAC and the IGAD, in partnership with UN agencies. It is interesting to note that a working group between the experts of the MASE and CRIMARIO (see Section 1.6) programs met for the first time only in December 2015 in Mombasa, under the co-presidency of the IOC and the EU delegation (Indian Ocean Commission, 2015, pp. 32–35). Another interesting example of convergence is to be found under the cross-regional financial envelope of the 2014–2020 RIP for ESA-IO that covers the implementation of the interim EPA with the ESA members. With a budget of 40 million euros, it supports the ESA countries with the implementation of the EPA provisions related, for example, to sanitary and phyto-sanitary standards.

On top of these regional programs, bilateral initiatives and specificities have also to be taken into consideration. The Comoros, benefit as a LDC from the EBA arrangement, meaning that Comoros have full duty-free and quota-free access to the EU market for their exports with the exception of arms and armaments. For the 11th EDF, the focal priorities of the National Indicative Programme for the Comoros are sustainable development of road and port transport infrastructures, vocational training, strengthening of the rule of law, as well as administrative and financial governance, for a total envelope of 68 million euros (EEAS, 17 May 2016). The Fisheries Partnership Agreement, covering the period from

1st January 2005 until 31 December 2011, has been tacitly renewed for a period of 7 years, but there is currently no protocol in force.

Cooperation between Madagascar and the EU has been, between 2009 and 2014, affected by the political events. In May 2014, the Decision that established in 2010 restrictive measures according to article 96 of the Cotonou agreement was abrogated. This normalization allowed the launching of the programming of the 11th EDF (2014–2020). The 2014–2020 National Indicative Programme for Madagascar was signed in November 2015. With a total amount of 518 million euros, cooperation is focusing on poverty alleviation (European Commission, 30 November 2015, pp. 4–5). The current protocol to the Fisheries Partnership Agreement was signed in December 2014 and covers the period from 1 January 2015 until 31 December 2018 with a financial contribution of 6 million euros.

For EU–Mauritius bilateral cooperation, the 2015–2020 National Indicative Programme has seen an important reduction of the financial envelope from 76 millions euros under the 10th EDF to 9.9 millions euros under the 11th EDF. This is due to the upgrade of Mauritius as an Upper Middle Income Country (European Commission, 23 June 2016). Tertiary education, research and innovation are the current priorities. In fact, the EU provided '371 million euros during the past 8 years to Mauritius in terms of bilateral aid mainly in the form [of] budget support' but 'most of these funds have been allocated to the sugar sector reform programme as part of the Accompanying Measures for the Sugar Protocol' (EEAS, 12 May 2016). The Fishery Partnership Agreement is currently being renegotiated.

As the World Bank classified, in 2015, the Seychelles as a High-Income Country, this led also to a reduction of the 11th EDF volume to 2.2 million euros. Current EU approach focuses on institutional capacities and innovative financing mechanisms. The EEAS confirms that Seychelles 'still qualifies for EU funding from various regional and horizontal baskets' and that the Fisheries Partnership Agreement 'contributes to Seychelles' efforts to promote sustainable use, good governance and sectoral support to the fishing industry.' The Protocol implementing the Agreement is in force until January 2020 and amounts 30.7 million euros (EEAS, 13 March 2016).

4.2. The Instrument for Development Cooperation: Maldives and Sri Lanka

Maldives and Sri Lanka are beneficiaries of the Instrument for Development Cooperation (DCI). EU–Sri Lanka and EU–Maldives relations are also linked to the emerging EU–SAARC framework for cooperation. It is worth mentioning that the DCI includes also an envelope of 845 million euros (2014–2020) for the Pan-African program that supports the objectives of the strategic partnership between Africa and the EU. In other words, synergies could be used to connect EU funds for Asian and African Indian Ocean islands.

Regarding EU–Sri Lanka cooperation the EU provided, over the past decade, approximately 760 million euros in assistance (EEAS, 13 May 2016). For 2014–2020, the financial envelope amounts 210 million euros and the main priority is integrated rural development (European Commission, 12 August 2014). Sri Lanka is also eligible to regional cooperation under the Asia Regional Multi-Annual Indicative Programme that promotes, for example, cross-border cooperation between Asian EU partners (Incl. Maldives, Indonesia and India), notably in the fields of trade, climate change, environment, border and migration management. After the cyclone Roanu in May 2016, humanitarian assistance was also provided and a common EU–UN project of 8 million euros (2016–2020) was launched in November to help Sri Lanka increase its trade competitiveness in regional and European markets.

The Maldives–European Community Country Strategy Paper 2007–2013, for which an envelope of 10 million euros was set aside, focused on poverty reduction (European Commission, 22 May 2007). The Maldives is, like Sri Lanka, eligible to the Asia Regional Multi-Annual Indicative Programme and is a member of the SAARC but EU–SAARC level of cooperation cannot be compared to the EU–ASEAN one. At the bilateral level, the archipelago benefitted from the EU's humanitarian assistance and specific actions in the field of climate change have been launched. The EU allocated, for example, 6.5 million euros to support the Government' climate change strategy. It is, however, obvious that the EU's relations with the archipelago are under-developed compared to the other Indian Ocean Islands. Although diplomatic relations were established 'in 1983, with the Commission Head of Delegation in Colombo being accredited as non-resident Ambassador to the Maldives' (EEAS, 26 May 2016), no bilateral agreement has been concluded so far. An EU statement, regarding the 2016 WTO Trade Policy Review of the Maldives, listed trade issues considered as being 'not very transparent and not trade-friendly' (EU mission to the WTO, 21 March 2016). In other words, a future bilateral agreement is not yet on the agenda.

4.3. The external dimension of the Interreg programs funded by the ERDF: La Réunion, Mayotte and their neighbors

We will in this part focus on the external dimension of the financial cooperation transiting *via* two EU's ORs: La Réunion and Mayotte, but it is important to understand, first of all, that contrary to the OCTs (the BIOT and the FSAL), the ORs are an integral part of the EU, the so-called acquis communautaire being fully applicable, although the specificities of these regions are taken into consideration. Following the 2009 referendum on the 'départementalisation' and a July 2012 decision of the European Council, Mayotte from 1 January 2014, ceased to be an OCT and became, like La Réunion, 'an outermost region of the Union within the meaning of Article 349 TFEU' (European Council, 11 July 2012, p. 131). Two legal bases, articles 349 and 355 TFEU of the Lisbon Treaty, have to be taken into consideration. The location of these legal bases in the 'general and final provisions' means that they do apply to the entire Treaty and are not linked to external relations chapters *per se*. Article 349 TFEU states that: 'taking account of the structural social and economic situation of Guadeloupe, French Guiana, Martinique, Mayotte, La Réunion, Saint-Martin, the Azores, Madeira and the Canary Islands', the EU Council shall adopt 'specific measures aimed, in particular, at laying down the conditions of application of the Treaties to those regions, including common policies.' These measures concern areas such as customs and trade policies, agriculture and fisheries policies, State aids and conditions of access to structural funds and to horizontal EU programs. These measures are adopted taking into account the 'special characteristics and constraints' of the ORs but 'without undermining the integrity and the coherence' of the EU legal order including the 'internal market and common policies.' Article 355 TFEU is important as it states that the provisions of the Treaties shall 'apply to the European territories for whose external relations a Member State is responsible.' Given the current list of ORs, France and Spain have a special interest of maintaining these EU constitutional provisions, but the key will be the budgetary arbitrations anticipating the BREXIT.

The ERDF funds the so-called Interreg programmes focusing on cross-border, transnational and interregional cooperation. As ORs, La Réunion and Mayotte (since 2014) are beneficiaries of the EU policies and financial assistance, including the EU structural and investment funds. These programs are very interesting for this topic as Interreg is built 'around three strands of cooperation: cross-border (Interreg A), transnational (Interreg B) and interregional (Interreg C)' and can associate third countries to these initiatives (http://ec.europa.eu/regional_policy/en/policy/cooperation/european-territorial/). Non-EU Indian Ocean islands and riparian states can thus benefit as well from this cooperation.

The 'Interreg V – Indian Ocean, 2014–2020' adopted on 23 September 2015 (European Commission, 23 September 2015) focuses on cooperation between La Réunion and Mayotte as well as the French Southern and Antarctic Territories (as OCT) and 12 countries in the Southern Indian Ocean: Comoros, Madagascar, Mauritius, Seychelles, South Africa, Tanzania, Mozambique, Kenya, India, Sri Lanka, Maldives and Australia. This overall program is somewhat particular as it is based on the association of two specific programs, as EU ORs may in a 'single programme for territorial cooperation, combine the amounts of the ERDF allocated for cross-border and transnational cooperation' (European Parliament and EU Council, 17 December 2013, Art. 3 (7)). The first one 'Inside TN Indian Ocean, Interreg V-A) France (Réunion) Pays de la Commission de l'Océan Indien' (European Commission, 16 June 2014a, p. 22) concerns *cross-border* cooperation between La Réunion and its closest neighbors grouped together within the IOC: Comoros, Madagascar, Mauritius and Seychelles. The second one: 'Interreg V-B) Indian Ocean, France, Several third countries and overseas countries or territories' (European Commission, 16 June 2014b, p. 23) is a *transnational* program relating to 'cooperation between La Réunion, Mayotte and the group of countries and territories that are programme partners.' In other words, this program is a 'key tool for regional cooperation on the part of La Réunion and Mayotte with the neighboring countries.' Apart from the technical assistance, five strategic priorities have been identified: research and innovation, trade, environment and climate change, natural and cultural heritage and high-quality training. The financial contribution of the ERDF is 63 million euros out of a total of 74 million euros. Out of the ERDF contribution, 41 million euros are earmarked for the cross-border cooperation and 21 million euros for the transnational cooperation.

What is interesting is that the Scattered Islands constitute since 2007 the fifth district of the FSAL. As such, they are considered as an OCT and are thus eligible to EDF funds. Under the 10th EDF regional component (2007–2013), Mayotte (still an OCT at that time) and the Scattered Islands benefitted from a 3 million euros joint project on sustainable management of their natural resources heritage (Eco Consult, 14 June 2011, p. 64). As Mayotte became an EU OR in January 2014, new opportunities are emerging under the 11th EDF-OCT Indicative Regional allocations (2014–2020) and 4 million euros have been earmarked for the Indian Ocean for 'observation, management, conservation of terrestrial and marine ecosystem' (European Commission, 22 February 2016).

The 'Interreg V A – Mayotte-Comores-Madagascar, 2014–2020' program focuses on *cross-border* cooperation between Mayotte and the neighboring islands of Comoros and Madagascar (European Commission, 16 June 2014a). Three priority areas have been identified: increasing trade; improving emergency services and the population's state of health and promoting access to education through mobility. A joint secretariat based in Mayotte assists the program, in conjunction with representatives from Comoros and Madagascar.

These initiatives are managed with the aim of setting up cooperation projects jointly financed by the EDF and the ERDF. The ERDF financial envelope is 12 million euros out of a total of 16. The potential to combine the external dimension of EU internal funds (ERDF) combined with the external instruments (EDF) are new opportunities to be considered by the African Indian Ocean islands.

5. Conclusion

At strategic level, the 2014 EUMSS and the June 2016 Global Strategy for the EU's Foreign and Security Policy have put the Indian Ocean on their agendas. Therefore, it should now be easier to define a proper EU comprehensive 'Strategy of the European Union in the Indian Ocean,' taking into consideration the specificities of its islands and promoting convergence and complementarities of the various scattered frameworks for cooperation while addressing current challenges like the sensitive territorial disputes. In this regard, the 2016 EU's Global Strategy made clear that the EU is seeking to further 'universalise and implement the UN Convention on the Law of the Sea, including its dispute settlement mechanisms.' In this respect, the 11th EDF has a specific cooperation priority with the IOC devoted to peace, security and regional stability in the Indian Ocean.

The trade dimension has also recently evolved after many years of, sometimes, difficult negotiations. The conclusion of the interim EPA with the ESA and the ongoing regional negotiation are therefore encouraging. Technical support and training will be needed to facilitate the smooth implementation of such agreements. Cooperation and exchanges could be envisaged with the Maghreb countries that concluded FTAs with the EU from the mid-1990s, Morocco and Tunisia currently negotiating more advanced agreements: the 'Deep and Comprehensive Free Trade Areas.' Links with other EPAs are to be taken into consideration as this cooperation could stimulate trade exchanges on a pan-African level and thus limit the Hub and Spokes effect (see Tovias, 2001, pp. 153–168). Also, it is key that partners understand that if the cost of reform is important, the benefit is first of all to have trade regulations and standards in line with the multilateral rules. Therefore, the current FTAs negotiations with Indonesia and India and their potential impacts have to be taken into consideration by the Indian Ocean islands. Of course, FTAs are to be considered, first of all, as tools for promoting sustainable development and prosperity for the mutual benefit of the partners.

The fact that the EU's regional financial envelope to South and East Africa and the Indian Ocean has more than doubled for 2014–2020 is clear evidence of the growing interest of the EU for the 'EA-SA-IO' regional framework for cooperation. This could help to create more complementarities between the main African regional organizations (AU, COMESA, EAC, IGAD, IOC, SADC). Regional cooperation in the Indian Ocean implies to cooperate with Asian regional groupings as well. IORA, as it comprises 21 members including Australia, India and Indonesia and 7 dialogue partners, could play a more important role in the future. As EU–ASEAN political and security cooperation is designed to enhance cooperation in multilateral *fora* and adopt when possible joint positions, this track should not be underestimated, as Indonesia remains an Indian Ocean island sharing many challenges with smaller ones. The SAARC is also key for the future as it includes not only Sri Lanka and Maldives but also India, as the EU is developing cooperation at the level of the harmonization of standards and regional integration. The

Europe–Asia Meeting of head of states or governments, a forum based on the informality of the dialogue, could also be taken into consideration. The fact the EU became, in 2012, the first organization to accede to the 'Treaty of Amity and Cooperation in Southeast Asia' could also potentially be relevant for some specific issues (EU Council, 26 April 2012). In sum, one of the main goals of any regional strategy should be to maximize complementarities and synergies between these regional organizations and frameworks.

Increasing cooperation between the ORs, OCTs and ACP countries is a priority for 2014–2020 and can be built on experiences such as the 'Islands project in the Indian Ocean' (2011–2014). With a budget of 10 million euros from the 10th EDF, it focused on 'economic, social and environmental development of the Comoros, Madagascar, Mauritius, the Seychelles and Zanzibar' and on 'better regional integration.' Combined ERDF resources *via* the participation of La Réunion, as OR and member of the IOC (*via* France) were also available (European Commission, 18 November 2014, p. 16). Last but not least, the BREXIT will imply a reduction of the EU funds for internal and external actions. On the other hand, in the Western Indian Ocean, the development of the external dimension of internal instruments (ERDF-Interreg) offers new opportunities. As it is through La Réunion and Mayotte that those projects are implemented, good neighborliness relationships between France and the Western Indian Ocean island states are essential. Given the potential of the Exclusive Economic Zones in terms of fisheries and energy resources as well as security issues such as piracy, illegal fishing and human trafficking (see Bouchard, 2013), this will be difficult to achieve but the EU is determined to further universalize and implement the dispute settlement mechanisms of the UN Convention on the Law of the Sea. Another issue will be to assess the impact of the EU's restrictive measures approach adopted vis-à-vis Madagascar, through the Cotonou agreement, and Sri Lanka, through the suspension of the GSP+. The EU approach regarding values and conditionality is facing more and more criticisms. As an example, at the meeting of the ACP–EU Subcommittee on Trade Cooperation, held in October 2016, the ACP states asked the following question: 'in what way does the strategy promote European values and why is reference made only to European and not to international values?' (ACP-EU, 4 October 2016).

Fostering international development cooperation is also crucial. The anti-piracy initiatives have proven to be incentives for fostering European (Ukraine and Norway participated to ATALANTA) and international cooperation, even if the involvement of countries like South Africa, India and China as proved to be difficult (Helly, June 2011). Fisheries, trade, environmental issues or immigration are among the many areas to be privileged for international cooperation, notably with the UN system. For instance, in 2011, the EU signed an agreement with the UN Department of Economic and Social Affairs for a grant to assist Small Island Developing States of the ESA-IO region in implementing the Mauritius Strategy for sustainable development. Another example is the Southern Indian Ocean Fisheries Agreement adopted in July 2006 at the Headquarters of the UN Food and Agriculture Organization. It entered into force in 2012 and has been signed by Australia, Comoros, the EU, France, Kenya, Madagascar, Mauritius, Mozambique, New Zealand and the Seychelles to ensure the long-term conservation and sustainable use of the fishery resources in the area (UN-FAO, 16 January 2015).

What is obvious is that the Indian Ocean is now more strategic for the EU as a whole. The development of an approach linking Africa, the Middle East and the Mediterranean is put forward in the 2016 EU global Strategy. This 'neighbours of the EU's neighbours' approach (Lannon, 2014, pp. 1–25) could provide new opportunities by better connecting the EU's policies in Africa and Asia, notably through the Maritime routes linking the Mediterranean to the Indian Ocean. But the design of an EU comprehensive strategy for the Indian Ocean as such is needed to maximize the impact of all its initiatives and to take into consideration the specificities of the Indian Ocean islands and archipelagos at large. It is thus also key for the EU to understand how the Indian Ocean islands perceive its actions in the region.

Disclosure statement

No potential conflict of interest was reported by the author.

References

ACP-EU Subcommittee on Trade Cooperation. (2016, October 4). *Summary record of the 73rd meeting.* ACP-UE 2117/16, Brussels.

Antrim, C. (2012, July). International law and order: The Indian Ocean and South China Sea. In D. Michel & R. Sticklor (Eds.), *Indian Ocean rising: Maritime security and policy challenges* (pp. 65–85). Washington, DC: Stimson.

Arbitral Tribunal. (2015, March 18). *Chagos marine protected area arbitration (Mauritius v. United Kingdom), Case 2011-03.* Retrieved from http://www.pcacases.com/pcadocs/MU-UK%2020150318%20Award.pdf

Bouchard, C. (2013). The Marine Nationale in the southwest and southern Indian Ocean. In A. Forbes (Ed.), *The Naval contribution to national security and prosperity: Proceedings of the Royal Australian Navy Conference 2012* (pp. 147–155). Canberra: Sea Power Center.

Bouchard, C., & Crumplin, W. (2011, December 19). Two faces of France: 'France of the Indian Ocean'/ 'France in the Indian Ocean.' *Journal of the Indian Ocean Region, 7*(2), 161–182.

Bouchard, C., & Crumplin, W. (2013, May 5). France as a Pertinent and Significant Indian Ocean Player. *FPRC Journal.* Foreign Policy Research Centre, New Delhi, India, No. 14 – Indian Ocean: A New Vision, pp. 88–100.

Brzezinski, Z. (1979, January 15). Iran: The crescent of crisis. *Time Magazine.* Retrieved from http://content.time.com/time/magazine/article/0,9171,919995,00.html#ixzz2tHbAjOuO

Chellaney, B. (2015). World's geopolitical center of gravity shifts to Indian Ocean. *Nikkie Asian Review.* Retrieved from http://asia.nikkei.com/Politics-Economy/International-Relations/World-s-geopolitical-center-of-gravity-shifts-to-Indian-Ocean

Chevalier-Govers, C. (2015). La mission EUCAP Nestor, et sa contribution à la lutte contre la piraterie maritime. In C. Chevalier-Govers & C. Schneider (Eds.), *L'Europe et la lutte contre la piraterie maritime* (pp. 75–90). Paris: Éditions Pedone.

CIA. (2017). World factbook. *Disputes-International.* Retrieved from https://www.cia.gov/library/publications/the-world-factbook/fields/2070.html

Cointat, C. (2010, February 17). *Les îles Eparses, terres d'avenir, Rapport d'information n° 299 fait au nom de la Commission des Lois*, Paris, France.

Cooperation agreement between the European Community and the Democratic Socialist Republic of Sri Lanka on partnership and development, 27 March 1995, OJ L 85/33. (1995, April 19).

Djibouti Declaration. (2016, May 15). *3rd Regional ministerial meeting for promoting maritime safety and security in the region ESA-IO*. Djibouti. Retrieved from http://commissionoceanindien.org/fileadmin/resources/MASE/ESA-IO_DJIBOUTI_DECLARATION_3rd_Regional_Ministerial_Meeting_for_Promoting_Maritime_Safety_and_Security.pdf

Eco Consult. (2011, June 14). *Region level evaluation – Overseas countries and territories* (104 p.). Retrieved from http://ec.europa.eu/europeaid/how/evaluation/evaluation_reports/reports/2011/1294_vol2_en.pdf

EEAS. (2013, December 23). *The EU fight against piracy in the Horn of Africa*. Brussels. Retrieved from http://www.eeas.europa.eu/statements/docs/2013/131223_03_en.pdf

EEAS. (2014). *Multiannual indicative programme 2014–2020 for Sri Lanka*. Brussels. Retrieved from https://eeas.europa.eu/sites/eeas/files/mip-20142020-programming-sri-lanka-20140812_en.pdf

EEAS. (2015, October). *Regional maritime security capacity building mission in the Horn of Africa and the western Indian Ocean*. Brussels. Retrieved from https://www.eucap-nestor.eu/data/file_db/factsheet/New_Factsheet_October_2015%20REV2_CPCC.pdf

EEAS. (2016, March 13). *EU relations with Seychelles*. Brussels. Retrieved from http://eeas.europa.eu/seychelles/index_en.htm

EEAS. (2016, May 3). *Fight against piracy*. Brussels. Retrieved from https://eeas.europa.eu/headquarters/headquarters-homepage_en/428/Fight%20against%20piracy

EEAS. (2016, May 12). *Mauritius and the EU*. Brussels. Retrieved from https://eeas.europa.eu/delegations/mauritius/1517/mauritius-and-eu_en

EEAS. (2016, May 13). *Sri Lanka and the EU*. Brussels. Retrieved from https://eeas.europa.eu/delegations/sri-lanka/1827/sri-lanka-and-eu_en

EEAS. (2016, May 17). *Comoros and the EU*. Brussels. Retrieved from https://eeas.europa.eu/delegations/mauritius/2075/comoros-and-eu_en

EEAS. (2016, May 26). *Maldives and the EU*. Brussels. Retrieved from https://eeas.europa.eu/headquarters/headquarters-homepage_en/2295/Maldives%20and%20the%20EU

EEAS. (2016, June). *A global strategy for the European Union's foreign and security policy*. Brussels. Retrieved from https://eeas.europa.eu/top_stories/pdf/eugs_review_web.pdf

EU Council. (2006, December 15). *Aceh monitoring mission*. Brussels. Retrieved from https://www.consilium.europa.eu/uedocs/cmsUpload/051130_background_info.pdf

EU Council. (2010, February 15). *Implementing regulation (EU) No 143/2010, temporarily withdrawing the special incentive arrangement for sustainable development and good governance provided for under Regulation (EC) No. 732/2008 with respect to the Democratic Socialist Republic of Sri Lanka*.

EU Council. (2010, October 7). *Communiqué of the 2nd regional ministerial meeting on piracy and maritime security in ESA-IO region*. Republic of Mauritius. Retrieved from http://www.consilium.europa.eu/uedocs/cms_data/docs/pressdata/en/foraff/116942.pdf

EU Council. (2012, April 26). *Council decision 2012/308/CFSP on the accession of the European Union to the Treaty of Amity and Cooperation in Southeast Asia*, OJ L154/1, June 15.

EU Council. (2012, July 16). *Decision 2012/389/CFSP of on the European Union Mission on Regional Maritime Capacity Building in the Horn of Africa*, OJ L 187, July 17, pp. 40–43, Brussels.

EU Council. (2013, November 25). *Decision 2013/755/EU on the association of the overseas countries and territories with the European Union*, OJ L 344/1, December 19, Brussels.

EU Council. (2014, June 24). *European Union Maritime security strategy*. Brussels. Retrieved from http://register.consilium.europa.eu/doc/srv?l=EN&f=ST%2011205%202014%20INIT

EU Council. (2014, July 22). *Decision 2014/485/CFSP amending decision 2012/389/CFSP on the European Union Mission on regional maritime capacity building in the Horn of Africa*, Brussels, OJ L 217, July 23, pp. 39–41.

EU Council. (2014, December 16). *European Union maritime security strategy – Action plan*. Brussels. Retrieved from https://ec.europa.eu/maritimeaffairs/sites/maritimeaffairs/files/docs/body/20141216-action-plan_en.pdf

EU Council. (2015, November 17). *Conclusions, 3426th Council meeting, foreign affairs* (p. 12). Brussels.

EU Council. (2016, June 7). *Implementing decision amending implementing decision 2014/170/EU establishing a list of non-cooperating third countries in fighting IUU fishing pursuant to regulation (EC) 1005/2008 establishing a community system to prevent, deter and eliminate illegal, unreported and unregulated fishing as regards Sri Lanka.*

EU mission to the WTO. (2016, March 21). *EU statement at the trade policy review of Maldives.* Geneva. Retrieved from https://eeas.europa.eu/sites/eeas/files/06_2016_03_21_statement_tpr_maldvies.pdf

European Commission. (2007, May 22). *Maldives – European community country strategy paper 2007–2013.* Brussels. Retrieved from https://ec.europa.eu/europeaid/sites/devco/files/csp-maldives-2007-2013_en.pdf

European Commission. (2012, January). *Fact sheet on the interim economic partnership agreements – Eastern and Southern Africa.* Brussels. Retrieved from http://trade.ec.europa.eu/doclib/docs/2009/january/tradoc_142193.pdf

European Commission. (2012, March). *Economic partnership agreement between the EU and the ESA EPA group.* Brussels. Retrieved from http://trade.ec.europa.eu/doclib/docs/2012/march/tradoc_149213.pdf

European Commission. (2014a, June 16). *Implementing decision 2014/388/EU setting up the list of regions and areas eligible for funding from the European Regional Development Fund under the cross-border and transnational components of the European territorial cooperation goal for the period 2014 to 2020*, OJ L 183/75, June 24. Brussels.

European Commission. (2014b, June 16). *Implementing decision 2014/366/EU setting up the list of cooperation programmes and indicating the global amount of total support from the European regional development fund for each programme under the European territorial cooperation goal for the period 2014 to 2020*, OJ L 178/18, June 18, Brussels.

European Commission. (2014, August 12). *Multiannual indicative programme 2014–2020 for Sri Lanka.* Brussels. Retrieved from https://eeas.europa.eu/sites/eeas/files/mip-20142020-programming-sri-lanka-20140812_en.pdf

European Commission. (2014, November 18). *Note for guidance on the funding of Joint EDF-EDRF projects 2014–2020, increasing cooperation between outermost regions of the European Union, African, Caribbean and Pacific countries and neighbouring overseas countries and territories.* Brussels

European Commission. (2015). *Regional indicative programme for EA-SA-IO 2014–2020.* Brussels. Retrieved from https://ec.europa.eu/europeaid/sites/devco/files/rip-ea-sa-io-signed-20150604_en.pdf

European Commission. (2015, June 4). *EU to support regional programmes in Southern, Eastern Africa and the Indian Ocean with more than €1.3 billion.* Press release IP/15/5114, Brussels.

European Commission. (2015, July 2). *New EU project helps increase maritime security in the Indian Ocean.* Web release, Brussels. Retrieved from https://ec.europa.eu/europeaid/sites/devco/files/2015-06-25-crimario-mombasa-press-release_en.pdf

European Commission. (2015, September 23). *Décision d'exécution C(2015) 6527 final.* Brussels. Retrieved from http://www.reunioneurope.org/DOCS/2014-2020_DECISION_PO_INTERREGV_REUNION.pdf

European Commission. (2015, November 30). *Programme Indicatif National Madagascar 2014–2020.* 11eme FED, Brussels. Retrieved from https://ec.europa.eu/europeaid/sites/devco/files/nip-madagascar-edf11-2015_fr.pdf

European Commission. (2016, February 22). *Report on the implementation of the financial assistance provided to the overseas countries and territories under the 11th EDF*, COM (2016) 79 final, Brussels.

European Commission. (2016, April 29). *The EU and Eastern and Southern Africa.* Brussels. Retrieved from http://ec.europa.eu/trade/policy/countries-and-regions/regions/esa/

European Commission. (2016, June 22). *Joint staff working document on the implementation of the EU Maritime Security Strategy Action Plan.* Brussels.

European Commission. (2016, June 23). *National indicative programme 2015–2020*, 11th EDF. Republic of Mauritius. Retrieved from https://eeas.europa.eu/sites/eeas/files/nip-mauritius-edf11-2016_en.pdf

European Commission. (2017, January). *Overview of economic partnership agreements*. Brussels. Retrieved from http://trade.ec.europa.eu/doclib/docs/2009/september/tradoc_144912.pdf

European Commission. (2017, January 11). *Delegated regulation (EU) amending annex III to regulation (EU) no 978/2012 of the European Parliament and of the council applying a scheme of generalised tariff preferences*.

European Commission. (2017, February 16). *European Union, trade in goods with ACP – Eastern and Southern Africa*. Retrieved from http://trade.ec.europa.eu/doclib/docs/2013/november/tradoc_151900.pdf

European Commission. (2017, April). *Overview of economic partnership agreements*. Retrieved from http://trade.ec.europa.eu/doclib/docs/2009/september/tradoc_144912.pdf

European Council. (2012, July 11). *Decision 2012/419/EU amending the status of Mayotte with regard to the European Union*, OJ L 204/131, July 31, Brussels.

European Parliament & EU Council. (2013, December 17). *Article 3 (7) of the Regulation 1299/2013 of the of on specific provisions for the support from the European Regional Development Fund to the European territorial cooperation goal*, OJ L 347/259, December 20, Brussels.

Gaymard, H. (2013, March 20). *Rapport sur le projet de loi, adopté par le Sénat, autorisant l'approbation de l'accord-cadre entre le Gouvernement de la République française et le Gouvernement de la République de Maurice sur la cogestion économique, scientifique et environnementale relative à l'île de Tromelin et à ses espaces maritimes environnants*, Paris.

Helly, D. (2011, June 17). *Lessons from Atalanta and EU counter-piracy policies* (14 p.). Brussels: EU ISS. Retrieved from http://www.iss.europa.eu/uploads/media/Atalanta_report.pdf

Indian Ocean Commission. (2015). *Rapport Annuel* (90 p.). République de Maurice. Retrieved from http://commissionoceanindien.org/fileadmin/resources/SG/Rapport%20annuel%202015.pdf.

Interim Agreement establishing a framework for an Economic Partnership Agreement between the Eastern and Southern Africa States, on the one part, and the European Community and its member states, on the other part. (2009, July 13). OJ L 111/1, 24 April 2012, Brussels.

International Maritime Organisation. (2016). *Djibouti code of conduct*. Retrieved from http://www.imo.org/en/OurWork/Security/PIU/Pages/DCoC.aspx

IRSEM. (2014). The comprehensive approach and the European Union: A case study of the Horn of Africa. In M. Langlois (Ed.), *Note de recherche stratégique*, N°10. Retrieved from http://www.defense.gouv.fr/content/download/285159/3671139/file/NRS_numero_10.pdf

Kaplan, R. (2011). *Monsoon – The Indian Ocean and the future of American power* (p. 9). New York, NY: Random House.

Kelegama, S. (2010). *EU trade policy and democracy building in South Asia* (p. 20). Stockholm: International Institute for Democracy and Electoral Assistance.

Kelegama, S. (2016, January 22). *EU – Sri Lanka trade & investment: Regaining GSP+*. Retrieved from http://eccsl.lk/sites/default/files/EU%27s%20Trade%20Policy%20on%20Sri%20Lanka%20-%20Dr.%20Saman%20Kelegama.pdf

Keohane, D. (2017). *Three's company? France, Germany, the UK and European defence post-Brexit*. Analyses of the Elcano Royal Institute, ARI 1/2017–5 January 2017. Retrieved from http://www.realinstitutoelcano.org/

Lannon, E. (2014). The neighbours of the EU's neighbours, the EU's broader neighbourhood and the arc of crisis and strategic challenges from the Sahel to Central Asia. In S. Gstohl & E. Lannon (Eds.), *The neighbours of the European Union's neighbours – Diplomatic and geopolitical dimensions beyond the European Union* (pp. 1–25). Farnham: Ashgate.

Observer Research Foundation. (2016). *Prospects for EU-India security cooperation*. New Delhi. Retrieved from http://www.iss.europa.eu/uploads/media/EU-India-Security-Cooperation.pdf

Osman, S. (2012). Tromelin: Une cogestion qui se fait attendre … . *Outre-Terre*, 2012/3 n° 33–34, pp. 651–655.

Présidence de la République Française. (2008). Commission du livre blanc sur la défense et la sécurité nationale 2008. *Défense et sécurité nationale – Le Livre Blanc*, Paris, La Documentation Française.

Raoof, A. (2014, March). *Still dispossessed – The battle of the Chagos Islanders to return to their homeland*. Minority Rights Group International. Retrieved from http://minorityrights.org/wp-content/uploads/2015/07/MRG_Brief_Chagosv2.pdf

Republic of Mauritius. (2016, November 18). *Chagos Archipelago an integral part of Mauritius*. The Government States, Mauritius. Retrieved from http://www.govmu.org/English/News/Pages/Chagos-Archipelago-an-integral-part-of-Mauritius,-the-Government-states-.aspx

Tovias, A. (2001). The optimum strategy for a spoke: Linking with other spokes or other hubs? In M. Maresceau & E. Lannon (Eds.), *The EU's enlargement and Mediterranean strategies* (pp. 153–168). Basingstoke: Palgrave-Macmillan.

UN-FAO. (2015, January 16). *Southern Indian Ocean fisheries agreement*. Retrieved from http://www.fao.org/fileadmin/user_upload/legal/docs/035s-e.pdf

Tropical cyclones and coastal communities: the dialectics of social and environmental change in the Sundarban delta

Debojyoti Das

ABSTRACT
Disasters caused by cyclones are a cyclical event in the Bay of Bengal delta seaboard. Periodically, cyclone disasters result in damaged houses and the loss of crops and livelihoods. They affect every type of social and economic infrastructure in the delta, which is inhabited by ostracized backward caste groups – seafarers, forest goers and landless peasants. The 1970 Bhola cyclone, for example, was the most catastrophic, generating a 9.1-meter storm surge at the mouth of the Ganges where it meets the Bay killing approximately 300,000 people. Often, these disasters are declared as 'natural' and 'acts of God.' This paper tests this epistemic viewpoint. I argue that cyclone-related disasters, like other calamities, cannot be merely viewed as 'natural' phenomena. Instead their embeddedness in the social and political relations shaping human habitation on the coastal seaboard endangers human settlement and has made the inhabitants vulnerable since the colonial land reclamation program began in the late eighteenth and early nineteenth century in Bengal. Through examination of competing discourses around 'natural disasters', I demonstrate how cyclones are portrayed as natural (rather than human-induced). The naturalization of disaster benefits powerful actors like politicians, civil engineers and contactors, among others. In analyzing the disaster narrative, I go beyond the textual and rhetorical components to include the socio-political and historical bases of the production of ideas of disaster in the Bengal delta. By focusing on the political and social causes of disaster, this paper does not in any way question the ontological reality of cyclones 'as dangerous and potentially very destructive natural hazards'; instead, it tries to demonstrate how disaster is naturalized in the different strands of state and epistemic discourse.

Introduction

Cyclones are not stand-alone natural phenomena, as the American environmental historian Ted Steinberg argues in his critically acclaimed book *Acts of God* (2006). Steinberg pointed out that politicians, bureaucrats and business leaders consistently seek to blame nature when calamity struck. He found such a response inadequate, arguing that their 'inert' conception of disaster was little more than a means of avoiding responsibility for the social and economic injustice that precedes and follows natural disasters. He claimed that disaster in America was not just a product of nature; it was also a product of the risk-taking, profit-maximizing culture of capitalism. Disasters are thus as much social catastrophes as they are material catastrophes (Endfield, Davies, Tejedo, Metcalfe, & O'Hara, 2009). In the northern Bay of Bengal delta, similar opinions are highlighted in media coverage during the aftermath of a cyclone. Blaming nature for a disaster's impact on human settlements and the built-up environment has become the business of politicians, scientific experts and bureaucrats. Geographer Anu Kapur, in her book *Vulnerable India* (2010), problematizes the concept of 'natural disasters' by arguing that its impact on environment and societies is at best an outcome of government apathy and human insensitivity in general.

These views have been persuasively echoed by Greg Bankoff and Joseph Christensen in their latest work titled *Natural Hazards and Peoples in the Indian Ocean World* where they argue that 'the origins of vulnerability and thus the root cause of disasters are to be found in the political structures, economic systems and social orders of the societies in which they take place' (Bankoff & Christensen 2016, p. 20).

I discuss in this paper that disasters resulting from cyclones, like any other natural calamity, are linked to socio-political conditions. This is a link I will look into further through the paper and try to determine that the origins of such disasters are beyond solely natural causes. I want to rethink the cyclone in the Sundarban delta as a trans-national disaster – as an event shaped, and in some sense created, by the unequal power relations characteristic of British imperial policies that intensified human settlement in the Bengal delta, thus intensifying the risk of cyclones for settlements and population (Figure 1).

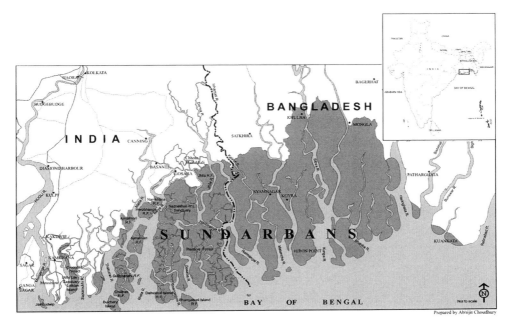

Figure 1. Map of the Sundarban delta. Source: http://www.wwfindia.org/about_wwf/critical_regions/sundarbans3/about_sundarbans/

Geographer David Harvey has pointed out that there is a dialectical relationship between nature, society and disaster that leads to environmental change with a substantial impact on marginalized communities who are forced to occupy these vulnerable places (Harvey, 1993, pp. 1–50). The theoretical slant that I take in this paper is based on the political economic-environmental approach, focusing on the historical-structural dimensions of vulnerability to hazard (Oliver-Smith, 1996, p. 303). The argument I propose here is not what causes events such as cyclones but their conceptualization in our discourses (Shaw, 2014). The paper is divided into three parts. In the first section, I engage with the history of British land reclamation and revenue program. This I follow up with the post-partition scenario. In the final section, I capture the contemporary situation in the delta by engaging with the life and experiences of people in the aftermath of the Aila cyclone in 2009.

The colonial and pre-colonial past: reclaiming wetlands and ecological change

In his preface to the book *The Revenuer History of the Sundarbans*, Kumud Ranjan Biswas observes that the Bengal delta, which now includes the metropolitan city of Kolkata (Calcutta), during the early eighteenth century, was three tiny villages lying on the outskirts of a wild country called the Sundarbans. It was covered with dense jungles composed of Sundari trees and the coastal mangrove forest. Their jungles were the habitat of reptiles, Bengal tigers and dangerous amphibians. The only people who inhabited these islands were sea pirates, salt makers and outcaste tribesman. It remained more or less inaccessible and hence unsettled.

However, this characterization may present a romantic view of the pre-colonial past (Eaton, 1994; Jalil, 1986; Mitra, 1914). No substantial permanent settlement was made in the area until the British Indian Government transformed the landscape for its imperial needs – freeing the region of its bandits and tigers, which were later controlled by forest and land revenue generation programs. It must be noted that the Sundarbans in the pre-colonial period were under the control of Hindu landlords locally known as 'twelve bhuyas' who were later crushed by the Mughals (Roychoudhury, 1965). They were replaced by more amenable *zamindars* and *talukdars* who were regarded by theoreticians of Mughal statecraft as officials appointed for collecting the revenue and administering the territory of the Parganas and Sarkars, as recorded in the manuals of Mughal administration (Roy, 1979).

From 1756, the East India Company, and later the British Raj, developed a keen interest in Bengal and its maritime waterways. This led to the construction of many canals, sewage gates and levees over the Ganges and its tributaries to harness hydropower, enable irrigation, build railways and to help facilitate inland navigation and river port facilities. The Sundarbans, on the other hand, was a wasteland that needed protection for mangrove afforestation and land reclamation to fulfill colonial revenue demand under the Bengal Presidency. Several experiments were carried out by pioneering British officials like Collector General Claud Russell (1770–1773)[1] and Tilman Hanckell, who was the Judge and Magistrate of Murli, Jessore (1788–1790).[2] But all of these early experiments failed to gain popularity on a mass scale until the British Indian Government took power and started granting leases in the early nineteenth century to Bengali *zamindars* who worked as local magnate-landlords and acted as intermediaries in revenue collection. To this end, the colonial government had to define the rights of the tillers and owners. An elaborate chain of rent-seeking patrons (*zamindars*, *talukdars*) and their clients (sharecroppers, landless laborers) were settled and regulated by the administration as migrant landless laborers flocked to take advantage of the land reclamation program initiated by the native *zamindars* and European investors and speculators, who were granted land on a lease basis. The Port Canning Company became a lead player in the land reclamation program along with other *zamindars* who wished to make windfall profits from wasteland reclamation and revenue settlement in *mouzas* (villages).

In the South 24 Parganas of present-day West Bengal, it became increasingly risky to clear and settle the Sundarban forest and mangrove swamp as the region, unlike Bakargang and Khulna, developed from south to north and the seaward side was more elevated than the interior. F.D. Ascoli in his book *The Revenue History of the Sundarbans* observes, 'the problems of the 24-Parganas Sundarbans are probably more complex than those of Khulna and Bakarganj' (1921, p. 187). This was primarily because in this part of the Sundarbans, the embankment and land reclamation program began at a rapid pace without an understanding of the geomorphology and fluvial pattern of the delta. As such, the islands were unable to mature and attain the required height so that tidal waves could not make easy inroads into them. According to the Ascoli report of 1921, land reclamation in the South 24 Parganas was an 'unnatural development' (Ascoli, 1921, p. 188).

In light of confrontation with the natural ebb and flow of tidal backwaters in the Sundarbans, there has been claim over nature between the colonial policy of land reclamation and the *zamindars* of the Sundarbans. Colonial revenue concerns and policies of extraction blinded the colonial government to the geomorphology and geography of island formation in the delta region. That rivers and tides played an important role in the ecological stability of the region was underemphasized within the policy of land reclamation. During my yearlong period of field research in the Sundarbans (2012–2013), I recorded similar narratives of land reclamation and settlement in Gosaba – land leased to Hamilton zamindari in the Sundarbans. The Hamilton Public Records contain zamindari files that record in detail the money spent on maintaining the embankments that were annually damaged by seawater storm surges, tidal waves and bank erosion in the active delta islands. In fact, Sir Daniel Mackinnon Hamilton, the patron of Gosaba, writes in his articles and speeches that maintaining the embankment was the prime duty of the estate officials (Bandopadhyay & Matilal, 2003). Mukunda Gayen, a local poet and writer in his midsixties, observes that since his childhood he has been noting the ebb and flow of the rivers on Dayapur Island. When Hamilton started his land reclamation program in Gosaba, it was an immature island. The need for a heavy embankment arose because the islands were much lower in height than the mean sea level, but sediment deposition was stopped once land reclamation started.

Villages like Gosaba and Dayapur, as well as other islands of the Sundarbans, continue to be part of the active delta in South 24 Parganas. Colonial policy and later post-colonial programs of land reclamation have determined the fate of these islands: the extension of road networks into these islands and the building of ports like Canning were later abandoned. In the late nineteenth century, it became clear that the Port Canning project had failed, and Governor-general Lord Canning ultimately abandoned it partly because of the river regime in the Matla that constrained the prospects of navigation, coupled with several shipwrecks that dampened the interest of investors. Portraitist Khitish Bishal, a resident of Canning, showed me his private museum collection that contains rare artifacts of the Sundarbans. In his repository, he had the bricks used by the Port Canning Company to build the Port that could not be operationalized because of problems caused by siltation and strong gale in the Matla. The fate of Diamond Harbour in the mouth of the Hooghly River has turned out to be the same. Subsequently, there are now plans to move the Kolkata port to Haldia, away from the mouth of the delta.

These colonial experiments to facilitate trade and maximize the production of capital in colonial Bengal brought the Empire's subjects and their go-between *zamindars* into intimate confrontation with coastal calamities. Who were the people most affected by these programs? The affected communities were the most vulnerable social groups, the Scheduled Castes of Bengal (Namasurdras, Pods, Mahisyas and Poundro Katriyas)[3] who worked as tenants, share croppers and bonded laborers of the *zamindars*. The vulnerability of Scheduled Caste agrarian peasants was historically constituted by their social position in Bengal *Samaj*. The high caste Hindus of Bengal settled mainly along the banks of the ancient active rivers, while the agricultural castes lived mainly in the intervening marshes and jungles. The descendants of the aboriginal races gradually extended the frontiers of cultivation to the southern and eastern swamps and forests, and today these represent the majority of the lower delta (Mukherjee, 1938). In order to reclaim the wastelands, embankment construction was executed by the *zamindars* through their deputies, locally known as *nayabs* (zamindar henchmen, managers). After the abolition of the zamindari in 1950, the Indian federal government was bestowed with the responsibility of protecting the embankments all over the Sundarbans. The elected government represented by upper caste Hindus was not interested in the welfare of its citizens who lived in marginal littoral spaces on the coastal seaboard. These people were the subaltern underclass, the untouchables – fishermen, honey collectors, seafarers, wood cutters, manual laborers and peasants, who were, up until recently, sharecroppers and tenants of the *bhadralok* landed gentry in colonial Bengal.

The political economy of embankment measures

In order to protect the reclaimed land for farming, embankment construction was pivotal in the success of settled agriculture in the Sundarban delta. Unlike the Law of Storm[4] (Baddeley, 1853; Blanford, 1868; Eliot, 1900; Grove, 1995; Paddington, 1849, 1853; Ross, 1869) that was developed by the colonial administration to help shipping and navigation with the financial support and assistance of British mercantile capital, the embankment projects were unplanned and 'complicated by lack of information on customary rights, diversity of interests and capacities of the private partners, and free riding' (Roy, 2010). This posed a larger threat to the defense of newly carved out settlements and agricultural fields in the delta region that were progressively salinized. The tenants who plowed these fields were made vulnerable by greedy moneylenders in the aftermath of cyclones. The expansion of the agrarian frontier in the Sundarban delta thus posed risks to life and property, and produced social, economic and physical vulnerability. All of these were not solely 'acts of God' or triggered by 'climate change' events. Rather the ecological changes in the Bengal delta brought about by colonial policies of land reclamation and weak embankment programs made the landscape vulnerable to tropical storms.

Several protagonists of the environmentalist discourse pay particular attention to the period 1880–1950, painting a dismal picture of public works on embankments (D'souza, 2006; Samanta, 2001; Singh, 2008). The motivation of the colonial state for doing so was partly economic – increasing tax income by reclaiming land. A riverbank became a potential source river water for irrigation, and embankments were needed for railway construction. In the main, however, the motive to spend public money on embankments was political: the desire to control peasant societies. In this respect, the embankment form of public works was no different from many other kinds of technologies for mass use that became 'tools of empire.'

According to Tirthankar Roy (2010) public works in this sphere gave rise to four kinds of social cost. First, they degraded the land: they prevented alluvial deposit formation and the natural cycle of soil enrichment in the flood plains. Second, embankments, in the long run, made floods more likely by hastening deposit formation on the riverbed. Third, embankments, by causing waterlogging, helped malaria spread in Bengal. Fourth, the railway embankments, which usually followed the course of rivers, often acted as obstacles to the natural drainage of floodwater. The environmentalist discourse further suggests that because of these damages, 'in the last quarter of [the 19th] century [the state's] role in controlling flood began to be critically examined' (Hill, 1997; Iqbal, 2007).

In the Sundarbans, the construction and management of embankments oscillated between the *zamindars* and the colonial state. The *zamindars*, who were granted land by the colonial government, took responsibility for embankment and dyke construction but often neglected embankment repairs and protection, thus compelling the colonial local administration to share the responsibility.[5] The future of these zamindaries depended on the robustness of embankments that blocked exceptionally high tides.

However, the opening up of these marshy wetlands for agriculture posed a new problem, exposing the peasants to the vagaries of tropical storms that intermittently ravaged settlements and farmlands. The state created a contractual setup of embankment management. Regulation 33 and two sections of Regulation 8 of the Code of 1793 divided all embankments in principle into two classes, one being 'public works' overseen by the Collector, and all others being managed by the zamindar (Roy, 2010). These intermediaries showed no interest in embankment measures of their own accord, and instead depended upon state subsidies and concessions as free riders. The burden was borne by the tenants (share croppers, bonded laborers and small peasants).[6] For example, L.F. Facus, in his settlement report of Khulna, writes that the untouchables (Pods and Namasudras) 'cleared the way, converting the jungle into paddy land' (Facus, 1927, p. 47). The neglect of embankment construction both by *zamindars* and the colonial state, and the constant shift of responsibility, affected the embankment program in the coastal seaboard badly and added to the economic and social vulnerability of the peasants working their land in the Sundarbans.

Simultaneously, the urbanization and industrialization of Kolkata in the settled part of the delta posed different challenges to land use, as the marshes and ponds in the suburbs of the city were quickly transformed into industrial and urban areas. In order to regulate the flow of the rivers joining the Bay of Bengal, canals were built and multipurpose River Valley Projects (MPRVPs) commissioned, like the flagship Damodar Valley Corporation (DVC) which was developed along the lines of the Tennessee Valley Corporation in the U.S.A. in 1941. This changed the hydrological regime of the rivers that joined the

Bay in the Sundarban delta through the construction of a controlled system of barrages, switch gates, check dams and reservoirs in the upper riparian areas of Bihar and present-day Jharkhand. These were supported by a number of thermal power plants. The DVC was commissioned to control floods and to provide inland navigation and electricity to the industries set up along the banks of the Hooghly River.

After India's independence, the Nehruvian policy was aimed at brisk industrialization and the increasing self-reliance of the Indian economy. Dam construction was seen as a symbol of scientific vigor and technological marvel, and it generated a sense of national pride among the political class and engineers (Klingensmith, 2007). It marked an era of MPRVPs that soon undermined the concerns of the littoral communities of Bengal. In the absence of both private and public interest in embankment construction, the embankments maintenance program suffered a setback, which left the area open to deltaic flooding, bank erosion and the consequent loss of livelihoods when cyclones struck. Partition also triggered refugee migration as the fresh immigrants from coastal East Pakistan (Jessore, Khulna, Barisal and Chittagong) were pushed towards the coastal belt of South 24 Parganas, their natural home, thus building population pressure on the littoral region.

A 70-year history (1880–1950) of land use for the three districts – 24 Parganas, Bakargang and Khulna – reveals massive transformation of the land. Between 1880 and 1950, cultivated land in these districts expanded by 45%. During this period, the human population of these districts increased from 5.6 million to 12.9 million persons. Large-scale land clearance occurred between 1940 and 1950, with cropland increasing by 23% (Sarkar, 2010; Richard & Flint, 1990). This reflects a response to two large traumatic events – the Bengal famine of 1943 and the massive movement of refugees in both directions across the newly created India–Pakistan border following the 1947 Partition.

The politics of embankment construction post-partition

In independent India, the 3500-kilometer embankment protecting 54 inhabited islands in South 24 Parganas, West Bengal, came about through the Irrigation Department. However, the Irrigation Department prioritized its embankment program and has been selective in devoting funds for riverine embankments on the coastal seaboard. The problem of flooding and erosion menaces the Ganga-Padma floodplain as it enters Malda and Murshidabad, because it not only engulfs thickly populated settlements in the Gangetic plains and results in the loss of fertile agricultural land, but also endangers national property like the railway, national highways, the feeder canal at Farakka Barrage and many places of archaeological, historical and religious importance (Irrigation and Waterways 1989, 1990 and 1991). However, the same flood management department is silent and non-active with respect to the problem of erosion in the Sundarbans. Since erosion and tidal surges here affect the poor peasant and Scheduled Caste communities who reside on the margins of the national imagination on reclaimed wastelands, the tragedies caused by super cyclones in the Sundarban coastal settlements do not attain national importance, and neither do they inform policy making on disaster management.

However, to say this is not to suggest that *bunds* (embankments) are not protected in the Sundarbans. The Irrigation Department's actual track record of embankment building and repair further explains the vulnerability of the coastal communities to sea surges and tropical cyclones. Soon after the Aila cyclone in May 2009, in a local newspaper circulated in the Sundarbans called *Badweep Barta*, the Communist Party of India Marxist led Left-front government was blamed for not maintaining the height of the Sundarban embankments (*Bawdeep* Barta, 2009). The newspaper reported:

> The Left-Front Government is in power for thirty-two years. Why did the Government fail in strengthening the embankments and increasing their heights? What did the Irrigation Department of the West Bengal Government do in taking care of the embankments in thirty-two years? After the Aila, the Left Government of West Bengal has planned to spend Rupees ten thousand crores in building and constructing the Sundarban embankments. However, this hardly boosts the morals and the poverty of Aila stricken islanders. In 2006 Rupees 85 Lakhs was spent in rebuilding 500 meters of embankment in Basanti block, the embankment collapsed in fifteen days. (*Badweep* Barta, 2009, translated from Bengali)

The local newspaper report hinted at the corruption surrounding the process of building embankments in the Sundarbans. While the Sundarbans' existing embankment may be ecologically unsustainable, the possibility of a ring embankment provides the engineers and contractors with an opportunity to make money. Decisions about how much of the land would be acquired for building new embankments are left entirely to the discretion of the engineers. They justify such acquisition on the pretext that it is they who are better able to judge what is 'good' for the purpose. With the help of contractors, the engineers acquire land for the purposes of building such ring embankments. Rarely are people compensated for the loss of their land.

Thus, the story of embankment protection in the Sundarbans is also one of continuous land acquisition without any compensation being offered to people. Here marginality does not simply result from the low priority assigned to people's problems, but also from the way in which their problems are addressed. Therefore, disasters caused by cyclones should not be viewed simply as a fundamental interruption to social and political life, but as another manifestation of pre-existing processes of power relations between the dominant and subaltern caste groups (De Wall, 2006).

Prasenjit sarkhel, in his study of embankments built under the Mahatma Gandhi National Rural Employment Guarantee Scheme, teases out another dimension to the embankment debate. His evaluation, based on econometric statistics generated from Irrigation Department reports, reveals that embankments constructed under this program remain vulnerable because of their inefficiency toward the public welfare (Sarkhel, 2009, p. 7). Hence we need to question the relevance of embankment programs that are not seen by the cyclone-affected community as effective measures.

Post-independence: the pressure of migration and the burden on the Sundarbans

The Partition of India transformed the power equation in West Bengal between the different caste groups. The upper caste lobby within the Indian National Congress successfully partitioned Bengal only to quell the Namasudra movement that was building a political platform in East Bengal in alliance with the Muslim League. Partition not only changed the demographic profile of Bengal but also signaled the dominance of the upper caste in the newly created West Bengal state of the Indian federation. The Namasudra movement weakened as Bengal was partitioned (Bandyopadhyay, 1997) and the majority of the lower caste people now had to migrate to West Bengal from East Pakistan. Their low social status and poor social network forced them to migrate out of Kolkata, which was occupied by the post-Partition upper caste and the land owning gentry who were the traditional *zamindars* and *bhadroloks* of Bengal. The *bhadrolok* families migrated to cities and towns and found high-ranking and white-collar jobs in public institutions, as they were forced to change their professions due to the abolition of the zamindari system in Bengal. Partition had a deep impact on the demographic profile of West Bengal as population pressure amplified with refugees arriving as new immigrants (Das, 2000; Samanta, 2001; Tan and Kudaisya, 2001).

Most of the 1947 Partition migrants first traveled to Kolkata, but subsequent migrants could not find shelter in the city and were transferred to refugee camps in Orissa and other parts of India (Mallick, 1999). Nonetheless, many migrants who belonged to the lower classes and had come from coastal Khulna, Barisal and Chittagong stayed back and later migrated to the Sundarbans. I discovered notes of petition made by the refugees for rehabilitation in the Hamilton zamindari. While interacting with officials in the land registration and records department in Gosaba, I was made aware of the land that was kept for refugee rehabilitation in the Sundarbans during the premiership of Pandit Jawaharlal Nehru, most of which has never been redistributed to the refugee settlers in Bengal but instead was taken by people under *benami* proprietorship.

The wave of refugee migration was seen by the upper caste population of Kolkata as a threat to their cultural status. The trail of migration continued even after the 1971 India–Pakistan War. The Congress government felt that with the creation of Bangladesh, the refugee problem could be resolved, but this was never realized (Sammadar, 1999). The additional influx of Hindu refugees, most of whom belong to the lower classes, has created additional pressure on the land, with most of the refugees settling in makeshift camps along railway lines and in public spaces. Some were rehabilitated in relief and rehabilitation colonies while most of them lived in illegal settlements (Chatterji, 2007).

In the 24 Parganas Sundarbans, migration began during the early nineteenth century when these lands were opened for settlement after experiments with land reclamation in Backargang and Khulna (Westland, 1871). We gather from the Hamilton Public Trust records that people migrated to this land from central India – Chota Nagpur, Khulna and other parts of South Bengal – in search of new land and freedom from the bondage of moneylenders. The progressive co-operative Hamilton zamindari also attracted upper caste families who joined the Education and Agricultural Department of Hamilton as schoolteachers, agricultural demonstrators, supervisors and medical staff. The peasantry was composed of lower caste tenants (from Khulna, Medenipur and tribal belts of central India) who were dependent on *khas* land (government land) on a *bhag chasi*, or sharecropping, arrangement with the estate, while many were given free land in return for clearing the forest. The population pressure, though minuscule in the beginning, grew rapidly after Partition and reached an upper threshold when immigrants started pouring in from East Pakistan and later Bangladesh.

The Congress party was not in favor of the new immigrants and this brought the Revolutionary Socialist Party and the Communist Party of India (Marxist) to the center stage of provincial politics. While the Communist Party was in favor of the refugee peasants and the entire working class it was not prepared to settle them in Sundarbans, on the grounds of protecting the Tiger Reserve. In 1979, it went on to forcefully evict the refugees who had settled in Marichjhanpi Island close to the Sundarban Tiger Reserve (Bhattacharjee, 2010;

Chatterjee, 1992; Jalais, 2005, 2011; Mallick, 1993, 1999; Pal, 2010). The resulting political violence over a small group of helpless refugee citizens did not challenge the political mandate of the Left government ruled by the microscopic minority of upper caste elites. The Left government, after its initial land reform and redistribution policies, was negligent in relation to bringing about rural development in the Sundarbans, and this continues today under the Trinomool Congress government. The political economy of the region is based upon a history of deep neglect and discrimination. This has been the trend followed by previous governments and continues even today, with no electricity or proper road or communication networks, and poor embankment management that periodically threatens settlements and agriculture in the region.

In the late 1970s, with the influx of Hindu immigrants from Bangladesh, marine fishing increased in the coastal towns of Kak Dwip and Namkhana. Land prices skyrocketed and many of the new immigrant settlers made money through the marine fishing trawler business. This period also saw the boom in shrimp farming in the region that attracted people of all ages and genders. Outside capital owners leased land from small peasants who were disillusioned with mono cropping, which produced little surplus. The shrimp farming business, which had been assumed to have a bright future, suffered a setback in the 1990s as the prawns developed a viral disease. The outside capitalist investors in shrimp farming now began to neglect the embankments, sluice gates and dug canals, finding the business unprofitable. The fish owners incurred huge losses due to the viral disease as export declined, and a new phase of land transformation began. As West Bengal did not have a single farm for prawn hatchlings, these had to be imported from Tamil Nadu, which raised the cost further. These abandoned aquaculture farms subsequently started getting converted into brick kilns that now dot the entire landscape along Barasat road on the outskirts of Kolkata. Ironically, the fishery fields are again leased out to outside capitalists against a higher lease rate and longer tenure than was the case for aquaculture lands. The shrimp farming and brick kiln industry has had a deep impact on the coastal environment, as the mangrove forests that had acted as a buffer to the cyclonic storms were systematically cleared (CSE, 2012). The Sundarban forest has been reduced to a great extent in human habitation areas as the land use has changed significantly.

With the declaration of the Sundarbans as a World Heritage site by UNESCO in 1987, it has been attracting an ever-growing number of foreign and domestic tourists. The tourism industry got a boost after the Leftist (Communist Party of India (Marxist)) government lost power in 2011 to the Trinomool Congress. The new government has been permitting local entrepreneurs and tour agencies to intensify eco-tourism with the sole motive of improving the revenue base of the delta. However, this has endangered the waterways and backwaters of the Sundarbans, as the pressure on the region's ecosystem builds up and mechanized engine boats ferrying tourists spill diesel oil, polluting the untouched backwaters. Similarly, cargo transport between Dhaka and Kolkata is carried out through the Sundarbans, with the heavy freight vessels carrying fly ash displacing thousands of liters of water every day, which creates pressure on the banks of the fragile islands that are vulnerable to bank erosion and tides. Unauthorized tourist resorts and hotels have expanded all over Gosaba island facing the Sajnakhali Forest Reserve, on government *khas* and private *rayat* land. They are placed dangerously close to the receding embankments and are vulnerable to embankment breaches.

Besides such unplanned anthropogenic intervention, big corporate houses and chit fund companies have invested in mega resorts in the region. The Gulshan group proposed in 2011 to build a tourist resort at a cost of over 100 crore rupees ($18 million) in Gosaba. The resort proposed to build multi-storeyed apartments and a helipad where the tourists could directly land in and take off from the resort. All such unplanned construction has made the lives of the villagers living in these islands precarious and increasingly vulnerable to tropical storms.

Gulshan Group Resort advertisement in Pakhiraloy, Gosaba Island, Sundraban. Photo credit Debojyoti Das.

The ecological nemesis: Cyclone Aila and its impact

On the 25th of May 2009, a severe cyclone named Aila hit the Bay of Bengal's coastal rim with a tidal surge of up to 6.5 meters, affecting eleven coastal districts. The seawater surge damaged and washed away over 1700 kilometers of embankments (Debnath, 2013). The tidal surge caused flooding over the entire region, increasing the salinity and pH of the water to high levels. It differed from preceding super cyclones in that the after-effects of the cyclone can be traced through people's livelihoods: particularly, the marginalized Scheduled Caste community of seafarers, petty peasants and the people who depend on foresting who were forced to migrate a long distance to gain employment soon after the cyclone. The timing of the cyclone during the pre-monsoon dry season turned out to be a catastrophe because the inundating seawater leached deep into the subsoil and vastly increased the salinity. The cyclone's impact was not unexpected due to years of the state neglecting to construct seaboard embankments and cyclone defenses through mangrove regeneration, making the built-up settlements and agricultural fields in the Sundarbans vulnerable to tropical surges.

The cyclone inundated people's homes, washed away villages, destroyed standing crops and cattle and led to salt deposition over fertile croplands, turning them into barren wastelands. The effect of Cyclone Aila on people's livelihoods and farming triggered the emigration of people from their farms for employment. The cyclone is deeply imprinted on the local communities' memories. Cyclone eyewitnesses and victims recollected the horrors of the cyclone that triggered the seawater inundation. The embankment breaches and the push of salt water from the sea surges resulted in flooding of the islands that remained for more than a week, paralyzing rescue and relief efforts. According to a report published by the Deccan Herald on 30th May 2010, more than 22,000 people living in the Sundarban delta were affected by Cyclone Aila in West Bengal alone (*The Deccan Herald*, 30 May 2010).

This was just one more natural calamity to add to the Sundarbans' disaster history. Politicians, policy-makers and non-governmental organizations in their rescue and relief reports declared Aila's devastation as incomprehensible and a natural calamity that humans only dared to imagine. In the aftermath of the cyclone, members of civil society organizations, religious groups and donor agencies like the World Bank and the federal government's Planning Commission staff visited the areas devastated by the cyclone. A local journalist had kept in his depositary a collection of photographs that he took soon after the devastation, and also showed us pictures of World Bank officials' and the Planning Commission Chairman Montek Singh Aluwalia's visit to the Gosaba island. They organized meetings and assured people of financial help. The Planning Commission announced Rs 2000 crores ($360 million) for repairing damaged houses, paying compensation to victims, and for building stronger concrete embankments and dykes on the island.

The disaster, as my informants revealed, had long been in the making. Decades of state apathy towards embankment construction, corruption and misuse of grants by *Gram Panchayat* (Village Council) meant that embankments were never properly built, nor were they managed to the standards set by the Public Works Department. Much of the embankment repair and restoration work was delayed and embankment grants embezzled by village henchman, contractors, politicians and officials involved in embankment construction. The devastation was primarily caused by seawater inundation following embankment breaches. Such breaches had happened in the past decade, affecting small areas and a few islands, but Cyclone Aila tested the embankment resilience and proved to be the most catastrophic cyclone in living memory.

The biggest damage was faced by the island's farmers and fishermen, as saline water remained in their cropland and fisheries, causing major damage to standing crops and killing fish. My respondents observed that the 1988 cyclone was much more severe than Aila and yet it caused little damage to their agricultural fields and inland fisheries were not flooded. Houses were damaged but their livelihood was untouched, and life returned to normal in the post-reconstruction phase. In the post-Aila scenario, not only were houses lost but communities living on the island lost their livelihoods. Villagers cited the timing of the cyclone as significant – as it was in the pre-monsoon season, the dry earth absorbed the saline water from the sea.

The natural disaster, as my respondents maintained, was manmade due to the neglect of embankment management by the state and village authorities. Storm surges, gales and low-pressure conditions are natural weather events in the tropical coastline annually.

Some of the low-pressure conditions result in catastrophic cyclones. Archaeological research based on excavations done by the Archaeological Survey of India, Kolkata, and by independent specialists like Krishnokali Mondol show that the islands have been immersed by sea water surges and fluvial processes that have created and destroyed sandbars since prehistoric times, and that natural disasters and geomorphic changes are an everlasting feature of a delta region vulnerable to tropical storms and bank erosion (Mondol, 2001; Banu, 2012).

The question that this naturally evokes in our minds is: why did Cyclone Aila become so disastrous? Was it a natural disaster wherein the state did not have the capacity to preclude its outcome? Or was it merely the lack of political will, or both? If we are to find answers to these complex questions we have to reflect back upon the long history of environmental change in the Sundarban delta. The goal is not to present an overly deterministic agenda of human–environment interaction, but to examine the politics of colonial intervention and colonial policy making, as well as the environmental changes that have occurred in the delta through the subsequent peopling of its islands.

The Cyclone Aila disaster is invariably linked to the human habitation of a region susceptible to riverbank erosion, a rising sea level and tropical storms. The vulnerability of such a landscape is increased as population numbers swell and governments deliberately avoid taking adequate disaster preparedness measures or measures aiding communities to live sustainably.

During my yearlong fieldwork in the Sundarbans (2012–2013), I conducted participant observation and interviews with state officials, policy-makers and NGO staff who were not aware on how to prepare for cyclone disasters. In one of my interviews, Gosaba's Block Development Officer (BDO) observed that their job was limited to project management. In the post-Aila disaster mitigation effort, they are engaged in monitoring the construction of a number of multipurpose cyclone structures built under the Prime Minister's National Disaster Management Relief Fund funded by the World Bank. When asked about how the block administration measures vulnerability, the BDO replied that the absence of *pucca* houses defines the degree of vulnerability of these islands. When I explained to them that the coastal belt still relied on the colonial weather forecasts and early warning system and that there was a need for a more modern early warning system at the block level, the BDO pointed to the higher lever authorities who take decisions on matters of disaster preparedness. In 2013, I was eyewitness to the disaster preparedness for Cyclone Mahasen, which coincidentally did not reach the South 24 Parganas Sundarbans. The block level authorities made an announcement in the villages of Gosaba block only after the cyclone touched the coastline and it was only by chance that everybody was safe as the cyclone changed its trail toward Myanmar after hitting the Bangladesh coastline.

When I enquired about the delay of the block officials to inform villagers of the coming cyclone, the BDO said that they still followed the colonial system of cyclone warning through telephone communication from the Deputy Magistrate's office in Alipur, Kolkata, and that delayed the process of public announcements on the eve of the cyclone. Adding to the bureaucratic red-tape, the provincial government was ill equipped, with no early warning system. Fishermen are the most vulnerable during cyclone disasters. One of the fishermen whom I interviewed mentioned that they relied on the Bangladeshi radio weather forecast, as this is more reliable at sea. Every year many fishermen lose their lives when cyclonic storms and strong gales drown their fishing vessels in high seas.

Cyclone Aila struck during daytime and did not produce high-speed cyclonic winds that would rip apart homesteads. Instead it produced sea surges. The impact of the cyclone was overwhelming due to embankment failures and the inundation of islands by seawater. In order to understand how Aila caused such widespread destruction in the Sundarbans, we must look at the history of human habitation, colonial policies of land reclamation and the ways in which Partition's forced migration has brought the coastal population into close proximity with potential cyclone disasters.

The impact of cyclone disasters is amplified due to the lack of resilience and the vulnerability produced by decades of neglect of embankment construction and a lack of vision in state disaster management programs, the result being that houses, cattle, standing crops and agricultural plots are all commonly lost to cyclones. The cyclone's impact is truly a manmade disaster in light of the fact that natural mangroves were degraded by human action, and particularly through the popularity of shrimp farming in the late 1970s. Even after Cyclone Aila, not much has been done to regenerate the mangrove forest, and neither have programs been developed and embankments and drainage systems built that suit the local environment. Vinod Bera, an eminent poet and intellectual of Sundarban, showed me his agricultural fields that were washed away by a flood and the land he has lost to the river. Local level developments like the filling up of small canals, streams and backwaters that join the main river have shown that it leads to heavy siltation that decreases the water holding capacity of the river channels and in return puts pressure on the islands.

The progress made in Sundarban villages over the decades was stalled by Cyclone Aila in 2009. Villagers explained that 10-meter deep seawater engulfed the islands and led to the salinization of cropland. Since 2009, double cropping has stopped and salt-water capillary action has destroyed every single food crop sown during the pre-monsoon season. A new trend in migration occurred following Cyclone Aila, from the village to the city. The loss of their livelihoods led to people migrating to Chennai, Gujarat, Andaman and Nicobar Islands and Delhi where they engaged themselves as manual laborers. Some have gained due to emigration; however, most of the migrants have entered a precarious life fighting with mosquitoes, falling sick, living in a poor environment and working too hard for low pay. Migrant villagers informed me that they have been at the mercy of middlemen who recruit villagers for contractual work and often run away with the wages. Incidences of the trafficking of women and children have come to light and in many distant villages, where *naam kirtan* (devotional chanting) and *jatra* (folk open air theater) were once revered, the sex trade and the viewing of pornographic adult videos have proliferated. The opening up of resorts has brought windfall profits to tour guides and hotel operators who run brisk business from November to March, while villagers participate as manual wage earners, cooks and night guards. However, many villagers now realize the negative impact of non-regulated tourism.

Poet Mukunda Gayen, a resident of Dayapur village, disclosed that tourism is only helping the outsiders who have opened up tourist lodges and resorts as well as the tour operators who depend on this business after the Cyclone Aila disaster. The regular visits of tourists have triggered noise and water pollution in the Sundarbans. They have also disturbed the village culture by bringing in urban habits such as drinking alcoholic drinks and wearing fancy clothes, which young villagers are keen to imitate. The other menace has been the use of mobile phones that promote conspicuous consumption and strain family incomes.

Activist Tushar Kanjilal who has been working among the villagers for the last four decades with his NGO, Tagore Society for Rural Development, explained when interviewed that change is an integral part of human evolution. In the Sundarbans, the devastation wrought by Cyclone Aila should not be seen as the end of life in the region. Rather, in one of his books he writes that the cyclone is a beginning for a new consciousness where people can grow through exploring their local traditions in order to fight back against the natural disaster through community participation and self-help. In the same vein, Sujit Sur, a retired schoolmaster from Gosaba, observes that in the Sundarbans, people have adapted to the harsh environment through their sheer hard labor and will to survive. Since medieval times, the region has witnessed many socio-political changes with the coming in of new kings, principalities and empires. Thus, it would be unfair to blame Cyclone Aila as the only major life-changing situation. This hybrid landscape has witnessed many changes and people have adapted over time to these life-churning events through their hard work. The emigration trend he observes will stop if people can eke out a living in the village by reclaiming the fertile land destroyed by saline water intrusion, a process that had already begun. During my stay in Gosaba and Kak Dwip, I witnessed many farmers engaging in double cropping while in Kak Dwip watermelon was again cultivated with brisk business.

Conclusion

The landscape of the Sundarbans is the product of two competing forces: the conversion of wetland forests to cropland, and the appropriation of the forests in reserves for biodiversity conservation such as mangrove megafauna and the protection of the endangered Bengal tiger. For two centuries, land-hungry peasants strove to transform the native tidal forest vegetation into an agro-ecosystem dominated by a paddy rice and fish culture (Richard and Flint, 1990). During the colonial period, their reclamation efforts were encouraged by *bhadrolok* landlords and speculators, who were themselves encouraged by increasingly favorable state policies (land grants, tax incentives, cadastral surveys and eventually colonization projects), designed by revenue officials to maximize the rate of transformation of wetland mangrove swamps to taxable agricultural land. In the post-independence period, the region further became populated with East Bengal refugees who mostly belonged to the lower caste population. The natural disasters that strike the Sundarbans such as cyclones Aila and Mahasen should not be interpreted as natural calamities triggered by global warming and tropical low pressure alone, as the effects of these cyclones have become catastrophic because of settlements that are defenseless to tropical storms. For too long the colonial policy was to build upon the notion of controlling the river and estuary regime in the Sundarbans by constructing embankments and *bunds* that failed, both because of state neglect and their ineffective construction. Here we need to understand that cyclones and tropical storms can be better managed by building the capacity for adaptation and resilience among local communities and by reducing those inequalities caused by social, political and economic marginalization of communities living along the coastal seaboard. Consequently, the naturalization of disasters by the epistemic community of 'experts' and policymaker's needs to be revised and critically examined when making policies for the future.

Notes

1. In the initial period, leases were granted by the Collector General, Claud Russell, to individuals during 1770–1773 on certain conditions. The lands were to be held free of rent for several years generally, after which they were to be subject to a yearly progressive assessment up to the full rate of 12, 8 or 6 annas per *bigha* according to their quality, which was to be determined by a survey conducted on the expiration of the fee period. Fresh measurement would take place once in every 10 years and necessary adjustments in the rent would be made. The land that came under this system of grants was known as *patitabadi taluks* – meaning the cultivation of wastelands.
2. Henckell's administrative tenure in the region (1783–1789) had to accommodate various factors at work-Magh piratical incursions, hostility of the neighboring *zamindars*, activities of the salt manufacturers and the operation of the weavers. Also the boundary dispute between the neighboring *zamindars* and the grantees in this region was not easy to solve. The boundary line was in a state of flux as it was subjected to periodic redefinition under the supervision of the various Collector Generals in this area. Hanckell thus failed in the benevolent paternalism adopted in his land reclamation program in Hankelgunj or Hingelgunj.
3. According to the Census Report of Bengal, 1921, 1931, edited by Thompson and Porter, Pods comprised 84% of the population in 24 Parganas, Khulna and Jessore while the Namashudras composed of more than 50% of the population in Bakarganj, Faridpur, Khulna and Jessore.
4. Henry Piddington, President of the Marine Courts of Enquiry at Calcutta, developed 'The Law of Storm.' Between 1830 and 1858, Paddington published in the *Journal of the Asiatic Society of Bengal* in the form of 20 articles under the title 'Law of Storm.' The law made its impact on navigation and safety for commercial freights in the Indian Ocean and Bay of Bengal after his death when it was further developed by the imperial metrological department staff and geologist working in the colony (see Eliot, 1900; Ross, 1869).
5. The issue has been discussed in many colonial accounts including Tirthankar Roy, in his book titled *Natural disasters and Indian history* (2012). Also look at the unpublished PhD thesis on the littoral region of Bengal by Ben Kingsbury submitter at the University of Wellington, New Zealand (2015), titled *An imperial disaster: The Bengal cyclone of 1876*.
6. J.C. Jack presents a typical descent from estate holders down to 160 petty tenure holders who in turn collected rents from 360 cultivating peasants. (1) A zamindar with an estate of 2000 acres and paying revenue of Rs 200, (2) Four *talukdars* each with a subordinate taluk of 500 acres and paying a rent of Rs 100 to the zamindar, (3) Twenty *osat talukdars* each with a revenue of 25 acres and paying a rent of Rs 25 to one of the 20 *takukdars*, and (4) 160 *nim hoaldars* each with a tenure of 12.5 acres and paying a rent of Rs 20 to one of the 80 *hoaldars* and he has sublet in turn to two cultivators in an ordinary *raiyati* lease stipulating a payment of Rs 55 rent apiece (see Jack, 1915, p. 52).

Acknowledgements

I would like to thank the two anonymous reviewers for their critical comments and constructive feedback.

Disclosure statement

No potential conflict of interest was reported by the authors.

Funding

This research has received funding from the European Research Council under the European Union's Seventh Framework Programme (FP/2007-2013)/ERC Grant Agreement [284053], for the project 'Coastal frontiers: Water, power, and the boundaries of South Asia,' with Dr Sunil Amrith as PI.

References

Ascoli, F. D. (1921). (2002) (reprint) *A revenue history of the Sundarbans: From 1870 to 1920* (Vol. 2). West Bengal District Gazetteers. Kolkata: Bengal Secretariat Book Depot.

Baddeley, R. F. H. (1853). On dust whirlwind and cyclones. *The Journal of the Asiatic Society of Bengal*, 21, 264–269.

Bandopadhyay, A., & Matilal, A. (2003). *The philosopher's stone: Speeches and writings of Sir Daniel Hamilton*. Calcutta: Das Gupta and Co.

Bandyopadhyay, S. (1997). *Caste, protest and identity in colonial India: The Namasudras of Bengal 1872–1947*. Surrey: Curzon.

Bankoff, G., & Christensen, J. (2016). Bordering on danger: An introduction. In G. Bankoff & J. Christensen (Eds.), *Natura Hazards and Peoples in the Indian Ocean World: Bordering on Danger* (pp. 1–30). London: Palgrave Macmillan.

Banu, G. (2012). *Pratna-Ithas o Shilpa Charca (A unique collection of selected essays on archaeology, art, history and culture of South Bengal)*. Baruipur: Baruipur Book Depot.

Barta, B. (2009). *Sammekshar Daitwa Kar? Battris bachharer sasane bund samanya unchu holo na keno* [Whose responsibility was the survey? Why wasn't the height of the bund slightly increased in thirty-two years]. West Bengal: Canning press.

Bhattacharjee, T. (2010). *Aprakishito Marichjhanpi (unpublished Marichjhanpi)*. Kolkata: Freethinkers.

Blanford, H. F. (1868). On the origin of a cyclone. *Proceedings of the Royal Society of London*, 17, 472–482.

Centre for Science and Environment. (2012). *Report on living with changing climate: Impact, vulnerability and adaptation challenges in Indian Sundarbans*. New Delhi: Centre for Science and Environment.

Chatterjee, N. (1992). *Midnight's unwanted children: East Bengali refugees and the politics of rehabilitation* (PhD dissertation). Brown University.

Chatterji, J. (2007). *The spoils of partition*. Cambridge: Cambridge University Press.

Das, S. K. (2000). Refugee crisis: Responses of the government of West Bengal. In P. K. Bose (Ed.), *Refugees in West Bengal: Institutional practices and contested identities* (pp. 106–151). Calcutta: Mahanirban Calcutta Research Group.

D'souza, R. (2006). *Dammed and drowned: Colonial capitalism and flood control in Eastern India*. New Delhi: Oxford University Press.

Debnath, A. (2013). Condition of agricultural productivity of Gosaba C. D block, south 24 Parganas, West Bengal, India after severe Cyclone Aila. *International Journal of Scientific and Research Publications*, 3(7), 1–4.

Deccan Herald. (2010). *Cyclone Aila affects agriculture in Sundarbans*. May. Retrieved January 1, 2015, from www.deccanherald.com › National.

De Wall, A. (2006). Towards a comparative political ethnography of disaster prevention. *Journal of International Affairs*. Retrieved January 1, 2015, from http://www.accessmylibrary.com/article-IGI-146073422/towards-comperative-politicalethnography.html.

Eaton, R. M. (1994). *The rise of Islam and the Bengal frontier 1204–1760*. Berkeley: University of California Press.

Eliot, J. (1900). *Handbook of cyclonic storm in the Bay of Bengal: For the use of sailors* (2nd ed. and 2 vols.). Calcutta: Government Press.

Endfield, G. H., Davies, S. J., Tejedo, I. F., Metcalfe, S. E., & O'Hara, S. L. (2009). Documenting disasters: Archival investigations of climate, crisis and catastrophes in colonial Mexico. In C. Mauchs & C. Pfister (Eds.), *Natural disasters: Case studies towards a global environmental history* (pp. 306–325). Plymouth: Lexinton Books.

Facus, R. L. (1927). *Final report on the survey settlement operation in the district of Khulna, 1920–26*. Calcutta: Government Press.

Grove, R. H. (1995). *Green imperialism: Colonial expansion, Tropical Island Edens and the origins of environmentalism 1600–1860*. Cambridge: Cambridge University Press.

Harvey, D. (1993). The nature of environment: Dialectics of social and environmental change. *Socialist Register, 21*, 1–51.

Hill, C. (1997). *River of sorrow: Environmental and social control in Riparian North India, 1770–1994*. Ann Arbor, MI: Association of Asian Studies.

Iqbal, I. (2007). The railways and the water regime of the Eastern Bengal delta, c1845–1943. *Internationals Asian Forum, 38*, 329–352.

Jack, J. C. (1915). *Final report of the survey settlement operations in the district of Bakarganj 1900 to 1908 (p. 52)*. Calcutta: Government Press.

Jalais, A. (2005). Dwelling on Morichjhanpi: When tigers become 'citizens', refugees 'tiger-food'. *Economic and Political Weekly, 40*(17), 1757–1762.

Jalais, A. (2011). *Forest of tigers: People, politics and environment in the Sundarbans*. Delhi: Routledge.

Jalil, M. F. S. (1986). *Sundarbaner Ithas* [Sundarbans history]. Dhaka: Bangla Publication.

Kapur, A. (2010). *Vulnerable India: A geographical study of disasters*. Delhi: IIAS and Sage.

Kingsbury, B. (2015). *An imperial disaster: The Bengal cyclone of 1876* (Unpublished PhD thesis). University of Wellington, New Zealand.

Klingensmith, D. (2007). *Dams, nationalism and development*. New Delhi: Oxford University Press.

Mallick, R. (1993). *Development policy of a communist government: West Bengal since 1977*. Cambridge: Cambridge University Press.

Mallick, R. (1999). Refugee settlements in forest reserves: West Bengals policy reversal and the Marichjhanpi Massacre. *The Journal of Asian Studies, 58*(1), 104–125.

Mitra, Satish. (1914). *Jassore Khulna ithas* [A history of Jassore and Khulna] (Vol. 1). Calcutta: Bengal Press.

Mondol, K. (2001). *Dokkhin Chobbishporgonar Loukik Deb-Debi O Murti Bhabna (Prothom Porbo)*. Kolkata: Nobo Cholontika [In Bangla].

Mukherjee, R. (1938). *The changing face of Bengal: A study of riverine economy*. Calcutta: Calcutta University Press.

Oliver-Smith, A. (1996). Anthropological research on hazard and disaster. *Annual Review of Anthropology, 30*(5), 303–328.

Paddington, H. (1849). A seventeenth memoir on the law of storm in India; being storm of China seas from 1842–1847, and some of the northern Pacific Ocean from 1797. *Journal of Asiatic Society of Bengal, 18*, 1–45.

Paddington, H. (1853). A twenty first memoir of the law of storm in the Indian and China Sea. *Journal of the Asiatic Society of Bengal, 21*, 283–328.

Pal, M. (Ed.). (2010). *Marichjanpi: Chinno Desh, Chinno Ithas* [Marichjanpi: Broken bond: Broken history]. Kolkata: Gangchil Publishing House.

Richard, J. F., & Flint, E. P. (1990). Long term transformations in the Sundarbans wastelands forest of Bengal. *Agriculture and Human Values, 7*(2), 17–33.

Ross, J. (1869). *The law of storm*. New York, NY: A Random and Co.

Roy, R. (1979). *Change in Bengal Agrarian society c1760–1850*. Delhi: Monahar.

Roy, T. (2010). The law of storm: European and Indigenous response to natural disasters in colonial India, c. 1800–1850. *Australian Economic History Review*, *50*(1), 6–22.

Roy, T. (2012). *Natural disasters and Indian history*. Oxford: Oxford University Press.

Roychoudhury, T. (1965). The agrarian system of Mughal India. *Enquiry*, Spring.

Samanta, A. (2001). Crop, climate and malaria: Ecological construction of an epidemic in colonial Bengal. *Economic and Political Weekly*, *36*(52), 4887–4890.

Sammadar, R. (1999). *The marginal nation: Trans border migration from Bangladesh to West Bengal*. New Delhi: Sage.

Sarkar, S. C. (2010). *The Sundarbans: Folk deities, monsters and mortals*. New Delhi: Orient Blackswan.

Sarkhel, P. (2009). *Vulnerability from embankment damage in Indian Sundarbans: Recent evidences from cyclone Aila* (SANDEE Working Paper). Kathmandu, Nepal: SANDEE.

Shaw, R. (2014). Nature, culture and disaster: Flood and gender in Bangladesh. In M. R. Dove (Ed.), *The anthropology of climate change: An historical reader* (pp. 223–234). Oxford: Willey Blackwell.

Singh, P. (2008). The colonial state, *zamindars* and the politics of flood control in North Bihar (1850–1945). *Indian Economic and Social History Review*, *45*(2), 261–294.

Steinberg, T. (2006). *Acts of God: The unnatural history of natural disasters in America* (2nd ed.). New York, NY: Oxford University Press.

Tan, T. Y., & Kudaisya, G. (Ed.). (2001). *The aftermath of partition in South Asia*. New York, NY: Routledge.

Westland, J. (1871). *A report on the district of Jessore, its antiquities, its histories and its commerce*. Calcutta: Government Press.

Index

Note: **Boldface** page numbers refer to tables & italic page numbers refer to figures. Page numbers followed by "n" refer to endnotes.

Aceh Monitoring Mission (AMM) 107–8
Ackroyd, John Henry 54
ACP *see* African Caribbean Pacific
'acquis communautaire' 119
Across the kalapani: The Bihari presence in Mauritius (Carter) 73
Acts of God (Steinberg) 128
Admiraal Evertsen 50
ADSU *see* Anti-Drug and Smuggling Unit
Africa–EU multidimensional policy framework 106
Africa–EU Strategic Partnership 106
African Caribbean Pacific (ACP) 113–14
African Union (AU) 87; African Maritime Transport Charter 109; Mission in Somalia 108
Agalega Ltd 58
'Agenda 21, Rio Declaration on Development and Environment' 85
Agrippine, R. 94
AIADMK *see* All India Anna Dravida Munnetra Kazhagam
Aila (cyclone) 138–42
AIMS *see* Atlantic, Indian Ocean, Mediterranean and South China Sea
All India Anna Dravida Munnetra Kazhagam (AIADMK) 21n9
Aluwalia, Montek Singh 139
America, disaster in 129
AMM *see* Aceh Monitoring Mission
Andaman and Nicobar Islands 32–4; access to facilities in 33; India's military capabilities in 32–3
Anti-Drug and Smuggling Unit (ADSU) 89, 90, 96
Anti-Piracy Unit (APU) of IOC 94, 117
Appanah, N. 73–5
AP-3C Orion 30, 37, 38

Article 198 TFEU 112
Article 355 TFEU 119
Article 349 TFEU 119
Arya Samaj 68
Ascoli, F. D. 131
ASEAN *see* Association of Southeast Asian Nations
Asia Regional Multi-Annual Indicative Programme 118, 119
Association of Southeast Asian Nations (ASEAN) 106
Athulathmudali, Lalith 7
Atlantic, Indian Ocean, Mediterranean and South China Sea (AIMS) 86
Auguste, Alexandre 52
Australian Defence Force Posture Review 38
Australian Defence White Paper (2016) 27
Australia's Indian Ocean territories 2, 26; island territories 29–30; regional defense partnerships 39–40; strategic changes 27–9; surveillance aircraft 30; *see also* Christmas Island; Cocos Island

Babbage, R. 36, 37
Badweep Barta 135
'Baixos dos Chagas' 46, 47
balancing, Sri Lanka foreign policy behavior 5, 7, 9–10, 19
bandwagoning, as Sri Lanka foreign policy behavior 5, 7, 10–14, 19
Ban Ki Moon 93
Bankoff, G. 129
Barbados + 5 review document (1999) 86
Basrur, R. 9
Bateman, S. 37
'Belt & Road Initiative' 28, 32
Bengal: Census Report of 143n3; partition of 135–6
Bera, Vinod 141
Bergin, A. 37
Berkeley, Henry 53
BIOT *see* British Indian Ocean Territory

INDEX

Bishal, Khitish 132
Bissoondoyal, Basdeo 76
Biswas, Kumud Ranjan 130
Blood, Hilary 57
Boeing P-8 maritime aircraft 40
Boswell, R. 60
Boucherat, Arthur 54
Brewster, D. 2
BREXIT 112–15, 119
Britain/British: land reclamation and revenue program 130–2; Royal Navy 27, 30; territorial claims 30
British Indian Ocean Territory (BIOT) 45, 46, 59, 107, 111–13
Brzezinski, Z. 107
bunds (embankments), in Sundarban delta: debate on 135; Irrigation Department 134; local newspaper report 135; political economy of 132–4; protection of 135; repair and restoration work 139; Sarkhel's study of 135; social cost 133; *zamindars* and colonial state 133

Caboche, Raoul 56
Canning 131
Cantino map 46
Car Nicobar Island 33
Carter, M. 2, 73
Ceasefire Agreement (CFA) 14
CEPA *see* Comprehensive Economic Partnership Agreement
Certeau, M. 66
CFA *see* Ceasefire Agreement
CGPCS *see* Contact Group on Piracy off the Coast of Somalia
CGS Barracuda 97, 98
Chagos Archipelago 2, 45, 111–13; Dutch shipping 46–7; experiences of Ilois 56–61; human settlement on 46–7; Mauritius–Britain dispute over 30; population of 54; post-1965 literature of 45; women workers' daily routine 56; *see also* Ilois, experiences of; labor history
Chan Low, J. 59
Chazal, M. (de) 76
Chellaney, B. 107
China: Maritime Silk Road initiative 15; Sri Lanka's foreign policy shift towards 8–9, 14–15
China, in Indian Ocean Region: anti-piracy operations 32; Belt & Road Initiative 28, 32; counter-piracy exercises 29; infrastructure development 31–2; naval presence 28–9, 32, 34, 39; 'String of Pearls' strategy 32
Chinese Harbor Engineering Company 13
Christensen, J. 129
Christmas Island 2, 26, 34; airfield at 38; Australia's ability to defend 36–8; distance between other locations and **35**; facilities in 41; immigration detention center 36; military infrastructure in 40; naval infrastructure on 37; proximity, to Southeast Asia 38–9; strategic value of 36; upgrades of infrastructure on 38–9
Claveyrolas, M. 2
Clémentin-Ojha, C. 73
CMR program *See* Critical Maritime Routes program
Cocos Island 2, 26, 34; Australia's ability to defend 36–8; distance between other locations and **35**; facilities in 41; military infrastructure 40; naval infrastructure 37; strategic value of 35, 36; upgrades of infrastructure on 38–9
colonization process 72
Colpitts, G. 96–7
command, communications, control, computers, ISR (C4ISR) 41
Common Foreign and Security Policy 107
Common Market for Eastern and Southern Africa (COMESA) 70
Common Security and Defence Policy (CSDP) 107; Aceh Monitoring Mission (2005–6) 107–8; CRIMARIO project (2015–19) 110–11; Djibouti Code of Conduct (2009) 108–9; Eastern and Southern Africa-Indian Ocean Region (2010) 109; EUCAP Nestor mission (2012–17) 110; EU Maritime Security Strategy (2014) 110–11; EU's Foreign and Security Policy (2016) 111; Naval operation (2008–18) 108
Communist Party of India (Marxist) 135, 136
competitive educational system 71
Comprehensive Economic Partnership Agreement (CEPA) 6, 9, 16–17, 19, 22n29
Contact Group on Piracy off the Coast of Somalia (CGPCS) 88–9, 92, 93, 99
continental approach 106
Cotonou agreement 106, 118
creolization process 67
CRIMARIO project (2015–19) 110–11, 117
Critical Maritime Routes Law Enforcement Agencies (CRIMLEA) 98; CRIMLEA I project (2010–14) 108–9; CRIMLEA II project (2014–17) 109
Critical Maritime Routes (CMR) program 108–11
Crooke, W. 73
cross-border cooperation program 120
CSDP *see* Common Security and Defence Policy
Cutlass Express Maritime Exercise 97, 98
Cyclone Aila 138–42
Cyclone Mahasen 140

dam construction 134
Damodar Valley Corporation (DVC) 133–4
Das, Debojyoti 3
DCA *see* Defence Cooperation Agreement

148

INDEX

DCI *see* Development Cooperation Instrument
Decaen, Charles 50
Declaration on Maritime Safety and Security 109
Defence Cooperation Agreement (DCA) 6, 13, 18
Defence White Paper (2016) 38, 40
DeSilva-Ranasinghe, S. 8
Development Cooperation Instrument (DCI) 106, 118–19
Devi, A. 74
DeVotta, N. 9
Dhowan, R K 32
Diego-Agalega Shipping Ltd 58
Diego Garcia 1, 27; British expedition at 48–9; French presence on 48; functions 30; harbor and products of 47; in US defence strategy 30–1
Diego Ltd 57–8
disaster 128; in America 129; natural 129; nature and society 130
Disaster Management Relief Fund 140
Dissanayake, Gamini 7
Djibouti Code of Conduct (2009) 108–9
Djibouti Declaration (2016) 93
DMK *see* Dravida Munnetra Kazhagam
Dornier Do 228 reconnaissance aircraft 33
Dravida Munnetra Kazhagam (DMK) 13, 14
drug trafficking by sea, Mauritius' response to 94–8
Duperrel, Victor 49–50
Dupont, Ivanoff 54
Dussercle, R. 55, 56
DVC *see* Damodar Valley Corporation

Eastern Africa, Southern Africa and the Indian Ocean (EA-SA-IO) 116, 117, 121
Eastern and Southern Africa (ESA) 113
Eastern and Southern Africa-Indian Ocean Region (ESA-IO) 109, 117, 122
'Economic and Social Transformation Plan' 88
Economic Partnership Agreements (EPAs) 106, 113–14
EDF *see* European Development Fund
EEC *see* European Economic Community
EEC–Asia relationships 106
Eelam War IV (2006–2009) 14, 15
EEZ *see* Exclusive Economic Zone
Elephant Pass 12
EPAs *see* Economic Partnership Agreements
ERDF *see* European Regional Development Fund
ESA *see* Eastern and Southern Africa
ESA-IO *see* Eastern and Southern Africa-Indian Ocean Region
ESDP civilian mission 107–8
EU–African Caribbean Pacific track 106
EU–Africa policy framework 106
EU–ASEAN Partnership 106
EU–Asia framework 106
EUCAP Nestor mission (2012–17) 110
EU–Indian Ocean islands frameworks: European Development Fund 116–18; Instrument for Development Cooperation 118–19; Interreg programs 119–21
EU Maritime Security Strategy (EUMSS) 110
EU–Mauritius bilateral cooperation 118
EUMSS *see* EU Maritime Security Strategy
Euro–Mediterranean track 106
European Development Fund (EDF) 116–18
European Economic Community (EEC) 105
European Regional Development Fund (ERDF) 117, 120, 121
European Union 28 (EU 28) 114, 115
European Union (EU) 3, 87, 92; Association of Southeast Asian Nations 106; Critical Maritime Routes program 108–9; development cooperation policies 107; and Eastern and Southern Africa 113, 114–15; Election Observation Mission 116; ESDP civilian mission 107–8; Foreign and Security Policy 111; geo-economic level 113–16; global strategy for 121, 123; humanitarian assistance 118, 119; inter-governmental policy framework 107; Maldives–Sri Lanka relations with 106, 118–19; NAVFOR-ATALANTA operation 108; New Asia strategy 106; Outermost Regions 106; policy perspective 106; South Asian Association for Regional Cooperation 106; strategic role limits 111–13; Wider Indian Ocean approach 105; *see also* Common Security and Defence Policy; EU–Indian Ocean islands frameworks
EU–SAARC framework for cooperation 106, 118
EU–Sri Lanka Cooperation Agreement 113, 115–16
Everything But Arms (EBA) treatment 114
Exclusive Economic Zone (EEZ) 17, 83, 122

Facus, L. F. 133
Farquhar, Robert 50
Faure, D. 89, 94
Faye, Dupuis de la 47
Fernand Mandarin 57
Fisheries Partnership Agreement 117, 118
Fonseka, Sarath 16
foreign economic policy, Sri Lanka 5
foreign security policy, Sri Lanka 5
Free Aceh Movement (GAM) 107
Free Trade Agreements (FTAs) 8, 11–12; EU–Indian Ocean Islands 107, 113–16; Indonesia and India 121
French Southern and Antarctic Lands (FSAL) 112
French Southern and Antarctic Territories (FSAT) 112

INDEX

French White Paper on Security and Defence (2008) 107
FSAL *see* French Southern and Antarctic Lands
FSAT *see* French Southern and Antarctic Territories

GAM *see* Free Aceh Movement
Gan Atoll naval base 33
Gandhi, Indira 9, 10
Gandhi, Rajiv 11
Gayen, Mukunda 131, 141
General Organization of People of Indian Origin (GOPIO) 70
Ghosh, A. 73–5
'Global Strike' concept 30
GOPIO *see* General Organization of People of Indian Origin
Gordon-Gentil, A. 70, 71
GOSL *see* Government of Sri Lanka
Government of Indonesia 107
Government of Sri Lanka (GOSL) 4, 6, 13; Framework Agreement 22n17
Grégoire, E. 70
Grenier, Vicomte 47
Greville 51
GSP plus ('GSP+') 115–16
'Gujral Doctrine' 11
Gulf of Aden 32; anti-piracy operations in 28
Gulshan group, tourist resort 138, *138*
Gunasena, J. T. S. 9
Gungah, Dookhee 75
Gwadar (Pakistan) 32

HADR *see* humanitarian assistance and disaster relief
Haitian Revolution 61–2
Hambantota Development Zone 15
Hambantota Port 13, 18, 21n15
Hamilton, Daniel Mackinnon 131
Hanckell, Tilman 130, 143n2
Hanning, W. J. 55
Harvey, D. 130
Hazareesingh, K. 77
Hindu communities, in Mauritius 67, 69, 72, 74, 77
Hindu reformist movements 68
Hindutva 69, 78n6
HMS *Frolic* 53
HMS *Rapid* 53
homogeneous community 67
Hookoomsing, V. 76
Houbert, J. 59
Hugon, Paul 52
humanitarian assistance 118
humanitarian assistance and disaster relief (HADR) 40

Ilois, experiences of 45, 46, 56–61; Chagossians cultural changes 60; Diego Company's assets 57–8; expulsion of 46; harsh realities of 57; marginalization of, in Mauritius 60; removal from Chagos 59–60
IMO *see* International Maritime Organization
imperial disaster, An: The Bengal cyclone of 1876 (Kingsbury) 143n5
India 21n12, 32; access to Cocos 40; Australian and US relationships with 39–40; base in Andaman and Nicobar Islands 32–3; Hambantota Port proposal rejection 13; Mauritius relations with 34; relationship with Seychelles 33–4; Sri Lanka's foreign policy calculus 6–7; US assistance in naval capabilities 34
Indian Air Force 32–3
Indian civilization 77
Indian colonization 68
Indian Navy 32, 36; P-8I Poseidon 32
Indian Ocean: sea lines of communication 91; size of 83
Indian Ocean Commission (IOC) 94
Indian Ocean Region (IOR) 1–2; Australia's strategic importance of 27–8; Britain's dominant power in 30; Chinese infrastructure development in 28–9, 31–2; Indian military infrastructure in 32–4; Japan's interest in 39; recent developments in 31; sea lines of communications *31*; strategic changes 26; strategic uncertainties in 40; United States military power in 28
Indian Ocean Rim Association (IORA) 87, 111
Indian Peace Keeping Forces (IPKF) 10, 11, 13
India–Sri Lanka Accord (ISLA) 10
India–Sri Lanka Free Trade Agreement (ISLFTA) 6, 9, 11–12, 16, 17
India–Sri Lanka–Maldives Maritime Agreement 6
'India's Sri Lanka Policy: Towards Economic Engagement' (Orland) 8
India–US Logistics Exchange Memorandum of Agreement 40
'Indira Doctrine' 11
Indo–Mauritian political elite 59
Indo–Mauritians relations 2–3, 67; bilateral relationships 69; center-of-the-world 70, 71; creolization process 67; economy 72; Gordon-Gentil, A. 70, 71; Grand Bassin in 77; Hindu communities 72; history 67; homogeneous community 67; Indian communities 68; national Independence 68; nation's destiny 76; overview 66–7; political legitimacy 69; population 67; rooting process 75; slave population 67
Indo-Pacific region, strategic change and uncertainty in 27–9
Indo-Sri Lanka Economic and Technology Cooperation Framework Agreement (ECTA) 23n29
Innova Ltd. 58

INDEX

intelligence, surveillance and reconnaissance (ISR) 40
International Maritime Organization (IMO) 17, 108
Interreg programmes 119–21
Interreg V A–Mayotte-Comores-Madagascar (2014–20) 120
Interreg V–Indian Ocean (2014–20) 120
IOC see Indian Ocean Commission
IOR see Indian Ocean Region
IORA see Indian Ocean Rim Association
IPKF see Indian Peace Keeping Forces
ISLA see India–Sri Lanka Accord
islands' general background 1–2
ISLFTA see India–Sri Lanka Free Trade Agreement
ISR see intelligence, surveillance and reconnaissance

Jack, J. C. 143n6
Jaffna Peninsula 12
Janata Vimukthi Peramuna (JVP) 12, 16
Japan, interest in Indian Ocean Region 39
Jathika Hela Urumaya (JHU) 16
Jathika Nidahas Peramuna (JNP) 16
Java 38
Jayewardene, J. R 18, 20n3; Ministry of Foreign Affairs 7; Sri Lankan foreign policy 9–10
Jean, Petit 55
Jeffery, L. 59, 60
JHU see Jathika Hela Urumaya
JNP see Jathika Nidahas Peramuna
Jones, T. T. 51
Journal of the Indian Ocean Region 1, 3
Jugnauth, A. 82, 88
JVP see Janata Vimukthi Peramuna
JY-11 3D radar system 17

kalapani 73, 76, 77
Kanjilal, Tushar 142
Kapur, A. 129
Kavaratti Island 33
Kelegama, J. B. 8, 9
Kelegama, S. 116
Kérulvay, Deschiens de 48
Koonjoo, P. 87
Kopp, C. 38
Kumaratunga, Chandrika Bandaranaike 21n5, 22n20; bandwagoning foreign policy 10–11; bilateral strategic linkages 9, 12–14; India–Sri Lanka Free Trade Agreement 11–12
Kumari Kandam 76
Kumari Nadu 76

labor history 46, 48; Berkeley, Henry 53; child mortality 55; grievances of workers 53–4; Le Normand 48–9; malnutrition 55; Peyton, Lumley 53; slave registration laws 52; Ver Huell, Maurits 50–1; women workers daily routine 56

La Bourdonnais, Mahé de 72, 76
Ladduwahetty, N. 8
Lagesse, M. 56
Lakshadweep Islands 33
Lal Pasina (Unnuth) 76
Lannon, E. 3
Lavoipierre, Maurice 57
Law of Storm 132
Le Favori ship 47
Le Mauricien 85
Lemoine, G. 70
Le Normand 48
Les Rochers de Poudre d'Or (Appanah) 73, 75
L'Express 85
Liberation Tigers of Tamil Eelam (LTTE) 10, 12, 14, 17, 21n9; suicide bomber 11
'Little India' see Mauritius
Lomé Convention 106
LTTE see Liberation Tigers of Tamil Eelam
Lucie-Smith, Maurice 57, 58

Maingard, René 58
making of the English working class, The (Thompson) 46
Malacca Strait 32
Malcolm, J. A. 3
Maldives–European Community Country Strategy Paper (2007–13) 119
Maldives–Sri Lanka relationships 106, 118–19
Mandarin, Fernand 58
Marine Police Investigation Unit 89
Maritime Domain Awareness (MDA) 17
maritime security 3, 82; responsibility for 88; Somali piracy 83; sustainability as 84, 85–7, 98; threat 85; see also Mauritius; Seychelles
MARSIC project 108–9
Mascarene islands 48, 50, 66; French settlement on 47
MASE program 117
Maurer, S. 60
Maurice Ile Durable project 88
Mauritian Hindu Federations 69
Mauritius 3, 33, 83, 98–9; Anti-Drug and Smuggling Unit 89, 90; anti-drugs trafficking governance structure 89, 90; copra imported to 55; drug trafficking by sea 89, 94–8; Government Information Service 85; heroin drugs 96; Hinduism in 67, 69, 77; illegal drugs in 95; Indian communities 68; India's relation with 34; maritime security 83–4; Mauritius Trochetia 95, 96; population 67, 83; Ramgoolam, Seewoosagur 69, 76; research methodology 84–5; securing maritime domain in 87–90; sustainable vision 88; see also Indo–Mauritians relations
Mauritius Conference 86
Mauritius Government 113
Mauritius Revenue Authority (MRA) 90, 96
Mauritius Trochetia 95, 96

151

INDEX

Mayer, G. 57
MDA *see* Maritime Domain Awareness
Medcalf, R. 2
Michel, J. 87, 91, 99n2
Miles, W. 60
Mishra, V. 77
Mondol, K. 140
Morgan, J. 93–4
Moulinié, Paul 58
Mozambique Channel 33
MRA *see* Mauritius Revenue Authority
multipurpose river valley projects (MPRVPs) 133, 134
Murday, Linganaden 3
museum collection 132

Namasudra movement 135
National Coast Guard (NCG) 89, 96; Action Plan leaflet 97; radar systems 98
National Democratic Alliance (NDA) 13
National Indicative Programme: for Comoros 117; for Madagascar 118
National Master Plan 97, 98
National Rural Employment Guarantee Scheme 135
Natural disasters and Indian history (Roy) 143n5
'natural disasters,' concept of 129
Natural Hazards and Peoples in the Indian Ocean World (Bankoff & Christensen) 129
Naval operation (2008–18) 108
NAVFOR-ATALANTA operation 108
NCG *see* National Coast Guard
NDA *see* National Democratic Alliance
Nehru, Jawaharlal 7, 136
neoclassical realism 7–8
New Asia strategy 106
Newton, Edward 53
Nicolay, William 52

Obock 32
Observer Research Foundation 111
Oceans and the Law of the Sea 87
OCTs *see* Overseas Countries and Territories
Operation Gateway 35
Organisation internationale de la Francophonie 70
Orland, B. 8
Overseas Countries and Territories (OCTs) 106

'participating delegations' 108
Partition of India 135
Patel, S. 61, 71
patitabadi taluks 143n1
Pattanaik, S. S. 9
P-8A Poseidon maritime reconnaissance 37, 38
Pero dos Banhos 46

Petit Cousin vessel 49
Petrusmok (Chazal) 76
Peyton, Lumley 53
Phayre, Arthur 53–4
Piddington, Henry 143n4
piracy 91; human consequences of 91; Seychelles' response to 91–4; Somali piracy 83, 88, 91, 99; tackling suspected cases of 92; threat 94
plantation society 67
Port Blair 32
Port Canning Company 131, 132
Premadasa, Ranasinghe 6, 18, 21n13; Sri Lankan foreign policy 10
Price, Richard 49

Quartiers de Pamplemousses (Gordon-Gentil) 70

RAAF *see* Royal Australian Air Force
Radhakrishnan, R. 61
Rajapaksa, Mahinda 4, 15, 22n28; national development agenda 8; turn towards China for armaments 14–15
Rajni Nayanthara Gamage 2
Rama's banishment: A centenary tribute to the Fiji Indians (Mishra) 77
Ramgoolam, Seewoosagur 59, 69, 76
RAND report 33
reciprocal instrumentalization 69
'Regional Coordination Mechanism' 109
Regional Indicative Programme (RIP) 116
Regional Maritime Centre for Fusion of Maritime Information (RMIFC) 94
Regional Maritime Centre for Operational Coordination (RMCOC) 94, 99
regional maritime security 117
Reunion Island 96, 97
Revenue History of the Sundarbans, The (Ascoli) 131
Revenuer History of the Sundarbans, The (Biswas) 130
revisionist theory 77
Revolutionary Socialist Party 136
Rio Summit 86
RIP *see* Regional Indicative Programme
RMCOC *see* Regional Maritime Centre for Operational Coordination
RMIFC *see* Regional Maritime Centre for Fusion of Maritime Information
Rochon, Abbé 47
Rogers & Co 58
Royal Australian Air Force (RAAF) 35, 37
Royal Navy 27, 30
Roy, T. 133, 143n5
Russell, Claud 130, 143n1

INDEX

SAARC *see* South Asian Association for Regional Cooperation
SAFTA *see* South Asian Free Trade Agreement
Saïd, E. 60
Samaranayake, N. 8
Samoa conference (2014) 86, 87
SAPTA *see* South Asian Preferential Trade Agreement
SAR *see* search and rescue
Sarkhel, P. 135
Scattered Islands 111–13, 120
SCG *see* Seychelles Coast Guard
Scheduled Castes of Bengal 132
sea lines of communications (SLOCs) 17
Sea of Poppies (Ghosh) 73
search and rescue (SAR) 40
Sewtohul, A. 69, 71, 72
Seychelles 3, 33–4, 57, 83, 98–9; anti-piracy governance structure 88, *89*; Contact Group on Piracy off the Coast of Somalia 92–3; maritime security 83–4; population 83; research methodology 84–5; response to piracy 91–4; securing maritime domain in 87–90; sustainable development mechanism 87
Seychelles Coast Guard (SCG) 88, 91–2
Seychelles Maritime Safety Administration (SMSA) 88–9
Seychelles Nation 85
Seychelles News Agency 85
Seychelles People's Defence Forces (SPDF) 88
Seychelles Supreme Court 92
Seychelles Sustainable Development Strategy (2012–20) 87
Sinohydro Company 13
Sino–US relationship 34
Sirisena, Maithripala 4
Six Degree Channel 33
SLA *see* Sri Lanka Army
Slave Abolition Act (1835) 52
slave registration laws 52
SLFP *see* Sri Lanka Freedom Party
SLOCs *see* sea lines of communications
Small Island Developing States (SIDS) community 85, 86
SMSA *see* Seychelles Maritime Safety Administration
social improvement 69
socio-cultural associations 69
Somali piracy 83, 88, 91, 99
Sookhoo, N. 59
South Asian Association for Regional Cooperation (SAARC) 70, 106, 121
South Asian Free Trade Agreement (SAFTA) 11
South Asian Preferential Trade Agreement (SAPTA) 8, 11

South 24 Parganas 131
spatial fabulation 76
SPDF *see* Seychelles People's Defence Forces
Sridharan, E. 21n4, 21n9
Sri Lanka Army (SLA) 10
Sri Lanka Freedom Party (SLFP) 6, 12
Sri Lanka–Maldives relationships 106, 118–19
Sri Lankan foreign policymaking 2, 4; balancing/bandwagoning strategy 5, 7, 19; bilateral strategic linkages 12–14; dynamics of 5; explaining shifts in 18–19; foreign economic policy 5; foreign security policy 5; historical overview 6–8; India–Sri Lanka Free Trade Agreement 11–12; Jayewardene and Premadasa administrations 9–10; Kumaratunga administration 10–14; neoclassical realism 7–8; policy recommendations 19; shift away from India 16–18; shift towards China 14–15; structural incentives 8; systemic and domestic factors on **19**; theoretical literature on 8–9
Sri Lankan Tamils 13
Steinberg, T. 128
Stoler, L. 61
strategic partnerships, creation of 106
Strategic Policing Plan (2015–18) 97
String of Pearls' strategy 32
Suez Canal 32
sui generis organization 111
Sundarban delta 3, 129, 142–3; agrarian frontier, expansion of 132; Aila cyclone 138–42; Bengal partition, impact of 135–6; *bhadrolok* families 136, 142; under British Indian Government 130; burden on 137; cargo transport 137; characterization of 130; colonial and pre-colonial past 130–2; cyclone's impact 141; Damodar Valley Corporation 133–4; embankment measures, political economy of 132–4; erosion in 134; fishermen 140; Hamilton Public Records 131; land reclamation program 130–1; landscape of 142; mangrove afforestation 130; map of *129*; political economy of 136–7; population pressure 136; post-independence 135–8, *138*; production of capital in 132; public works in 133; refugee migration 136; shrimp farming business 137; *talukdars* 130, 143n6; tidal backwaters in 131; Tiger Reserve 136; vulnerable social groups 132; as World Heritage site 137; *zamindars* 130–3, 143n2; *see also bunds* (embankments), in Sundarban delta

Tagore Society for Rural Development 142
Talbot, Robert 58
Tamil Nadu, Sri Lankan Tamils and 13

INDEX

Tanzania 32
TFEU see Treaty on the Functioning of the European Union
Thompson, E. P. 46
Topaz vessel 91
Torabully, K. 75
transnational cooperation program 120
transnational networks 72
Treaty of Rome (1957) 106
Treaty on the Functioning of the European Union (TFEU) 112, 119
Trouillot, M. 62
Trump, Donald 28
24-Parganas Sundarbans 131, 136

UK–US agreement 113
UNF see United National Front
UN human rights conventions 116
United Kingdom, security dimension of maritime domain 87
United National Front (UNF) 14
United National Party (UNP) 6, 10, 12
United Nations Development Programme 85
United Nations Office on Drugs and Crime (UNODC) 92, 97, 99
United Nations Security Council (UNSC) 15, 91; Resolution 1851 92
United People's Freedom Alliance (UPFA) 16
United States 39–40; Central Intelligence Agency 95; defence strategy, Diego Garcia in 30–1; encouraged India's role in IOR 39; military power in Indian Ocean Region 28; naval power in Indian Ocean 27; 'Nixon doctrine' 39
United States Navy 33

United States Strategic Command 30
Unmanned Aerial Vehicles (UAVs) 33
Unnuth, A. 76, 77
UNODC see United Nations Office on Drugs and Crime
UNP see United National Party
UNSC see United Nations Security Council
UPFA see United People's Freedom Alliance
Uyangoda, J. 21n4

Van Onselen, C. 46
Vaughan, M. 67, 70, 71
Ver Huell, Maurits 50, 51; depiction of slave and oil-making machinery *51*
Victory vessel 95
Voyage à Rodrigues (Clézio) 71
Vulnerable India (Kapur) 129

Walker, I. 60
welfare state policy 69
West Cocos Island 35, 37, 38
'white shipping' information sharing agreement 40
Wickremasinghe, Ranil 22n19; Sri Lankan foreign policy 14
Wider Indian Ocean approach 105, 110–11
Wiehe's report 58
Wilson, Harold 59
'World Drug Report' 94
World Food Programme 108

Yaoundé II Convention 106

Zanzibar Archipelago 1
Ziethen, A. 61